YOUR RIGHTS
AT WORK

Second Edition

Darien A. McWhirter

JOHN WILEY & SONS, INC.

NEW YORK • CHICHESTER • BRISBANE • TORONTO • SINGAPORE

In recognition of the importance of preserving what has been written, it is a policy of John Wiley & Sons, Inc., to have books of enduring value published in the United States printed on acid-free paper, and we exert our best efforts to that end.

This publication is designed to provide accurate and authoritative information in regard to the subject matter covered. It is sold with the understanding that the publisher is not engaged in rendering legal, accounting, or other professional services. If legal advice or other expert assistance is required, the services of a competent professional person should be sought. *From a Declaration of Principles jointly adopted by a Committee of the American Bar Association and a Committee of Publishers.*

Library of Congress Cataloging-in-Publication Data

McWhirter, Darien A. (Darien Auburn)
    Your rights at work / Darien A. McWhirter. — 2nd ed.
        p.   cm.
    Includes bibliographical references and index.
    ISBN 0-471-57693-X. — ISBN 0-471-57692-1 (pbk.)
    1. Labor laws and legislation—United States—Popular works.
    2. Employee rights—United States—Popular works.   I. Title.
KF3319.6.M39   1993
344.73′01—dc20
[347.3041]   92-16643

*For
Page Keeton,
former dean of the
University of Texas Law School,
in grateful recognition
of his dedication
to the teaching
of law*

Preface

This book is written primarily for three groups: employees, employers, and managers. Its function for all three groups is to provide a general overview of employment law *before* employers do something that might cause an employee to sue and *before* an employee is seriously thinking about suing. It is also intended to provide all three groups with a ready reference concerning what the law is in this fast-changing area. Many disputes could be avoided if both sides knew what the law in this area really is and how it might apply to their unique situation.

Managers are truly the people in the middle. They may at some point in their careers be sued by an employee and at another point desire to sue their employer. They should read this book with both possibilities in mind.

The temptation with a book like this is to read only the part of particular interest at the moment. I urge readers to avoid this temptation and to read through the entire book once before focusing on a particular section. Even people with a specific problem in mind may be surprised to find that more than one section is relevant to their problem. Also, while the book is divided into chapters, each chapter in a particular section assumes that the reader has read the preceding chapters in that section.

Why a second edition? Since the first edition was published in 1989, hundreds of important cases have been decided in this area and dozens of significant statutes have been passed at both the state and federal level, the most important of these being the federal Civil Rights Act of 1991 and the federal Americans with Disabilities Act of 1990. While these and other new statutes are discussed at length in this book, it is important to realize that we never really know what a statute means until the judges interpret it and apply it to the facts of particular cases.

It is also important to remember that while this book can provide an overview of employment law, there is no substitute for the advice of an attorney when the time comes. Although I have worked very hard to be as accurate as possible in describing statutes and court decisions, there is always the possibility of error. There is also the possibility that a judge may not agree with my interpretation when *your* case comes up. No one should rely on a specific statement about the law made in this book without consulting an attorney.

A book like this cannot be written without the help of many people. My teachers at New College (Florida), Yale University, and the University of Texas Law School provided me with the educational background for writing this book. Dozens of legal scholars have written articles and books on the subjects discussed, and I have consulted these whenever possible. My editor, John Mahaney, and the copy editor for this second edition, Martha Urban, provided many valuable suggestions.

I would like to thank the librarians at the Santa Clara County, University of Texas, and University of California law libraries for the use of their excellent facilities.

I would particularly like to thank the hosts of dozens of radio and television talk shows around the country for allowing me to appear and discuss these issues on the air. The questions and concerns of hundreds of callers to these shows are reflected in this second edition.

DARIEN A. McWHIRTER

*Fremont, California
and Austin, Texas
September 1992*

Contents

ONE
CONTRACT RIGHTS

TWO
RIGHTS AFTER BEING FIRED

THREE
CIVIL RIGHTS

FOUR
CONSTITUTIONAL RIGHTS

13. The Right to Privacy 165

The judge ruled that the teacher's right to bear children out of wedlock was greater than the school district's need to protect children from the sight of an unmarried, pregnant schoolteacher.

FIVE
RIGHTS UNDER WAGE, HOUR, AND LABOR LAWS

14. Wages and Hours 183

They were "on call" and could not go to the movies or out to dinner. The judge ruled that they were "working" and had to be paid for their "on call" time.

SIX
RIGHTS AFTER INJURY

Introduction

As we sit in the United States in the last decade of the twentieth century, we can't help but marvel at all the things that have happened during this century. The twentieth century saw two world wars and a 40-year cold war that finally ended in December 1991, with the demise of the Soviet Union. At the same time it has been a century of continual progress in the area of social reform.

A century ago there was no worker's compensation, no Social Security, no unemployment compensation, no civil rights laws, and no laws protecting the rights of union members. A century later the question is not whether we should have such laws but how can we make these laws more effective and the agencies charged with enforcing them more efficient. We live in the house that President Franklin D. Roosevelt built. During the 1930s, his New Deal administration passed the basic legislation creating Social Security and protecting union bargaining. However, during the last half century, the main concern of the federal government has been fighting wars, both hot and cold. As the nation turns back to the issues discussed in this book, it is apparent that another coat of paint and a new room addition will simply not do. What is needed is a basic remodeling.

The main impetus for this remodeling is the feeling, held by too many Americans, that the present system is simply not fair. Why do people born between 1917 and 1926 have their Social Security retirement benefits calculated differently from those of everyone else? Why do disabled railroad workers receive full compensation for their disability, in some cases amounting to a million dollars, while most disabled American workers never receive more than a hundred thousand dollars under state worker's compensation? Why does a minority worker who has never been the victim of actual discrimination

1

receive the benefit of "affirmative action" at the expense of a white worker who has never received any benefit from the old discriminatory system? Why does immigration law keep out some people while nurses, teachers, and farm workers are allowed in under special rules? One has to wonder what the wages and working conditions of nurses, teachers, and farm workers would currently be if new competitors for these jobs had not been continually imported into the country over the decades.

The American people heard much about quotas as the Civil Rights Act of 1991 was debated. What they did not hear is that even if American employers wanted to impose voluntary quotas in order to make their work force a true reflection of the relevant labor pool, there would be no way to go about it. There is no agency in the United States capable of telling an employer how many people of each race and sex within the relevant labor pool are qualified to work in each position. There is also no agency with the authority to decide what the "relevant labor pool" is!

In the 1930s, FDR envisioned a simple system in which everyone would have a union, and the union would deal with all their problems. Today, less than 10 percent of the nongovernment work force belongs to a union, and too many issues are simply beyond the ability of union and management to solve. The idea of a simple system in which disputes between employers and employees are handled quickly and inexpensively by arbitration has been replaced by a crazy quilt of laws that could find the same employee and employer facing off in half a dozen different forums. What was a system dominated by the federal government in the 1930s became a system dominated by the states in the 1970s and 1980s. In many employment cases, the first issue to be resolved is which set of laws control—the federal or the state? Too often the answer is neither or both.

During the second half of the nineteenth century, the basic employment law of the various states developed in a "we" versus "them" environment. In the East, the "we" was generally considered to be employers, and the legal system moved to protect the "we" from the "them"—in this case, new immigrants and former slaves. Most of the states east of the Mississippi River developed a set of legal principles designed to make sure "we" won. I call these states "pro-boss" states. Most of these states have evolved out of this mentality, but a dozen still cling to the old legal concepts developed during this era. The existing pro-boss states are Delaware, Indiana, Ohio, New York, Pennsylvania, and Rhode Island in the North; Alabama, Georgia, Florida, Louisiana, Mississippi, and North Carolina in the South.

Many of the western states saw things differently, as the descendants of the first settlers found large corporations moving in to exploit the natural resources of their states. Some of these western states developed legal concepts to protect workers and continue to pass laws that most states would never even consider. Over time, however, these "pro-employee" western states had to compete for new companies and, as a result, have evolved a legal position that tries to accommodate fairly the interests of both sides. By the 1990s, most states, east and west, deserve to be called "fair" states.

Throughout much of the debate over employment issues in America, a fundamental point goes unmentioned, that is, the newly developing economic system in the United States. America is no longer dominated by corporations owned by wealthy men and their descendants. By the end of the 1990s, half of the common stock in the United States will be owned by pension funds. Less than a thousand pension fund trustees around the country will exercise the powers of ownership without any real guidance from the actual owners. We will have met the enemy, and it will be us!

The fundamental purpose of the American employment system often gets lost. It is to provide the best person for each job, and a job for each person that takes full advantage of his or her singular abilities and interests. The American employment system is, at bottom, a free market system that does not seem to function very well. If it were functioning correctly, the following should have happened: as the wages for particular occupations rose, more people would be trained to fill those positions and, over time, everyone would be making similar wages. The opposite has occurred during the last half century. The wage differential is significantly greater now than it was when the postdepression economic expansion began. What is the cause of this lack of response by the free market—lack of educational facilities? misdirected educational resources? lack of information? the continuing effects of discrimination? misguided government policies? During the 1950s and 1960s, no one worried too much because everyone was becoming better off. That was not the case during the 1970s and 1980s, as average Americans saw their standard of living stagnate and then decline.

The American employment system impacts every problem in American society, and is impacted by them. The major disadvantage that American car manufacturers face when trying to compete with their Japanese counterparts is the higher cost of U.S. employee health care and pension funds. During 1990 and 1991, the majority of workers on strike in America were striking over who would pay for health insurance and how much coverage they would receive.

During the 1980s, America declared war on drugs and tried to fight addiction with guns, jails, and discharge for addicted workers. Many employers are only now finding out that, in many states, those fired employees are entitled to unemployment compensation and, in some cases, are suing their employers under handicap discrimination laws.

Most states and the federal government now have laws outlawing discrimination against handicapped people in the workplace. If you talk to employers, you find that most do not want to discriminate against handicapped people. They do it because they can't afford to pay the health insurance premiums that result when an insurance pool has too many handicapped people in it. Of course, nothing in either state or federal law addresses that very real cause of handicapped discrimination.

This is a book written primarily for employees thinking about suing their employers and employers who think they might be sued. During the twentieth century, setting up systems to allow everyone to sue everyone else has become the American solution to every problem. However, it is a solution that generates problems. Lawsuits are expensive. For every employee who actually receives a day in court, two dozen are turned away by attorneys who simply do not think their case is worth the time and trouble involved in taking it through the American legal system. That means that most workers who feel they have been victimized by the system receive no redress for their grievances while employers face potentially devastating legal costs and damages when the wheel of fortune finally comes around to them.

Americans are used to thinking about efficiency when talking about private companies but not when talking about legal, governmental, or social systems. This will have to change. Our employment law system is inefficient, if efficiency is measured in terms of resolving actual disputes between employees and employers. Our medical system is inefficient, if efficiency is measured in terms of dollars spent and health care received. Our unemployment system is inefficient, if efficiency is measured in terms of placing workers in the most suitable job for their individual talents.

If we were to say to the average American something that we will be able to say in a very few years, "OK, you now own all the major corporations in America, how do you want them to go about hiring and firing people?" I do not know the exact response, but I do know that the average American would not say, "Oh, I like it just the way it is, thank you very much!"

PART

ONE

CONTRACT RIGHTS

1

We All Have
a Contract

Every employee has an employment contract. Most do not have a written or even an oral contract. The contract is "implied" from words and actions. For example, if an employer in the business of digging ditches says to a worker, "Hey, want a job?" and the worker responds, "Yeah," they have an employment contract. That brief conversation implies that the employer will pay a reasonable wage, the location of the work is the town they are standing in, and the service to be performed is manual labor.

The difficult question is: How long is this contract supposed to last? Centuries ago the English judges assumed that the parties to an employment contract intended the contract to last one year. American judges do not make that assumption. They assume the parties intended the contract to be *at-will*, meaning the employee works "at the will" of the employer. The employer can fire the employee at any time for no reason. The employee can quit at any time for no reason.

The law works like your home computer. If you do not tell the computer something specific, the computer program "defaults" to the command most people want. The law does the same thing; it defaults to what the judges think most people intend when they enter into an employment contract. There are four basic terms that every employment contract has: wages, place of performance, work to be performed, and amount of time the contract is to last. The "defaults" for employment contracts are: the wages are reasonable wages; the location of the job is the place where the employee is; the work to be performed is anything the employee is capable of doing; and the length of time is at-will (*Mallory*).

During the 1980s, many people in California came to believe that California was different, that once employees were hired they could only be fired for good cause. On December 29, 1988, the California Supreme Court put an end to this notion, ruling that employees in California without contracts (written, oral, or implied) are at-will employees and can be fired for any reason or no reason at all just like employees in every other state (*Foley*).

In some states, if the salary is stated as "so much per year," the judges assume that means the employer intended to hire the employee for a whole year. In a recent Tennessee case, the employer quoted a salary as so much per year and the court enforced a one-year contract (*Ball*). In a recent Illinois case, the letter confirming the job said "guaranteed salary for twelve months of $750 per week ($39K per annum)." The judges ruled this implied that the employer intended to hire the employee for one year (*Berutti*). Some states have statutes dealing with this. For example, a Georgia statute says that stating wages as so much per a period of time creates the presumption that the employee has been hired for that period of time (Ga. 34-7-1).

The judges have no trouble assuming the two parties intended that reasonable wages would be paid or that the employee would do whatever he or she was capable of doing. They have a lot of trouble assuming the parties intended the contract to last for any specific length of time. The time element can be one of three: at-will, for a definite term, or for an indefinite term.

What does it mean to have a contract for an indefinite term? In 1896 the Minnesota Supreme Court enforced a contract that said the employee had a job as long as he did his work efficiently and owned 50 shares of company stock. The court said the employee could not be fired as long as he met those conditions (*McMullan*).

In fair states, written contracts for an indefinite term will be enforced. The judges in some pro-boss states think there is no such thing as a contract for an indefinite term; if contracts do not run for a specific period of time, then they are interpreted to be at-will.

Even in fair states, at-will is what the legal system defaults to. If the judge cannot figure out how long the employment contract is supposed to last, it is at-will. The vast majority of employees in America are at-will employees.

Written Term Contracts

Judges in all states will enforce an employment contract that runs for a definite length of time if it is in writing. An employee with a written term contract has a big advantage over an at-will employee. The employer cannot fire the employee during the term of the contract except as spelled out in the contract. Most contracts say that the employee can be fired only for "good cause."

Even if the contract does not specifically say this, most judges assume that this is implied in any written employment contract. Union contracts are really nothing more than written term contracts that cover a large number of employees for a specific period of time.

There is a special problem that comes up with written contracts. Often the two parties have negotiated for a long period of time before the final contract is signed. It is hard to tell if the final written contract is intended to supersede all the prior discussions or if those discussions are intended to be part of the final agreement. That is why many people put a clause in the final written contract that specifically says it supersedes everything else.

What if the contract does not specifically say this? Then it is up to the judge to decide if the parties intended the final written contract to supersede the letters and conversations that came before it. Judges in pro-boss states tend to decide that the parties intended the final contract to be the entire agreement (*Pranzo*). In fair states the judges are more likely to find that the two parties did not intend the last written contract to be the whole agreement.

The case of Professor Martin Lewis, M.D., illustrates this problem (*Lewis*). Dean Clarence Peiss tried over several months to recruit Lewis to teach at Loyola University in Chicago. On September 20, 1979, the dean sent a long letter to Lewis with numbered paragraphs dealing with things like salary and tenure. In this letter the dean promised to submit Lewis for tenure at the first opportunity. Negotiations continued and, on February 18, 1980, the dean sent another long letter to Lewis promising to submit Lewis for tenure in September 1981. Lewis accepted and on May 14, 1980, he received an appointment letter that stated his salary and appointed him professor of pathology from July 1980 through June 1981.

The dean did not submit Lewis for tenure in September 1981 as he had promised. Lewis did not receive tenure and was fired after three years. The university and the dean argued that the letters the dean sent in September 1979 and February 1980 should not be considered part of the contract. They argued that the contract consisted only of the one-page appointment letter. The court found that the appointment letter was not "expressive of the complete agreement and understanding of the parties" and ruled that the letters from the dean were part of the contract.

Employees should avoid signing contracts that say the written document contains the entire agreement when in fact it does not. An employee in the position that Lewis was in should insist that the president of the university sign a contract that really contains the entire agreement, including all the promises the dean has made. Employers should make sure that supervisors are not making promises the employer does not want to keep. Also, if the employer intends the final written contract to supersede all prior negotiations and promises, then the contract should say so.

How long can a written employment contract last? In California, employment contracts cannot run for more than seven years (Calif. Labor Code Sec.
2855); in Louisiana, they are limited to five years (Art. 167, 2746 La. Civ.
Code); and in North and South Dakota, they are limited to two years (N.D.
34-01-02; S.D. 60-2-6). In other states there is no limit set by statute but
the judges might not enforce an employment contract if it ran for too long a
time. Seven years is probably safe because under old English law, employment
contracts were limited to seven years.

Oral Term Contracts

Oral contracts for a specified term are just as enforceable as written contracts
if they do not violate the *Statute of Frauds*. The first Statute of Frauds was
enacted in England in 1677. Today every state has its own version. This
statute requires certain agreements to be in writing before the judges will
enforce them. Technically, these statutes usually require that there be *something written and signed* by the party being sued. The provision that causes
the most trouble in an employment setting is the requirement that an oral
contract must be capable of being performed completely within one year
from the day the agreement is made or it is not enforceable. An oral agreement
to employ someone for more than one year would not be enforced in most
courts because of the Statute of Frauds.

This provision has caused a lot of hardship to employees. Generally, judges
in pro-boss states strictly enforce the Statute of Frauds (*Gatins*). Judges in
fair states will find a way around the Statute of Frauds if enforcement of the
statute would cause too great a hardship to the employee. For example, in
one case an employee was hired in Los Angeles for a one-year job in Hawaii.
He quit his California job and moved his family to Hawaii only to be fired
2½ months later. Technically, the one-year contract violated the Statute of
Frauds because it ran for more than one year from the time the agreement
was made. (An agreement made on December 30, 1989, to employ someone
through December 31, 1990, technically violates the Statute of Frauds because it cannot be completed within one year of its making.) In this case, the
Supreme Court of Hawaii enforced the oral contract, saying "injustice can
only be avoided by the enforcement of the contract" (*McIntosh*).

Courts will generally enforce specific oral promises that have been made
to employees. In a 1991 case, the boss promised in 1967 that the employee
would become president of the company. The employee was fired in 1987
without having been made president. The South Dakota Supreme Court said
that it would enforce this oral promise (*Larson*). In a Kentucky case, an
employee was promised that she would not be fired if she appeared nude in

Playboy magazine and was then fired when the magazine came out. The court said this violated the oral promise that had been made to her and allowed her to sue for damages (*Hammond #2*). In a 1992 case, the employer told the employee that if he worked for nothing the employee would inherit the ranch when the employer died. The employee worked without pay for 40 years and the Oklahoma Supreme Court enforced the promise when the employer died (*Crossman*).

Employers who do not intend to give employees oral contracts should instruct their supervisors accordingly. Employees should think twice before relying on an oral contract, particularly if it will run for more than a year from the time of the agreement.

Some people think an oral promise will not be enforced by a court unless there is some independent witness to the conversation. That is not true. If it is a case of the employer's word against the employee's word, then it is up to the jury to decide who is telling the truth (*Bernoudy*).

Oral Contracts for an Indefinite Term

Oral employment contracts that run for an indefinite term run into two problems. The first is the Statute of Frauds. The second is the reluctance of some judges to enforce employment contracts for an indefinite term.

In fair states, the judges will not allow the Statute of Frauds to interfere with the enforcement of an oral employment contract for an indefinite period of time if there is any way the contract could end within one year of its making. In one Idaho case the court enforced a promise to employ the worker as long as the factory was in operation. The judge reasoned that the factory could close within one year so there was no Statute of Frauds problem (*Whitlock*). In an Oregon case the employer promised the employee a job for as long as there was "production to run." The court said the production could run out within one year and enforced the promise (*Seibel*).

What if the employer makes an oral promise that the employee will not be fired except for good cause or that the employee has a lifetime job? In many fair states the courts will enforce this promise despite the Statute of Frauds because the employee might die or give the employer good cause to fire him or her within one year. The question is not, Did the contract end within one year? The question is, Is there any way the contract could have ended within one year? Most courts will not enforce an oral promise to employ someone until retirement because "until retirement" is a definite period of time, more than one year and, therefore, violates the Statute of Frauds (*Baxley; Burton*).

Judges in the pro-boss states will enforce an oral promise to employ someone for an indefinite term only if the employee can prove not only that the promise was made but also that the employee gave up something special ("special consideration") in exchange for the promise. Promises of permanent employment, promises of lifetime employment, and promises to fire only for good cause are all promises to employ someone for an indefinite term.

When Mr. Romack gave up a civil service job with the state of Indiana on the oral promise of permanent employment with a private company, the Indiana Supreme Court said giving up a job where he could only be fired for good cause was enough "special consideration" and enforced the promise (*Romack*). In Alabama (another pro-boss state), the supreme court ruled that moving from one place to another or quitting a job is enough "special consideration" to allow enforcement of these kinds of oral promises (*Murphree*; *Scott*).

Most fair states do not require special consideration, but they do require that it be reasonable to interpret what the employer said as a promise to employ the person for an indefinite term. The Kentucky Supreme Court ruled in 1983 that if the employer simply says that the job will be "permanent," this usually means that the job is not a "temporary" one, and the Kentucky courts would not rule that anything else was intended without "special consideration" or some other reason to believe the employer really meant to employ the person for an indefinite term. On the other hand, the Kentucky Supreme Court said promises to hire someone for life or to fire them only for good cause will be interpreted to mean exactly what most employees would think, that they have a job until they die or provide the employer with a good reason to fire them (*Synthetic Rubber*).

Courts in fair states have recently ruled that telling workers that they have a job "as long as they want it" or "as long as they sell" is like saying they have a "permanent job" and will not be enforced without something more than this simple statement by a manager (*Rowe*; *Addison*; *Merritt*). On the other hand, telling someone that he or she will be fired only for "good cause" is a promise that will be enforced without the need for special consideration (*Richards*; *Berube*; *Whitlock #2*).

This doctrine of American law has caused problems for a number of Japanese companies recently. These companies are not used to the idea that workers have rights. In Japan, employers can tell employees that they have a lifetime job one day and fire them the next day without any legal consequences. That is not the case in the United States. Arthur Shebar says that when he threatened to quit Sanyo, his Japanese bosses told him he had a job for life and that he would never be fired without good cause. Mr. Shebar says that a few months after that statement was made, these same managers told him to "clean out his desk" and get out of the building. The New Jersey Supreme Court said that oral promises of lifetime employment and promises to fire only for good cause are enforceable in New Jersey without any need for special consideration (*Shebar*). The supreme courts of Connecticut and New Mexico haved ruled that it is up to the jury to decide what these kinds of statements mean, and no special consideration is needed (*Coelho*; *Kastenbaum*).

Implied Employment Contracts

We have seen that most employees have an implied employment contract. The employee has simply accepted the job. Generally, if no specific term has been agreed to, the judges assume that the parties intended to have an at-will employment contract. This is not always true, however. In fair states the judge will look at the negotiations of the two parties, the nature of the employment, and all the circumstances of the job before deciding whether or not the implied employment contract is at-will (*Allegri*).

Two California Appeals Court cases frightened a lot of employers. These judges ruled that if an employee has worked for the same employer for many years, that alone implies that the employee has something more than an at-will employment contract (*Cleary*; *Walker*). No other state has gone along with these California decisions. While most fair states are willing to look at all the circumstances to see if something more than at-will has been implied, it takes more than just a great many years on the job to find something other than at-will employment.

Judges in both fair and pro-boss states will not find that lifetime or fire-only-for-good-cause employment has been implied unless enough of the right kind of "very special consideration" exists. However, if the employee has given up something special, the judges figure something more than at-will employment must have been intended, even though the parties did not discuss it.

This is illustrated by a recent Indiana case (*Speckman*). David Speckman was the director of the Brookside Community Center for the city of Indianapolis. He was fired in December 1979. When he threatened to sue over this firing, the city rehired him in March 1981. Speckman was fired again in February 1982. This time he did sue. The court held that implied in his March rehiring was the promise that the city would fire him in the future only for good cause. Giving up his right to sue over the December firing was enough "very special consideration" to support a finding that he had an implied promise from the city to fire him only for good cause in the future.

A Pennsylvania court ruled in 1991 that giving up a high-paying job, selling a house, and moving to another state provided the very special consideration needed to allow the jury to decide that something more than at-will employment was implied. The court enforced an implied contract of seven years of employment (*Cashdollar*).

Remember this is a problem only because there is no written contract. Even pro-boss judges will enforce an employment contract if it is in writing and for a definite term. For example, an Ohio Appeals Court enforced a written employment contract that promised to employ the worker until he was 65, was unable to work, or failed to perform his duties. The court said this was a written contract for a specified term, which ended on the employee's 65th birthday (*Boundy*).

To summarize: Both fair and pro-boss states will enforce written employment contracts for definite terms. Judges in most fair states will enforce written contracts for indefinite terms. Judges in most pro-boss states will not, finding them to be at-will contracts.

Both fair and pro-boss states will enforce oral employment contracts for less than one year. Both will generally not enforce oral employment contracts for more than one year because of the Statute of Frauds. Judges in fair states may ignore the Statute of Frauds if they feel that justice and equity require them to.

Some fair states and all pro-boss states require "special consideration" before enforcing oral promises to hire people for an indefinite period of time. More and more fair states are no longer requiring "special consideration" in these cases.

Finally, given the right circumstances, both fair and pro-boss states may find an implied promise to fire someone only for good cause. Judges will not find these kinds of implied contracts without some "very special consideration" (see Table 1.1).

In the past, employers did not worry too much about the oral or implied promises their supervisors made. Employers should start worrying. More and more employees are winning these lawsuits, and more and more states are changing long-standing legal doctrines that used to protect lazy employers with careless supervisors. Most employers would find it to their advantage to give their employees some kind of written contract. The contract could be for a specific term, or it could specify that the employee is hired at-will. Without a written contract, an employer may well find that employees have been given oral or implied contracts that run indefinitely.

A Promise to Give a Contract

What if the employee does not actually have a contract because the employer promised to give him one but did not? There is a general rule in American

Table 1.1 Enforcement of Employment Contracts

	Fair States	Pro-Boss States
Written contract, definite term	Contract enforced	Contract enforced
Written contract, indefinite term	Contract enforced	Some enforce, some consider to be at-will
Oral contract, definite term, less than one year	Contract enforced	Contract enforced
Oral contract, definite term, over a year	Not enforced unless fairness requires it	Not enforced
Oral contract, indefinite term	Some enforce; some require "special consideration"	Require "special consideration"
Implied contract, indefinite term	Require "very special consideration"	Require "very special consideration"

law that promises to enter into a contract in the future will not be enforced. However, judges in the fair states will enforce a promise to enter into an employment contract if it would cause too great a hardship to the employee not to do so.

In a recent New Mexico case, Marie Eavenson was offered a job. She quit her existing job, but when she showed up for work the new employer refused to hire her as promised. The New Mexico Supreme Court enforced the promise to hire her (*Eavenson*). Courts in Michigan and Texas have recently ruled the same way in similar cases (*Filcek*; *Roberts*).

In an Arizona case, Mr. Lindsey was hired as the basketball coach at the University of Arizona. He was given a one-year written contract but was orally promised that the contract would be renewed for at least three more years. The Arizona Appeals Court enforced this promise and affirmed the jury's award of $215,000 in damages (*Lindsey*).

What if the employee came to work because the employer promised to sign a written employment contract but the employer never got around to it and eventually fired the employee instead? Judges in the fair states will enforce an oral promise to give a written employment contract if they are reasonably certain what that written contract would have contained (*Alaska Airlines*; *Lovely*).

It is much harder for an employee to win a case involving a promise to give an employment contract in a pro-boss state. In every state it is always a good idea for an employee to get a written employment contract for a definite period of time *before* quitting their old job.

The Problem of Authority

When employees want to enforce a contract against a corporation, they come up against a fundamental question: Did the person making the contract for the corporation have the authority to do so? Courts will enforce a contract against a corporation if the person making the contract had actual or apparent authority to make the contract. The chairman of the board, acting pursuant to a vote of the board of directors, has the most actual authority. Generally, the president of the corporation also has actual authority to sign a contract and bind the corporation.

The idea of "apparent" authority was developed to keep corporations from having someone who seemed to have authority sign contracts that the corporation could get out of later. Judges will generally hold a corporation to promises made by people with apparent authority. Someone has apparent authority if a reasonable person under the circumstances would think that person had authority to bind the corporation.

Sheila Rancourt worked at a hospital in Waterville, Maine, for 16 years. She says that in March 1984 her supervisor, Dr. Littman, told her that she would "never have to worry about losing her job." She was fired three months later. The Supreme Court of Maine held that Dr. Littman did not have actual or apparent authority to bind the hospital to a lifetime employment contract (*Rancourt*). Other courts would not have agreed. If employers do not intend for supervisors to have this kind of authority, they should make that clear to the employees.

The Duty of Loyalty

Courts in every state have ruled that implied in every employment contract is a promise by employees that they will be "loyal" to their employer. This means that the employee owes an allegiance to the employer in situations in which the employer's interests are at stake. In one case, the employee diverted business from his employer to a competitor, which obviously violated the rule (*SHV*). In another case, the employee formed a company to rent generators to the employer without telling the employer he owned the company. This also violated the duty of loyalty (*Odeco*).

Many of these cases involve employees who are planning to go into business for themselves. While employees can "prepare" to form a competing company, they cannot do it in a way that is detrimental to their current employer. In a 1989 case, the employee talked to his current employer's customers about doing business with his new company and to current employees about coming to work for his new company before he had left the employer. The Colorado Supreme Court said this was a violation of the duty of loyalty (*Mulei #2*). In a 1991 case, an employee solicited many of his employer's key executives to come to work for his new company before he quit. The Massachusetts Supreme Court said this was a violation of the duty of loyalty (*Augat*).

Employees that violate the duty of loyalty can be sued for the damages they caused to their employer. They also have to give back any pay they received from the employer during the period when they were being disloyal (*Hill #2*; *Roberto*).

Good Faith and Fair Dealing

Some courts have begun to hold that employers owe a duty of loyalty to their employees, which these courts call a duty of "good faith and fair dealing." For example, in a 1990 case the written contract gave the employer total power to alter sales quotas and compensation rates without notice and without reason. The New Jersey Appeals Court ruled that this would still have to be done in "good faith" and for "legitimate business reasons" so as not to deprive the employee of fair compensation for his labor. The court felt that to rule otherwise would make the contract an "illusion," something courts avoid doing if they can (*Nolan*). The California Supreme Court ruled in 1988 that employers in California owe this duty of "good faith and fair dealing" to their employees, and employees can sue for contract damages if the duty is violated (*Foley*).

2

Employee Handbooks Are Contracts in Most States

During the 1980s, a great battle was waged in the state courts of America over whether the promises made in employee handbooks are enforceable in court.

In the 1920s and 1930s, employee handbooks appeared that spelled out the retirement, sick-leave, and fringe-benefit plan of the company. Judges found these to be promises of compensation and enforced them. There was no change in the at-will status of the employees. They could still be fired at any time for no reason. All these handbooks did was to spell out what the benefits would be as long as the employee remained with the company. Today, these retirement and benefit plans are enforced by a federal statute, the Employee Retirement Income Security Act (ERISA), which will be discussed in Chapter 19.

In the 1960s and 1970s, employee handbooks began to appear that either promised employees that they would be fired only for "good cause" or set out a particular discipline procedure that the employer promised to follow.

The judges in several pro-boss states had no trouble dismissing these handbooks as unenforceable. Because the two sides had not signed the handbook before beginning the employment relationship, pro-boss judges ruled that employee handbooks were not contracts and, therefore, were not enforceable in court.

In 1980, the Supreme Court of Michigan held that when an employer distributes an employee handbook that spells out the reasons employees can be discharged, the employer has given up the right to fire employees for other reasons (or no reason). The court said this was so even though the handbook is "signed by neither party," "can be unilaterally amended by the employer," and "the employee does not learn of its existence until after his hiring." In other words, the Michigan Supreme Court did not care that the usual contract procedures had not been followed. It found this to be a contract. When the handbook was distributed, because the employees were at-will, they could have quit. Instead, they continued to work. The employer had made an offer that the employees accepted by not quitting (*Toussaint*).

In 1983, the Supreme Court of Minnesota agreed. The court made the employer follow the disciplinary procedure contained in the handbook (*Pine River*).

Some courts appear reluctant to enforce these handbook provisions because they do not understand why employers would write such things in a handbook. There is a concept in the law that judges should not hold insane or retarded people to their promises. Some judges seem to think that any employer who would give out handbooks promising to follow certain discipline procedures, or to fire employees only for good cause, must be either insane or retarded. Several recent cases illustrate the reasons employers give out employee handbooks.

In one case, Canadian Pacific Airlines was trying to keep unions out at the time it issued the handbook. The Supreme Court of Hawaii found this to be a "sane" reason for giving out a handbook, and enforced its provisions against the company (*Kinoshita*).

In another case, the Supreme Court of Illinois was faced with a handbook that appeared to set up a system similar to a civil service system (*Duldulao*). Employees were given a 90-day probationary period, at the end of which they became permanent employees who could be terminated only after certain procedures had been followed. The court found that Saint Mary's Hospital had to compete for competent employees with government hospitals that provided their employees with civil service protection. Presumably Saint Mary's would have had to pay higher wages or offer some other inducement if it could not have provided a system similar to that of the government hospitals. The Illinois Supreme Court enforced the promises made in the handbook.

Given these precedents, the Supreme Court of South Carolina had no trouble enforcing the promises made in employee handbooks (*Small*). The South Carolina Supreme Court dealt with the argument that if courts enforce handbooks, companies will stop putting them out by saying: "If company policies are not worth the paper on which they are printed, then it would be better not to mislead employees by distributing them."

By the summer of 1992, 36 state supreme courts (all but two in fair states) had ruled that employee handbooks are enforceable in court (see Table 2.1). Only four state supreme courts have specifically ruled otherwise: Delaware, Massachusetts, Missouri, and New York. Missouri and Massachusetts are the only fair states to have ruled against enforcing employee handbooks. It is difficult to know what the other pro-boss states will do. Ohio and Alabama have broken ranks and enforced employee handbooks. Pro-boss states in the South may well find these handbooks enforceable because these courts do not like unions; and if employers can write enforceable employee handbooks, this can be used as a weapon in the war against unions.

Having an enforceable handbook can work in the employer's favor. In one case, the employee said he had been told (an oral contract) that he had a job for as long as the employer got federal funding (indefinite term). The Virginia Supreme Court ruled that this oral statement was overridden by a handbook provision that said the employee worked at the discretion of the executive director (*Miller*). However, the Michigan Supreme Court ruled in a similar case that these kinds of contradictory statements create an ambiguity (which is the employer's fault), and therefore it would enforce whichever promise benefited the employee the most (*Bullock*).

Once a state supreme court decides employee handbooks are binding contracts, several interesting questions arise. Once the handbook is distributed, can it ever be changed, at least as regards employees who have worked under that particular handbook? Does the employee have to read the handbook before he or she can sue to enforce its provisions? Are provisions in the handbook that set out how the handbook will be interpreted enforceable? What if the handbook seems to promise the employees the moon but has a disclaimer that says the handbook is not a contract?

If a handbook is a binding contract for an indefinite term, and states that employees can be fired only for good cause or for specific reasons listed in the handbook, then how can the employer alter that provision without violating that promise? Of course, if the original handbook specifically said that the employer reserved the right to make changes in the future, that would be different. We usually suggest that employers put a date on the handbook. They should make it the 1995 handbook and state therein that the employer will revise it at the end of that period. However, this could cause problems in some pro-boss states. If a pro-boss state supreme court is refusing to enforce employee handbooks because they appear to be employment contracts for an indefinite time period, then putting a date on the handbook may make it enforceable. As always, employers should consult their attorneys before making any changes in the employee handbook.

What if the employer has not put a date on the handbook or specifically reserved the right to make changes? The supreme courts of Iowa and Michigan have ruled recently that because these handbooks are "unilateral contracts" (written by one side only), they can be changed at any time by the employer without any need for new or special consideration. Employees

Table 2.1   Employee Handbooks

Employee Handbooks	Are/Are Not	Enforceable Contracts
Alabama*	Are	(Hoffman)
Alaska	Are	(Jones #3)
Arizona	Are	(Leikvold; Loffa)
Arkansas	Are	(Gladden; Crain)
California	Are	(Hepp)
Colorado	Are	(Keenan; Churchy)
Connecticut	Are	(Finley)
Delaware*	Are not	(Heideck)
District of Columbia	Are	(Wheeler; Howard U.)
Florida*	Supreme court has not ruled	
Georgia*	Supreme court has not ruled	
Hawaii	Are	(Kinoshita)
Idaho	Are	(Watson)
Illinois	Are	(Duldulao; Mitchell)
Indiana*	Are not	(Shaw)
Iowa	Are	(Cannon)
Kansas	Are	(Morriss)
Kentucky	Are	(Synthetic Rubber)
Louisiana*	Supreme court has not ruled	
Maine	Are	(Libby)
Maryland	Are	(Staggs; Castiglione)
Massachusetts	Are not	(Action for Boston)
Michigan	Are	(Toussaint)
Minnesota	Are	(Pine River)
Mississippi*	Supreme court has not ruled	
Missouri	Are not	(Johnson #4)
Montana	Are	(Gates; Kerr)
Nebraska	Are	(Lutheran; Johnson #3)
Nevada	Are	(Southwest Gas)
New Hampshire	Are	(Panto)
New Jersey	Are	(Woolley)
New Mexico	Are	(Vigil; Boudar; Lukoski)
New York*	Are not	(Weiner; Sabetay)
North Carolina*	Supreme court has not ruled	
North Dakota	Are	(Aasmundstad; Sadler)
Ohio*	Are	(Mers; Hedrick)
Oklahoma	Supreme court is not sure	(Hinson)
Oregon	Are	(Simpson)
Pennsylvania*	Supreme court has not ruled	
Rhode Island*	Supreme court has not ruled	
South Carolina	Are	(Small)
South Dakota	Are	(Osterkamp)
Tennessee	Supreme court has not ruled	

*Pro-boss state. The law is constantly changing. Consult an attorney about your situation.

Table 2.1—*Continued*

Employee Handbooks	Are/Are Not	Enforceable Contracts
Texas	Supreme court has not ruled	
Utah	Are	*(Berube)*
Vermont	Are	*(Sherman; Larose; Benoir)*
Virginia	Are	*(Hercules Powder)*
Washington	Are	*(Thompson)*
West Virginia	Are	*(Heck's)*
Wisconsin	Are	*(Ferraro)*
Wyoming	Are	*(Mobile Coal; Leithead)*

accept the new contract in the same way that they accepted the old contract, by continuing to work (*Cannon*; *Question*).

Does the employee have to read the handbook in order to have it enforced? A number of state supreme courts have specifically said that it does not matter; they will enforce the handbook against the employer whether the particular employee read it or not (*Toussaint*; *Kinoshita*). The New Jersey Supreme Court said these handbooks should be interpreted "in accordance with the reasonable expectations of the employees," and that it should be presumed that employees have read the handbook (*Woolley*). Your state supreme court may not agree. Judges in your state may say an individual employee cannot have relied on the handbook until that individual employee actually read the handbook. Employees who work for companies with employee handbooks should get a copy as quickly as possible (before accepting employment if possible), make a note of when they read it, and keep a copy.

What if the handbook has special provisions calling for the employee to follow a special grievance procedure in disputes over the handbook? In 1990, the Ohio Supreme Court ruled that the employee had to follow the grievance procedure set out in the handbook in order to enforce the handbook provisions against the employer (*Nemazee*). Courts in Maryland have come to the same conclusion (*Dearden*; *Dwiggins*).

How should terms in the handbook be interpreted? Generally, state courts have said that they should be interpreted the same way that they would be interpreted if they were in a "normal" employment contract. For example, in a 1990 case, the handbook said the employee could be fired only for "good cause" after he had completed the 90-day probationary period. The Illinois Supreme Court said that it was up to the jury to decide if the employee really did what he was charged with doing and if that infraction constituted good cause for dismissal. The employer could have specifically said in the handbook that it reserved the right to decide what "good cause" meant, but it had not done so. Therefore, the jury would make that decision just as it would with any other employment contract (*Mitchell*). The Washington Supreme Court

Employers Should Avoid Using the "P" Words

Probationary Employee
Permanent Employee
Progressive Discipline

is the only supreme court to rule otherwise. It said that the jury is to decide if the employer reasonably believed the charges made against the employee to be true and if that belief was supported by substantial evidence. In Washington, the jury is not to decide for itself if good cause existed for dismissal (*Baldwin*).

What if the handbook has a disclaimer? In a Maryland case, the Johns Hopkins Hospital handbook made a number of promises but also had a disclaimer that said: "This handbook does not constitute an express or implied contract. The employee may separate from his employment at any time; the Hospital reserves the right to do the same" (*Castiglione*). The Maryland Appeals Court held that because of this disclaimer the hospital did not have to live up to its promises made in the handbook. The North Dakota Supreme Court has ruled the same way in a similar case (*Eldridge*).

This idea of disclaimers creates an interesting problem. Usually, if one person hands another person a contract that makes all kinds of promises but then takes them all back, we call that an ambiguous contract. Generally, judges interpret ambiguous contracts against the person who created the ambiguity.

The Fifth Circuit Court of Appeals held that an employer cannot "taketh" with a disclaimer what he or she appears to "giveth" in a handbook (*Aiello*). The case involved Linda Aiello, an 18-year employee with United Air Lines. When she was transferred from Ft. Lauderdale to Dallas, she was allowed to receive a reimbursement from the company for the cost of moving her two cars. She drove one car from Florida to Texas at a cost of $201.70. She submitted a bill for twice that amount, figuring it would cost about the same amount to move the other car. She was fired for asking to be reimbursed for expenses she had not yet incurred.

United Air Lines had an extensive collection of employee handbooks. The Transfer and Relocation Handbook did not specifically forbid putting in a request for an anticipated expense. The General Handbook said that employees would be fired only for good cause. The jury in this case specifically found that Linda Aiello had an express written employment contract (the handbooks) that required good cause for dismissal, and that she had not been fired for good cause.

The Fifth Circuit judges said that United Air Lines could not act as if these handbooks were binding contracts most of the time and then fall back on a general disclaimer when things did not go its way. Essentially, these judges said that employers cannot use a handbook with a disclaimer as an instrument of fraud on the employees.

The Kansas Supreme Court was also faced with a handbook that said employees could be fired only for good cause but had a disclaimer that said "nothing in this policy manual should be construed as an employment contract" (*Morris*). The Kansas Supreme Court said this kind of general disclaimer was not enough to negate the specific promises made in the handbook.

Handbooks given to public employees have been enforced even in states that are not sure whether they will enforce handbooks for private employees (*Myrtle Springs*). These courts enforce government handbooks because they have the same legal force as any other government regulations.

Employers should not rely on general disclaimers, and they should not make promises in the employee handbook that they do not intend to keep. If an employer wants to reserve the right not to follow the discipline procedure, then it should say so in the discipline procedure itself.

Not following handbook provisions can cause problems for an employer. In one case, the company did not follow its own progressive discipline policy (verbal warning, written reprimand, suspension and, finally, discharge). Instead, it fired the employees at the first sign of misconduct. The Eighth Circuit Court said that this could be seen as evidence that the company merely used this misconduct to cover up its real reason for the firing, namely, that the employees were union members (firing people just because they are union members is a violation of federal law) (*Wells Dairy*). In a Pennsylvania case, the court ruled that because the employer did not follow its own progressive discipline policy, the employee was automatically entitled to unemployment compensation (*Brady*).

Employers should not make changes in employee handbooks without consulting an attorney and without considering both the legal and management ramifications of the changes. If you do not mean it, do not say it.

3

Special Contract Issues

If Employees Invent Things

A number of special problems arise if employees invent things. What happens if employees bring their inventions with them when they start a new job? The question of who owns these inventions should be dealt with in the employment contract. If not, then the employee owns them.

Take the case of Mr. Michels. When he came to work for Dyna-Kote Industries, he brought with him several chemical formulas that he had developed. There was a written employment contract, but the question of who would own these formulas was not mentioned. When he left Dyna-Kote, the company sued, trying to get the formulas back. The Indiana Appeals Court held that the formulas belonged to Michels when he came to work and, because there was nothing in the contract to the contrary, they still belonged to him when he left. The fact that he let the company use them while he worked for the company was irrelevant (*Michels*).

What if the employee agreed to sell her idea to the company but no price was ever agreed on? In one case, Ms. Tate, a surgical nurse at the University of Minnesota, came up with the idea of covering the tips of metal surgical clamps with a plastic cover so that the suture material would not break when held by the clamps. She told her idea to a company called Scanlan International, which developed the product. Tate and Scanlan never agreed on what her royalty would be. At one point the company offered her a total payment of $3,000 in lieu of royalties. She sued and the jury felt a reasonable total royalty for her, given the circumstances, would be $520,313 (*Tate*).

If an employee develops an invention on company time, who owns the invention? If the employee was hired to design a specific invention, the employee must assign the patent to the employer. Otherwise, the company has what is called a *shop right* to use the product without paying the employee a royalty, but the invention belongs to the employee unless there is an agreement to the contrary (*Aetna-Standard*). That is why an employer who has employees who invent things should require them to sign a written employment contract that deals with this issue.

What if employers try to claim some right to inventions created by the employee after the employee has left? They usually cannot unless they can prove that the employee did most of the inventing before leaving. What if the employer has a contract with the employee that says the employer owns whatever the employee invents, even after the employee stops working for the employer?

While working for Ingersoll-Rand, Armand Ciavatta signed an agreement promising to assign to the company any inventions he conceived within one year of ending his employment with the company. The New Jersey Supreme Court refused to enforce the agreement. Since the invention was not conceived until two months after Ciavatta left Ingersoll-Rand, this was not a case of someone working on an invention at the company and then quitting to patent it for himself. Because of this fact, and the fact that no company trade secrets were used, the New Jersey Supreme Court did not feel the legitimate interests of the company were harmed. Ciavatta owned the invention, not Ingersoll-Rand (*Ingersoll-Rand*).

Any employee who invents something at work should talk to an attorney. If there is no written contract dealing with this question, the employee may own the invention, not the employer.

A number of states have specific statutes that deal with these kinds of questions and limit the way these agreements can be written (Kan. 44-130; N.C. 66-57.1; Wash. 49.44.140; Cal. Labor Code 2870; Minn. 181.78; Utah 34-39-1). Only an attorney familiar with the laws in your state can make sure your rights (employee or employer) are protected.

If Employees Write or Create Things

A copyright is just that, the right to copy something. If you buy a book, you have the right to read it, lend it to someone else, and burn it up. You do not have the right to copy it. Only the author has that right. The key question is, Who is the author?

Under the U.S. Copyright Act, the author is the person who creates something in a tangible form (writes, paints, sculpts). The moment the thing is put in a tangible form, it is protected by the U.S. Copyright Act. Authors should routinely put a copyright notice on everything they create (the word *copyright*, the year, and your name). Anyone who is going to sell copies to the public should register with the copyright office. You can get the form at many post offices. (In some situations, notice and registration are not required; but why not be safe?)

Under the copyright law, if an employee writes or draws something that is "within the scope" of his or her employment, the employer is considered to be the author and owns the copyright (17 U.S.C. Sec. 101). If the person doing the work is an independent contractor, instead of a regular employee, then the independent contractor owns the copyright. Throughout this book we will be talking about employees and independent contractors. Basically, people who go to work every day and do whatever the employer tells them to do are considered to be employees. If they are hired to do a particular job unrelated to the employer's main business, like fixing the plumbing, they are considered to be independent contractors.

Of course, an independent contractor can sell the copyright to someone else, but the Copyright Act provides that anyone who sells a copyright can sue and get the copyright back 35 years later. If you write, paint, sculpt, and so on, you should keep track of the copyrights you sell. You may want to get them back and sell them again in your old age.

If there is any question about whether someone is an employee or an independent contractor, the issue of who owns the copyright should be dealt with in a written contract. A recent case illustrates how important this is (*Easter Seal Society*). The Easter Seal Society hired a company to film some Easter Seal Society events. The film was edited and used on a national Easter Seal telethon. There was no agreement about who owned the copyright on the film. The company later sold the film to a movie producer who used it in an adult movie called *Candy, the Stripper*. The Easter Seal Society sued and lost. The Fifth Circuit Court said the Easter Seal Society should have had a contract with the company that spelled out who would own the copyright to the film. They did not, so the copyright belonged to the company that made the film, not to the Easter Seal Society. The company was an independent contractor, not an employee, and therefore owned the copyright. In 1989, the U.S. Supreme Court agreed with this interpretation of the copyright law (*Reid*).

Agreements Not to Compete

Many employees are asked to sign agreements not to compete with their employers for a certain period of time after the employment relationship ends. Whether these agreements will be enforced usually depends on two factors: first, does the employer really have an interest that needs protecting or is he simply trying to limit competition? and, second, is the agreement reasonable as to the length of time, geographic area, and activities the employee cannot engage in?

In the 1980s and 1990s, more and more courts have refused to enforce these kinds of agreements unless the employer has a "legitimate business interest" to protect. Generally, courts will allow employers to use noncompetition agreements to protect three things: (1) trade secrets, (2) the cost of special training given to the employee, and (3) the goodwill of the company. In each case, however, the employer has the burden of proving that the particular interest involved could only be protected by a noncompetition agreement and that the agreement is reasonable given the particular interest that the employer wants to protect.

Most courts will allow the use of noncompetition agreements if there are trade secrets to protect, but they must qualify as real trade secrets. In 1991, the Georgia Supreme Court ruled that a list of customers with whom the employer does business is not a trade secret (*Smith*). A Texas Appeals Court refused to enforce a noncompetition agreement against a former company vice-president, ruling that customer names and product prices do not qualify as trade secrets (*Numed*).

Some employers have argued that they need to expend money to provide special training and should be protected if they do so. In 1991, a Florida Appeals Court said that this could qualify as a protectable interest but the training must be "extraordinary." In this case, the employee was a car mechanic who was learning by doing and that kind of training did not qualify (*Hapney*).

Most employers who try to impose noncompetition agreements on employees argue that the employee has become identified with the company and in a very real sense is now part of the goodwill of the company. If these employees contact the employer's customers soon after leaving, those customers might associate them with the company, which is not fair. The question then becomes whether an employee is really associated with the company in the minds of the employer's customers and, if so, how long it will take for the "goodwill glow" to wear off. In 1990, the Nebraska Supreme Court refused to enforce a noncompetition agreement because it tried to prevent the employee from soliciting or working for anyone, not just former clients of his employer. Since other people who had not done business with the employer would not be affected by the goodwill glow of this former employee, this was an unreasonable noncompetition agreement (*Vlasin*). In a Minnesota case, the employer argued that the interest it was protecting was goodwill and that it would take three years before customers no longer associated this employee with the company. The Minnesota court would enforce the agreement for only one year, believing that the goodwill glow would wear off in that time (*Dean Van Horn*). Two courts have recently ruled that if the employer has no "regular customers," there is no goodwill to protect (*Williams*; *Steamatic*).

The second major requirement is that the agreement must be reasonable as to time, area covered, and activity prevented. In 1989, the supreme courts of Virginia and North Carolina ruled that two years was a reasonable period of time (*Rector*; *Whittaker*). Generally, the employee must be prevented from working only in areas in which the employee worked for the employer (particularly if the argument is that the employee is identified with the goodwill of the company). In one recent Georgia case, the agreement tried to keep the employee from working in states that he had not worked in for the employer. The Georgia Appeals Court refused to enforce the agreement (*Kem*). An Indiana Appeals Court refused to enforce an agreement that had no geographic restriction at all (*Com. Bankers*). If the concern is goodwill, then the agreement should prevent soliciting former customers of the employer; it should not prevent the employee from working in the business "in any capacity" (*National Settlement*).

A few courts have gone further, ruling that these agreements will not be enforced if they keep employees from engaging in the only trade they know. The Alabama Supreme Court has gone the farthest down this road, ruling that the employee must be left with the ability to make a living (without having to move out of the state) before a noncompetition agreement will be enforced (*Chavers*). Needless to say, most noncompetition agreements signed by employees are not enforced in Alabama because of this requirement.

During the 1980s, the Texas Supreme Court looked as if it was about to join the Alabama Supreme Court in making it all but impossible to enforce noncompetition agreements against former employees. In 1989, the Texas legislature passed an amendment to the Texas Business and Commerce Code (subchapter E, sec. 15.50) making these agreements enforceable if they contain "reasonable limitations as to time, area, and scope of activity" and do not "impose a greater restraint than is necessary to protect the goodwill or other business interest" of the employer (*DeSantis*).

In some states, such as Montana, Nevada, North Dakota, and Oklahoma (either by statute or court decision), agreements not to compete are simply not enforceable against employees (*State Med.*; *Bayly*). In other states, statutes limit these kinds of agreements to particular groups. For example, in Colorado only "executives, managers, and professional employees" can be bound by noncompetition agreements; doctors cannot be bound (Colo. 8-2-113). In California, only owners and partners can sign legally enforceable noncompetition agreements (Cal. Bus. & Prof. Code sec. 16600 to 16602).

Many employers have stopped using traditional noncompetition agreements and have found the courts more willing to enforce more limited types of agreements. The Connecticut Supreme Court enforced an agreement that kept the leaving employee from soliciting any customers he had serviced at the old firm. The court said that this was a nonsolicitation agreement, not a noncompetition agreement, and enforced it (*Weiss*).

Employees should avoid signing noncompetition agreements if at all possible. Employers who want to have enforceable noncompetition agreements should consult an attorney.

Stock Options

Some employees are given stock options. How does a stock option work? Suppose the stock of the company is presently selling for $10 a share. The company recognizes that if the price of the shares goes up over the next five years, it will be due in part to the hard work of the employees. Suppose the employer gives the employees the option of buying a certain number of shares during the five years at $12 a share. If in five years the stock is selling for $20 a share, the employees can exercise their option, buy at $12, sell at $20, and make money.

These plans are filled with potential problems. In some states a contract for a stock option has to be in writing because it involves the sale of securities.

Also the employee may be fired before the time comes to exercise the option. In one case, the employee was fired five days before he had the right to buy stock under the stock-option plan. The Georgia Appeals Court ruled against the employee because the option plan said the option rights were granted "without restriction on the right of the company to terminate optionee's employment" (*Lowe*).

Commissions

The biggest problem with commissions comes when the sale has been made but the salesperson is fired before the goods are delivered. Should the salesperson still get the commission? To most people the answer would seem obvious. A commission is payment for making the sale and should be paid even if the salesperson is fired before delivery. It was not so obvious to many American judges until a decade ago.

In a landmark case, Mr. Fortune's contract with the National Cash Register Company called for a payment of 75 percent of the commission when he made the sale and the rest after delivery. Fortune made a $5,000,000 sale but he was fired before the machines were delivered. He sued for the rest of his commission. The Massachusetts Supreme Court ruled that in every employment contract is the implied promise from the employer to act in *good faith*. The court held that NCR could not fire Mr. Fortune just to deprive him of his commissions (*Fortune*).

This principle has come to be called the *procuring cause doctrine*, which says that employees who make the sale get the commission, even if they are fired before delivery (*Scheduling Corp.*; *Kreinz*).

Bonuses

Bonus plans can often be difficult to enforce because they are so vague. However, a fair court will not let that deter it from enforcing these plans. After all, the plan is usually vague because the employer made it that way. For example, Mr. Lessley was recruited out of college. At the 1980 job interview, the employer described his "golden handcuffs" bonus plan. He promised to set 10 percent of the income from each project aside to be distributed among the key employees. The exact distribution plan was left up to the employer. Did this make the promise too indefinite to be enforced? The Supreme Court of Kansas did not think so. The 10 percent was certain. The only question was which key employees got what part of the bonus fund. The employer had promised to distribute the bonus based on the quality and quantity of work put into each particular project. The Kansas Supreme Court said that implied here was the promise to exercise this discretion "honestly" and "faithfully." The court felt a judge and jury would be capable of figuring out what a faithful employer would do under the circumstances (*Lessley*).

Some bonus plans are tied to employee suggestions. In one Texas case, Lone Star Steel Company had a suggestion plan that said the employee would be entitled to 5 percent of whatever the company saved in a year because of the suggestion. John Scott, a brick mason, believed he could redesign the brick pits where steel is soaked to cut down on the number of times these pits would need maintenance. Throughout the 1970s he pushed his idea with management and on the day after Christmas, 1979, he was allowed to try out his design. He eventually rebuilt all of the pits. The number of pit cleanouts fell from 212 in 1979 to 62 in 1980. Three hundred thousand more tons of steel were processed during 1980, with $60 million of extra profits as a result. Ultimately Lone Star Steel decided to give John Scott nothing for his suggestion. He sued and a jury felt that $3 million was a fair reward (*Lone Star*).

Judges in fair states will enforce stock-option plans, profit-sharing plans, or bonus plans if there is any reasonable way to figure out what the employee deserves to get under the plan. Judges in pro-boss states do not work quite as hard to enforce these plans. In all states, the employees might find it worthwhile to hire an attorney to look over the plan before they work extra hard only to end up with nothing.

4

Writing and Breaking Employment Contracts

If the Employee Breaks a Written Employment Contract

What happens if an employee breaks a written employment contract by quitting before the term is up?

The Employee Cannot Be Sent to Jail

Half a century ago many states had laws, called Labor Contract Acts, which provided that employees working under a written term contract could be put in jail if they tried to quit before the term was up. The U.S. Supreme Court declared those statutes unconstitutional in 1944 (*Pollock*). From time to time, you hear on the news that a union leader has been put in jail. That relates to special laws that apply only to union leaders. No one else is going to jail for breaking a written term employment contract.

The Employee Cannot Be Ordered Back to Work

When the U.S. Supreme Court overturned the Labor Contract Acts, the Court said an employee cannot be made to choose between working and going to jail. That violates the Thirteenth Amendment's ban on involuntary servitude. When a judge orders employees back to work, they are being forced to choose between going to work or going to jail for contempt of court. A judge cannot do that. Again, special rules apply to unions. (Whether these special rules violate the Thirteenth Amendment has not been decided by the U.S. Supreme Court.)

The Employee Cannot Be Stopped from Working for Others

Most employees cannot be prevented from going to work for another employer, even though there is still time left on a written contract, unless the employee is a movie star or a famous singer. From time to time, you hear about some actor or singer who has broken a written term contract. The judge cannot order them to sing or act for the company they had originally agreed to sing or act for (that would be involuntary servitude), but the judge can order them not to sing or act for anyone else. Even the High Court of New York has agreed that a judge can do this only if the employee is "unique or extraordinary" (*ABC*). The idea is that when the employer hired this unique employee it was not just buying an employee but was also trying to deprive the competition of this unique commodity. Employees such as Olivia Newton-John or the San Diego Chicken have to worry about this. The rest of us do not (*MCA Records*; *KGB*).

The Employee Can Be Sued for Money

The employee can be sued for money, but normally not a lot of money. The employer can sue only for the money it has really lost because the employee quit before the end of the contract term. Also, the employer has a duty to mitigate damages. That means the employer has to go out and hire someone else. The employer must bargain with that new employee and pay a reasonable salary. The employer can sue for the difference between what it was paying the former employee and what it has to pay the replacement until the contract term runs out.

The employer can also sue the employee for the cost of finding a replacement. This might involve an employment-agency fee and the cost of flying in a couple of candidates for interviews. Given the high cost of lawsuits, it is almost never going to be worth it to an employer to sue an employee who has broken a written employment contract.

Once in a very great while, an employer will try to sue the employee for a lot of money, arguing that because the employee quit, the employer had to go out of business or suffered some other terrible loss (this is called consequential damages). The Tenth Circuit Court has ruled that an employer can sue an employee for these kinds of damages only if the employee is "unique or irreplaceable" (*Eckles*). Again, movie stars have to worry about this; the rest of us do not.

If the Employer Breaks a Written Employment Contract

What happens if the employer breaks a written employment contract? While employees usually break contracts by giving the employer good cause to fire them or by quitting, there are many things an employer can do that might constitute a breach of the contract.

Demotion or Reassignment

If the employer demotes or reassigns the employee, that may be enough. In a New York case, Mr. Rudman was a textbook author who ran a small publishing company. He sold his company to Cowles Communications and signed a written employment contract that put him in charge of the division that published his textbooks. When Cowles tried to put other people in charge of that division, Rudman quit and sued. The High Court of New York said that a significant reduction in rank or duties constitutes a breach of contract. Rudman had every right at that point to quit and sue for his damages (*Rudman*).

Some companies handle this problem by "promoting" people out of the way. It is not a breach of contract to give someone more money and a better title. That is why some organizations have so many vice-presidents.

Employees who have been demoted or reassigned in violation of a contract should talk to an attorney right away. If they wait for months, the judge may say that they accepted the demotion and waived their right to sue.

Do Nothing

Most people cannot sue if the employer decides to make them sit and do nothing. In a few cases the courts have said that part of what the employee bargained for was the chance to build up a reputation and the employer damaged that chance by not letting the employee work. These cases usually involve people in show business. In 1930, an actor in England was hired for the lead in a play. When the producer wanted to cast him in a smaller part, the actor sued and won (*Herbert*). A California court recognized that a radio disc jockey got more than just money from being on the air; he also increased his reputation (*Colvig*).

Employers in show business deal with this problem by putting what is called a "pay or play" clause in employment contracts. This clause says that the employer has the right to ask the employee to sit and do nothing and the employee agrees that this is acceptable. This kind of clause is now turning up in employment contracts for professionals and executives outside of show business.

es, the employee has been fired. An employer has a right to fire a ~~...... contract~~ employee if good cause exists. What constitutes good cause is not always easy to determine. If someone is incompetent or insubordinate or habitually comes to work late, most judges would consider that good cause. Beyond that it can get complicated. Mr. Schuermann was accused of (and fired for) having an affair with the wife of another employee (*Schuermann*). The district judge ruled in favor of Schuermann, finding that this was not good cause to fire someone. The South Carolina Supreme Court sent the case back for trial. There was some evidence that Schuermann's employer had specifically told him not to have "affairs inside the company." The South Carolina Supreme Court felt that the jury should decide whether the employer really told him this and, if he did, whether breaking this rule was enough to constitute good cause for dismissal.

Money Damages

Generally, an employee with a broken employment contract sues for money. There is a special rule that some courts use when an employment contract has been broken. The judge will not let the employee sue for "future lost wages," only wages that would have been earned by the time of the trial (*Lewis*).

Not all courts follow this special rule. In a case involving the breach of an employee handbook, the Michigan Supreme Court upheld an award of $100,000. Most of the money was for lost future wages (*Renny*). In another case involving the breach of an employee handbook, the Supreme Court of Nevada upheld an award of $382,000 (*K Mart*). Most of this was to compensate for lost future wages.

While the employee has a duty to look for another job (mitigate damages), he or she does not have to take any job that comes along. For example, Shirley Maclaine had a contract with Twentieth Century Fox to star in a movie musical. Fox admitted breaking the contract but argued that Shirley Maclaine had to mitigate damages by accepting their offer to star in a Western instead. The court said Shirley Maclaine did not have to accept significantly different employment and a Western is significantly different from a musical. Shirley Maclaine got the money and did not have to make the Western (*Parker*). While employees have to look for another job, they do not have to take a significantly different job or a job in a different city.

Mental Anguish

Money for lost wages is usually about all an employee who sues for breach of contract is going to get. In rare cases, employees may receive damages for mental anguish if they can prove that they really suffered anguish and that the employer was "willful or wanton" in breaking the contract (*Hoffsetz*). Courts are generally willing to find the behavior willful or wanton if the employer acted not out of business necessity but simply to harm the employee.

In 1991, a Colorado Appeals Court upheld an award of $250,000 for mental anguish damages. The discharge procedures set out in the handbook were not followed, and the employee was not allowed to personally discuss her termination with her employer. The court felt that this constituted a willful, wanton, and "insulting" breach of contract (*Allabashi*).

Punitive Damages

In many states, punitive damages are never awarded in breach-of-contract cases. That is not the case in all states. In a recent California case, the jury awarded $8 million in punitive damages to Raquel Welch. Ms. Welch had been fired from the movie *Cannery Row* in an attempt to make her the scapegoat for the problems that the movie company was having making the movie. The jury felt that that kind of behavior should be punished (*Welch #2*). In a 1991 Vermont case, the employer made false allegations against a fired employee in an effort to avoid paying the severance bonus required by the written employment contract. The bonus did not have to be paid if the employee was fired for cause. The jury awarded $200,000 in punitive damages, and the Vermont Supreme Court upheld the award (*Ainsworth*).

Reinstatement

A contract employee is almost never going to get a court to order the employer to give the employee his or her job back.

Stipulated Damage Clauses

As you can see, it is often hard to figure out what the employee has lost by being fired and what the employer has lost if the employee quits. Because of this, a clause is often put in the contract that spells out how much each side has to pay if they break the contract. This is called a stipulated damage clause. The amount specified has to be a realistic estimate of what the real damages will be. It cannot be a penalty used to punish the person breaking the contract.

Employees would like a clause that says the employer has to pay the rest of the salary called for in the contract. Courts, at least those in fair states, will enforce a clause like this. In one case, the Wisconsin Supreme Court enforced a clause that required the employer to pay the rest of the salary to the employee. The court said that because of this clause, the employee did not have to mitigate damages by getting another job. Because the real damages to the employee, including damage to reputation and mental anguish, are hard to calculate, the court felt that this was a reasonable estimate of damages (*Wassenaar*).

Quantum Meruit

In a few cases, it turns out that there is no enforceable contract. The court will still make the employer pay the employee the reasonable value of his or her services for any work the employee has actually performed. This is called *quantum meruit*, which is Latin meaning "the value of the work." Once the employee has done work, the employer has to pay, even if the contract turns out to be unenforceable.

In one case, a young dentist worked for an older dentist. The employment contract ran out in 1980 but the young dentist continued to work until 1982. The court awarded the young dentist money for the reasonable value of his services using *quantum meruit* (*Johnston*).

Writing an Employment Contract

Having read this chapter, both employers and employees are in a position to write an employment contract. Both should consult an attorney before signing any employment contract. Anyone writing an employment contract should follow the rules given here.

1. *Never Copy an Employment Contract out of a Book.* On several occasions an employee has come to me with a written employment contract that was very favorable to the employer. The employee had copied the contract out of a book, and both employer and employee had signed it without reading it. A sample contract will be provided at the end of this chapter that was written to favor the employee, but even that contract should not be blindly copied. This is one time when you can pay a little for an attorney now or a lot for an attorney later.

   The same advice goes double for employers. For example, in one case the employer copied a noncompetition agreement out of a book and had the employee sign it (*Riffert*). There was nothing in this agreement about a geographical limit. Apparently, it kept the employee from competing anywhere in the world. Even the pro-boss judges in Pennsylvania would not enforce a noncompetition agreement like that.

2. *Write the Contract in Plain English.* Both employers and employees are generally going to be better off with plain English. Most legal mumbo jumbo has been twisted over the last century to favor employers, and is now being twisted again to compensate for this bias. The result is that both parties will generally be better off avoiding legal mumbo jumbo altogether. If either side does not understand what an employment contract means, it should be rewritten. Otherwise, a lot of judges simply will not enforce it. On the other hand, if the contract is written in plain English, California judges will enforce it even if it means the employee loses, and Delaware judges will enforce it even if it means the employee wins.

3. *Make Sure the Four Basic Terms Are Covered.* The four basic terms of an employment contract are time, service, compensation, and location. Make sure your contract says how long it is going to run. Generally, both parties will be better off if the contract runs for a definite number of years. You have seen that in some states if the contract is not for a definite term, the court will not enforce it. The contract should spell out what the employee is going to do and what the employer is going to pay. The place where the work will be done should also be specified in the contract.

4. *Consider Integration Clauses Carefully.* An integration clause says that the written agreement is the entire agreement and supersedes all prior agreements, either written or oral. In some situations, the employee may want to put in an antiintegration clause that says: *This is not the entire agreement of the parties. All prior written and oral statements made by the employer or his representatives are also a part of this contract.*

5. *Consider Arbitration Clauses Carefully.* Many employment contracts have an arbitration clause that says the parties will submit any disagreement about the contract to an arbitrator. Generally, employers like arbitration clauses; employees do not.

6. *If Profits Are Supposed to Be Shared, Get an Attorney.* If the contract is simple, you may be able to write it yourself. If the employee is supposed to get part of the profit, a stock option, complicated commissions, special bonuses, or anything else that will be difficult to calculate, both sides should get an attorney. This is another situation in which both employers and employees can pay a little for an attorney now or a lot for an attorney later.

7. *Be Exact whenever Possible.* Avoid using vague phrases. If you know the exact day the employment is to begin and the exact amount of the salary, put it in the contract.

8. *Consider a Stipulated Damage Clause.* You have seen that a stipulated damage clause can help when the contract is broken and it is difficult to figure out what the real damages are. Consider putting a stipulated damage clause in the contract.

9. *Consider a Choice of Law Clause.* A choice of law clause says the contract will be interpreted under the legal doctrines of a particular state. If an employee is going to put a stipulated damage clause in, he or she may want to say that the law of Wisconsin will be used to interpret the contract, because the Wisconsin Supreme Court has approved the use of these kinds of clauses in employment contracts. Which state employers should pick will depend on the kinds of clauses that they put in the contract.

Now we shall see a sample contract that favors the employee. It is a contract for a fictitious client who is supposed to be a computer genius and has a number of special concerns.

The contract is written using the pronouns *I* and *you*, and those pronouns are defined at the beginning. A contract written this way is easy to read. You will notice that the contract uses the word *shall* a lot. The word *shall* in a legal document means something must be done.

You will also see a special sentence in the contract that says the employee is not "unique." You have learned that bad things can happen to "unique" employees.

There is a sentence that requires the employer to pay if the employee gets sued because of his work. That is called *indemnification*.

Also included is a requirement that if one side has to complete a trial and wins, the other side has to pay the attorney fees. This can be dealt with in a number of ways. This client wanted to deal with it this way.

It is usually best, if one party to a contract has a right, to give it to the other party as well. Remember, we may have to convince a judge that this is a fair contract. Giving a right to both sides helps us do that.

Remember the problem of authority. It is best to get the signature of the chairman of the board, with a statement from the secretary of the corporation that the board of directors voted to authorize that signature. In most employment situations, that is not going to happen. The signature of the president of the corporation will usually be sufficient in most situations.

The law does not require notarization or witnesses. However, in some states, if the contract is notarized it can be filed in the county records and acts as a lien on the employer's property to guarantee the payment of wages under the contract. Your attorney will advise you on this. Also, it never hurts to have a contract signed by witnesses.

A Sample Employment Contract

In this employment contract, the pronoun *you* refers to XXX Corporation, a Delaware corporation with its principal office in New York. The pronouns *I* and *me* refer to Fred Smoot, an individual residing at XXX St., Austin, Texas. The pronouns *we* and *us* refer to both the XXX Corporation and Fred Smoot.

I. EMPLOYMENT

You agree to employ me as a computer researcher. I agree to work for you as a computer researcher.

II. TERM

You shall employ me for five (5) years beginning on May 1, 1989, and ending on April 30, 1994.

III. DUTIES

I shall be a computer researcher. I shall do research into advanced computer architectures.

You shall furnish me with a private office above the first floor that has at least two hundred (200) square feet of space. This office will also have a window to the outside of at least nine (9) square feet.

You shall allow me access to the office twenty-four (24) hours a day.

You shall not impose any dress code on me or restrict me to certain working hours. I shall do a reasonable amount of work at the office if that is possible. You shall allow me to work at home when that is necessary because you have allowed too many distractions to interfere with my work at the office.

I shall not divulge any trade secrets to anyone without your permission. You will tell me when something I am working with is a trade secret.

IV. COMPENSATION

You shall pay me one hundred thousand dollars ($100,000) a year. You shall pay me in bimonthly installments on the first day and the fifteenth day of each month.

V. FRINGE BENEFITS

You shall provide me with fringe benefits equal to what you provide to other employees doing similar work. At a minimum you will provide me with medical insurance that pays for all medical expenses over five hundred dollars ($500) in any one year. If I am injured or disabled, you will pay me my full salary until I recover or Social Security begins paying me benefits. If I am sick you will pay me my full salary until I recover. The injury, disability, or illness does not have to be job-related.

You will provide me with a defined-contribution retirement fund. You shall take ten percent (10%) of my salary every paycheck, match that amount with company funds, and deposit the entire amount into my retirement fund. The fund shall be administered by a financial institution that is mutually agreeable to both of us. This fund will meet the requirements of the Internal Revenue Service so the amount taken out of my paycheck is not taxable as income to me. This retirement fund will vest, completely, immediately upon deposit.

VI. EXPENSE REIMBURSEMENT

You shall allow me to incur reasonable business expenses. You shall provide me with a company American Express card so that I do not have to do more than a reasonable amount of paperwork in accounting for these expenses. You shall allow me to attend at least three (3) computer conferences during each year of this contract. You shall reimburse me for the expenses involved in going to these conferences.

You shall reimburse me for all reasonable moving expenses I incur because I must move to your Dallas office. You shall not transfer me from the Dallas office without my express written permission. If I do agree to a transfer, you shall reimburse me for those moving expenses as well.

You shall indemnify me. You shall pay for all damages and attorney's fees that result from any lawsuits that arise out of my employment with you.

You shall allow me to present papers at computer conferences and universities. I shall keep any income I derive from these presentations. The time I spend attending conferences and presenting papers shall not be deducted from my vacation or personal leave.

You shall reimburse me for all business travel expenses. You shall send me on business trips only with my permission. I shall decide how much I travel, where I travel, what form of transportation I take, and where I stay when I travel.

VII. VACATION AND PERSONAL LEAVE

You shall allow me four (4) weeks' vacation for each year of this contract. I shall decide when to take my vacation. I do not have to give you advance notice of when I plan to take a vacation.

You shall allow me ten (10) normal working days as personal leave for each year of this contract. Personal days are days that I may take off to take care of personal business.

I shall be eligible for my vacation and personal leave from the first day I work for you.

You shall allow me to take off any days that are official holidays of the corporation. These days will not count as vacation or personal-leave days. At a minimum, official holidays will include: Christmas Day, New Year's Day, the Fourth of July, Labor Day, Memorial Day, Thanksgiving Day, and the day after Thanksgiving Day.

All unused vacation and personal-leave days shall carry over to the following years. You shall pay me my full salary for any vacation days I have not used when this contract ends.

VIII. TERMINATION

You may terminate my employment for good cause only. Only a judge and jury shall determine if I actually did what you accuse me of. Only a judge shall determine if my actions are good cause for termination. What you think I did and what you think constitutes good cause are irrelevant.

I may terminate this contract if you give me good cause to do so. I shall have good cause to terminate this contract if you merge or consolidate with another company.

You shall not require me to take any physical or mental examination. You shall not require me to take a drug test, a lie detector test, or any other test.

IX. STIPULATED DAMAGES

We both agree that the actual damages in a breach of contract case will be difficult to ascertain. Both of us may suffer damage to our reputations. It will be difficult to ascertain whether I get a comparable job or you have recruited a comparable employee. The expenses I incur in searching for another job, and you incur in recruiting a replacement, will be difficult to ascertain. Because of this we agree that the following stipulated damages are fair and reasonable. If I break this contact I shall pay you five thousand dollars ($5,000) to compensate you in full for your damages. If you break this contract you shall pay me the salary that remains to be paid under the terms of this contract. You shall not have to continue to provide me with fringe benefits or put money into the retirement fund.

X. BREACH OF CONTRACT

If for some reason a court will not enforce the stipulated-damages clause, then we both agree that our remedy will be limited to money damages. Neither you nor I shall ask for an injunction or court order of any kind. If either of us has to complete a trial because the other party has breached this contract, then the losing party shall pay the attorney's fees for the winning party.

You and I agree that I am not unique or irreplaceable. Other people are capable of doing my job.

XI. ASSIGNMENT

Neither you nor I can assign this contract without first obtaining the other's written permission. You agree that the president of the corporation has authority to act for the corporation in all things that relate to this contract.

XII. GOVERNING LAW

Both of us agree that Wisconsin law shall be used to interpret this contract.

XIII. CONCLUSION

This contract supersedes all other agreements between you and me. This contract contains our entire agreement.

Neither you nor I shall amend or alter this contract without the written permission of the other party.

If a court decides any of the provisions in this contract are void or not enforceable, the other provisions shall remain valid.

It shall not be a waiver if you or I fail to sue because of a breach of this contract. We may sue later for that breach or any other breach.

The titles in this contract serve only as a guide to the reader. They are not part of the substance of this agreement.

DATE—YOUR SIGNATURE—MY SIGNATURE

Employer Alterations

An employer would probably remove some of the items concerned with office size and fringe benefits. An employer would probably ask that stipulated damages be the same amount for both parties and might require disputes over the contract to be handled by arbitration. An employer who wants to add special clauses concerned with trade secrets, patents, copyrights, and competition should consult an attorney.

PART
TWO

RIGHTS AFTER
BEING FIRED

5

Unemployment Compensation

The Past

After the Great Depression, many economists felt that America needed a program to provide temporarily unemployed workers with money so that consumer spending would not drop drastically and recessions would not turn into depressions.

The Social Security Act of 1935 set up a federal unemployment compensation system. "Oh no," people cried, "not another giant federal bureaucracy!" In response to this outcry, the federal government agreed to waive most of the federal unemployment tax in any state that set up its own unemployment system. Every state did just that. The focus at the time was on a national depression that had hit every state. No one was looking to a time in the 1980s when some states would go through severe recessions while other states would have booming economies.

Employees versus Independent Contractors

Throughout this book the distinction between employees and independent contractors is important. Employees are covered by unemployment compensation, worker's compensation, and federal and state wage, hour, and labor laws. Independent contractors are not. The test used to decide whether someone is an employee or an independent contractor changed during the 1980s in response to employers who tried to stretch the concept of independent contractor too far. The old test, which looked to a variety of factors such as whether or not the person brought personal tools and the amount of supervision the person was subject to, led to some ridiculous cases in the late 1980s.

A 1987 case involved Cathy Adler, whose duties at the Lonely Lady Club included working an eight-hour shift, six days a week. During her working hours, Adler was required to dance three times for about 15 minutes each time, and was also expected to solicit private dances and drinks. Her employer argued that she was an independent contractor (she brought her own "tools" and most of her pay was in the form of tips), but the Alaska Supreme Court disagreed, finding her to be an employee (*Jeffcoat*).

In a 1988 case, a crab-packing company argued that its employees were really independent contractors because they brought their own tools (a crab knife) and worked under minimal supervision. The Fifth Circuit Court found them to be employees and declared that from then on a new test would be used. The question would no longer be whether workers brought their own tools or worked under minimal supervision. The question would be: Are the workers really in business for themselves? Do they work for a lot of different people and are they really specialists who are called in to solve a special problem? If the answer is no, then they are employees, not independent contractors (*Seafood*). In 1989, the California and Idaho supreme courts adopted the same test in cases involving cucumber pickers and dog handlers who brought their own tools and worked under minimal supervision. The courts found them to be employees (*Borello*; *Partello*).

This new test has been called the "relative nature of the work" test, but it might better be called the "are they really independent entrepreneurs" test. A 1990 Missouri case involved a group of people who put up siding on houses. They did 80 percent of their work for one company, and their business would not have survived without that work. The Missouri Appeals Court said the new test is: Are the workers engaged in an entrepreneurial enterprise with a degree of economic independence such that the business could survive without any relationship with this particular company? The answer was no, so they were employees (*McDonald #2*). In 1991, the Illinois Supreme Court said that before someone could be considered an independent contractor they must: (1) work outside the employer's control; (2) work outside the employer's usual business; and (3) be engaged in an independent profession (*Bradley #2*). If all three conditions are not met, the workers are employees, not independent contractors.

State Unemployment Compensation Programs

While every state has to meet minimum federal standards, there are differences from state to state. You will want to contact your state unemployment agency with any specific questions you may have. Throughout this chapter we are talking about the "average" state unemployment system.

Calculating Benefits

The amount an unemployed worker is entitled to receive every week is determined in a bizarre way. Suppose the worker is laid off in April 1989. Most states do not look at what he or she earned during the last full quarter of work (January to March), but look instead to the four quarters before the last full quarter. In this case that would be the four quarters of 1988. This four-quarter period is called the Base Period. Of these four quarters in the Base Period, the quarter with the highest wages is chosen. Let's suppose our fictional worker earned $4,000 during the best quarter in the Base Period. Divide this amount by 25 to get $160. That is our fictional worker's basic weekly compensation payment. The worker receives his or her best quarter of wages spread out over 25 weeks. There is a maximum weekly amount that differs from state to state. Some states require the worker to have earned a certain total amount over the entire Base Period to be eligible to receive compensation at all. Other states require the worker to have earned a minimum amount of money a week for a minimum number of weeks to be entitled to compensation. Weeks spent on sick leave count toward this total (*Lopata*; *Wiersma*).

Most agencies take a percentage of the total amount of wages earned during the entire Base Period, usually 27 percent. That is the maximum the agency will pay out to a worker in unemployment compensation.

The amount of unemployment compensation depends on the amount of wages the worker earned while working. Even meals and lodging provided by the employer count as wages for calculating benefits (*Vermont Camping*).

The purpose of the unemployment compensation system is to keep consumer spending up and to provide financial help to people who are temporarily unemployed. If a worker has been fired but has income from other sources such as a pension, complex rules determine whether he or she can collect unemployment compensation.

Who Can Get Benefits

People who quit usually cannot get unemployment compensation. There is an exception that we will discuss in a moment, but don't count on it. An employee about to quit should consider consulting an attorney first. In some states, a worker who quits is disqualified from receiving unemployment compensation until he or she has worked for another employer for a certain period of time, usually six weeks. But there are exceptions to this. For example, the

Ohio statute said if the worker quits to take another job and starts the new job within one week of quitting, the worker has to work only three weeks at the new job to be eligible for compensation. In one case the employee worked two weeks and received one week's severance pay. The Ohio Supreme Court, following the rule that these statutes are to be liberally interpreted, held that the severance pay counted and the employee had worked the required three weeks (*Radcliffe*).

While almost every worker in the United States is covered by unemployment compensation insurance, a few are not. In some states, people who work for religious organizations are not covered. In many states, agricultural workers are not covered.

Some years ago an enterprising teacher filed for unemployment compensation during summer vacation. That caused most states to amend their statutes. Today, in most states, if teachers have "reasonable assurance of employment" for the coming school year, they cannot get unemployment compensation during the summer. They do not have to have a signed employment contract.

What if the teacher has been fired but is getting paychecks during the summer because he or she had the pay spread out over the summer? The Ohio Supreme Court held that a teacher who was receiving delayed paychecks during the summer, and who had no reasonable assurance of employment for the fall, was entitled to receive unemployment compensation during the summer (*Cook #2*).

Generally, substitute teachers who work from day to day are entitled to unemployment compensation during school vacation periods (*Soliman*; *Hopewell*).

Extended Benefits

There are several provisions for extending benefits beyond the usual 25 weeks. If unemployment in the state reaches a certain level, people on unemployment may be entitled to extended benefits. Also, the Federal Trade Act of 1974 (19 U.S.C. sec. 2101) allows employees who have been laid off because of foreign competition to receive extended benefits. These employees may also be entitled to money to help them retrain for another occupation (*Poll*; *Jones #2*).

Denial of Benefits

There are three main reasons why people are denied unemployment compensation benefits: they were discharged for misconduct; they quit without cause; or they are unemployed because of a labor dispute.

Discharged for Misconduct

Most unemployment compensation statutes deny benefits to anyone who is discharged for misconduct. Whether an employee engaged in a kind of misconduct that disqualifies him or her from getting unemployment compensation is the subject of most unemployment compensation hearings.

Incompetence is not misconduct. Making mistakes or not having the necessary job skills is not misconduct. However, if the employee has demonstrated an ability to perform in the past and stops performing competently, that would be misconduct. Also, if the employee lied on a job application, causing the employer to think the employee had the necessary job skills, that would also constitute misconduct (*Zadworny*; *Northwest Foods*; *Attisano*).

Negligence is not misconduct. In one case, the employee was fired after having three accidents in five months. The Pennsylvania Appeals Court ruled that this was not misconduct because there was no evidence of a "conscious disregard of the employer's interests" (*Colonial Taxi*). A Washington Appeals Court explained that intentional or deliberate actions are required for misconduct to be present. An employee who had an accident because he was preoccupied with personal problems was not guilty of misconduct (*Darnielle*).

Many cases involve the use of obscene language by employees. The general rule is that one incident of vulgarity is not enough to constitute misconduct. Courts in Oregon and Minnesota have ruled that one isolated incident of vulgarity ("I've had enough of this shit") or hothead behavior (throwing the hammer on the ground) is not misconduct (*Bunnell*; *McCoy*). However, if the one incident is directed toward a supervisor or customer, it may be seen as misconduct (*Dye*; *Myers*). Courts usually look to the surrounding circumstances to see if the vulgarity was justified or provoked. In one case, Sara Kowal was put in a room with two other employees and yelled at by her supervisor. When the supervisor finally asked her if she liked her job, she threw a writing tablet at him and told him to "shove it up his ass." The Pennsylvania Appeals Court did not think that, given these circumstances, this was misconduct. The judges felt that "forty-five minutes of harassment" by the supervisor constituted "justifiable provocation" for Ms. Kowal's behavior (*Kowal*).

The issue with absences is usually whether the employee had a reasonable excuse. Being late to work because of heavy traffic or missing work because of illness is not misconduct (*Mendez*; *Manatawny Manor*).

Failure to obey reasonable employer rules is usually considered misconduct. These cases run the gambit from falsifying time cards to spitting on the floor and from sleeping on the job to threatening to shoot a co-worker (*Burlington*; *Bowers*; *Grant*; *Thompson #2*).

On the other hand, refusing to settle a worker's compensation claim, disputing the ownership of an invention with the employer, having wages repeatedly garnished, or defending against attack by a co-worker is not misconduct (*Dunkle*; *BMY*; *Great Plains*; *Peeples*).

Some of the cases would seem silly were it not for the fact that someone's unemployment compensation hung in the balance. In one case, Kristen Hurst was fired because she ate some cookies that were about to be thrown away. The court said Hurst had not engaged in misconduct. Taking something of no value is not theft (*Hurst*).

One female employee was subjected to so much verbal and physical abuse by a co-worker that she grabbed a 25-pound roast beef and threw it at him (they worked in a meat market). The New Jersey Appeals Court found this to be a spontaneous reaction to "persistent, unremitting, and sexually offensive" behavior, not a deliberate attack, and therefore not misconduct (*Demech*).

Just breaking the employer's rules in not enough. As one court said, if it were, "then the employer would need only to establish rules so complex or so strict that any employee would ultimately fail to live up to every provision" (*Safety Med.*). The rules must be reasonable and generally enforced.

Employers often get themselves into trouble by having handbooks that list what is considered misconduct and what discipline procedure the employer intends to follow. In a Pennsylvania case, the employer did not follow its own discipline procedure so the employee got unemployment compensation (*Brady*). In an Indiana case, the particular offense was not listed on the "discharge causing" list in the company handbook so the court awarded unemployment compensation (*Cablevision*).

A few states make a distinction between gross misconduct and regular misconduct, with the employee losing only a few weeks of unemployment compensation if the misconduct is not "gross" enough (Ala. 25-4-78; Alaska 23.20.379; Md. Labor Code sec. 8-1001; W. Va. sec. 21A-6-3).

In most cases, the courts are not enforcing some esoteric legal doctrine. Misconduct means what most people think it means in the circumstances. Employers and employees who use a little common sense should not have any problem. See Table 5.1 for a summary of what is and is not misconduct in most states.

Off-Duty Behavior

The biggest problem for many courts at the end of the 1980s was the extent to which off-duty behavior constitutes misconduct. The general rule is that employers are not gods and cannot expect to control their employees' lives both at work and away from the workplace. In a 1989 case, the New Mexico Supreme Court ruled that having purple hair was not misconduct. The em-

Table 5.1 What Is Misconduct?

Is Misconduct	Is Not Misconduct
Failure to perform work after having demonstrated ability to do the work	Incompetence; genuine inability to do the work
Deliberate damage to equipment; willful failure to follow safety rules	Accidents; negligence; errors that are not the result of reckless conduct
Unreasonable or excessive use of obscene language in violation of employer's rules	Isolated incident using obscene language
Excessive and unjustified absences and tardiness; failure to inform supervisor	Justified absences and tardiness
Lying; stealing; using equipment without permission of supervisor	Age; physical condition; illness; pregnancy
Failure to obey reasonable rules and follow reasonable orders	Failure to obey unreasonable rules and follow unreasonable orders
Unjustified assault on co-worker or supervisor	Justified assault on co-worker; self-defense
Spending too much time socializing at work after being told not to	Associating with co-workers or marrying co-worker in violation of employer's rules
Refusal to work on the weekend	Refusal to work on the employee's Sabbath day

ployee worked at a fast-food restaurant and none of the customers had complained (*Apodaca*).

Many of the recent cases involve drugs and alcohol. One employer had a rule against any off-duty consumption of alcohol, drugs, or tobacco. When the employee was seen consuming alcohol off-duty, he was fired. The Indiana Appeals Court said that the off-duty conduct must be shown to have a direct effect on work. The employer did not prove any effect on work in this case so the employee received unemployment compensation (*Best Lock*).

The difficult question has been whether simply flunking a drug test is misconduct. The general answer is that a drug test only reveals off-duty conduct, and there must be proof that the off-duty conduct (drug taking) has an effect on the workplace. That is what the Kansas Supreme Court said in 1989 when the employer fired the employee simply for flunking a drug test. Because there was no reason to believe that the employee was impaired at the time, there was no misconduct (*National Gypsum*). This has been difficult for many employers to understand. If someone smokes one marijuana "joint" on Saturday, that person is going to flunk a drug test on Monday. However, there is no reason to believe that the very small amount of "drugs" left in the blood is going to impair the person's work performance any more than drinking a beer on Saturday would impair one's work performance on Monday. Courts in Oklahoma, Oregon, Virginia, and Louisiana have come to the same conclusion as the Kansas Supreme Court and have ruled that simply flunking a drug test without evidence of an effect on work is not misconduct (*Grace Drilling*; *Veneer*; *Blake*; *Marine Drill*). In 1991, a Utah Appeals Court ruled that simply smoking marijuana away from work was not misconduct (*Swider*).

Of course, in some jobs any amount of drugs in the blood could be seen as misconduct. The Nevada Supreme Court felt that one employer was justified in firing an employee who flunked a drug test even though the amount of drugs in the blood was very low. The employer manufactured explosives (*Clevenger*).

The same rule applies to alcohol. Simply having some alcohol in the blood is not enough. There must be evidence that the level of alcohol was so high that it would impair work performance. If there is no evidence that work was affected, there is no misconduct (*Longmont*; *Keay*).

Quitting without Cause

The general rule is that people who quit their jobs do not get unemployment compensation. However, there is an exception in most states. If the employee has a good enough reason to quit, he or she can still get unemployment compensation. The states do not always agree on what is a good enough reason, but there are some general principles (see Table 5.2).

If the employer changes the duties of the employee, that may be a good enough reason to quit. Mr. Shingles was hired to be the pharmacist in a store near his home. Eventually the employer made him a floater, which required him to work at 12 different stores. On some days he had to commute 90 miles. Shingles quit, and the court allowed him to receive unemployment compensation. The court felt that this was enough of a "substantial unilateral change in employment" by the employer to justify giving unemployment compensation to the employee (*Shingles*). In other cases, the courts ruled that a nurse who was demoted with a substantial reduction in pay had good reason to quit, as did a museum curator who quit rather than take the two half-time clerical jobs offered by the employer (*Ponderosa Villa*; *Holbrook*).

Not all "unilateral changes" in working conditions justify quitting. A temporary reduction in pay while the workplace is being renovated, not getting a big enough raise, and not being willing to commute to the new plant location are all not good enough (*Rodeen*; *LaBlanc*; *Lee*).

Some courts seem particularly willing to find good cause for quitting when the employer has gone back on a promise to the employee. An Indiana

Appeals Court felt that not living up to the promise to train, promote, and give a raise to the employee justified quitting (*Gathering*). In another case, the employee took the job only because of the promise of eight hours a week of overtime work. When the employer failed to live up to that promise, the employee quit and the Minnesota Appeals Court allowed him to receive unemployment compensation (*Danielson Mobil*).

Most courts will allow employees to quit to protect their health and safety. The High Court in Maryland allowed a teacher to quit because he was being harassed mercilessly by a gang of students (*Paynter*). Quitting because the draft from the air conditioner caused sinus headaches was good enough in another case. The employer refused to let the employee move her desk to avoid the draft (*Goettler*).

The battle between smokers and nonsmokers causes problems. In one case, the court allowed an employee with allergic bronchitis to quit rather than work around people who smoked cigarettes (*Lapham*).

Generally, the employee must have a real health or safety problem, must inform the employer about the problem, and must be available to work if the employer corrects the problem (*Allen #2*).

Employees can quit rather than endure sexual or racial harassment. In most cases, the employee should report the harassment to upper management and give them a chance to correct the problem before quitting (*St. Barnabas*; *Umbarger*). If the supervisor is doing the harassing, this may not be necessary. Both New Jersey and Minnesota appeals courts have allowed women who were sexually harassed by their supervisors to quit without going to upper management first (*Doering*; *Heaser*). Employees who cause racial or sexual harassment are generally considered to have committed misconduct and are therefore not entitled to unemployment compensation (*Reitmeyer*).

As noted earlier, some states require someone who has quit to take another job to work at that new job for a minimum number of weeks before being entitled to unemployment compensation. Not all states feel that way. Alice Brennan quit to take a new job only to have the new employer change his mind and not hire her. The Pennsylvania Appeals Court ruled that the promise of a better job was good cause to quit and allowed her to receive unemployment compensation. The Idaho and Vermont supreme courts ruled the same way recently in similar cases (*Brennan*; *Schafer*; *Howard*).

Most states say the reason for quitting must be related to the job. Personal reasons do not qualify. This is illustrated by a 1987 U.S. Supreme Court decision concerning pregnant women. The Court ruled that a state does not have to give preferential treatment to pregnant women. If a woman has to quit her job because of pregnancy, a state is free to deny her unemployment compensation because the reason for quitting was personal and not job-related (*Wimberly*).

Table 5.2   What Is Good Cause to Quit?

The employer has significantly changed the employee's duties or compensation.

The employer has gone back on a promise made to the employee when the
   employee was hired.

The job is endangering the employee's health or safety.

The employee is the victim of sexual, religious, or racial harassment.

While most states will not allow an employee to quit for personal reasons, every state is different. Employees should consider consulting an attorney before giving up. They may find that there is a special provision in their state that applies to their situation. For example, the Washington statute allows people to quit because of domestic responsibilities. In one case the Washington Supreme Court allowed a person to collect unemployment compensation because she quit to move in with her new spouse (*Yamavchi*).

Sometimes it is hard to tell whether the employee quit or was fired. In one case the employee gave his two-week notice and the employer decided to go ahead and fire him before the two weeks were up. The court said the employee had been fired and was thus entitled to unemployment compensation (*Westport*). In another case the employer said, "How would you like to leave here?" and the employee replied, "Sounds like a wonderful idea." The court said that employee had quit and was not entitled to unemployment compensation (*Keast*). This can be particularly difficult when the employee resigns and then tries to take back the resignation. In one case Richard Nichols wrote a memorandum that said he would resign effective January 2, 1985, unless there was a change in management. There was a change in management but the employer would not let him take back his resignation. The court said the resignation was conditional, and since the condition happened, he had not resigned, he had been fired (*Nichols*). In another case the employee tried to revoke the letter of resignation before the deadline but the employer would not let him. The court said that an employee can revoke a resignation anytime before the actual date of separation unless the employer has taken real steps to replace the worker (*Pa. Labor*).

Unemployed because of a Labor Dispute

Most unemployment compensation statutes have some provision concerning people who are unemployed because of a "work stoppage" or "labor dispute." Often whether or not the employee gets unemployment compensation depends on how the court interprets these phrases. The Indiana Appeals Court said that once the strikers make an unconditional offer to return to work, the "labor dispute" is over; if the employer does not take them back, they can collect unemployment compensation (*Allen*). The Vermont and Maryland supreme courts have ruled that during a strike or lockout the key question is whether or not there has been a "stoppage of work," which means that if the factory is still producing, the strikers get their unemployment compensation; if it is shut down, they do not (*Sinai Hosp.*; *Pfenning*).

In Pennsylvania, the rule is that employees who are on strike do not get unemployment compensation, but employees who are locked out do. It is not always easy to know which is which. When 22,000 employees of the Philadelphia School District walked off the job, the Unemployment Compensation Board said it was a strike and refused to pay them unemployment compensation. The Pennsylvania Supreme Court said it was a lockout because the school district had refused to live up to the union contract (*Odgers*).

The Duty to Be Available for and Seek Suitable Work

One of the purposes of unemployment compensation is to give an unemployed worker time to find a job that matches his or her skill level. Society is not really well served if skilled workers are forced by necessity to take the first menial job that comes along. At the same time, unemployed workers have to look for work. They cannot just sit around and do nothing, or spend their time on personal projects. One worker spent 40 hours a week remodeling his parent's home. The court ruled that spending full time on a project like that did not constitute "being available for work." He did not get compensation (*Bergstedt*).

Some courts say that the employee has to be "attached to the labor force." That means ready, willing, and able to work. Workers who are not mentally, emotionally, or physically able to work are not entitled to unemployment compensation. Unemployment insurance is not temporary disability insurance (*Kuna*; *Taylor*).

What kind of job is suitable? is often the key question. It depends on the worker's training and experience, the location of possible jobs, and the probability that the employee will actually find work in his or her usual occupation. Three cases involving teachers illustrate the point. One teacher refused to accept a substitute-teacher position that paid 40 percent less than her previous job. Another teacher refused to take a 10-hour-a-week position as a part-time tutor. Yet another refused to look for any kind of work other than teaching, even though it was during the summer. In each case, the courts said the teacher was within her rights to refuse work of lesser skill and pay (*Eddings*; *Simpson #2*; *DaSilva*).

Persons can go to college and get unemployment compensation. The key is whether they are reasonably available for work. Often, if the workers had managed to go to college and work before being laid off, they will get unemployment compensation. Of course, they must be "available for work" and "actively seeking work." In one case, the worker was enrolled in school from 8:00 A.M. to noon. He contacted three or four employers a week and was willing to quit school if he found a job. The New Hampshire Supreme Court ruled that he was entitled to receive unemployment compensation (*Blanchard*).

Unemployment Taxes

Employers pay taxes into the unemployment system based on the wages they pay out and the amount of money the unemployment compensation agency has to pay to their former employees. That gives employers an incentive to keep former employees from getting unemployment compensation payments.

Income Taxes

The money a worker receives as unemployment compensation is subject to federal income tax. The unemployment compensation agency will not withhold any money for the IRS, so remember to save for April 15th.

Claims Procedure

To file a claim, the first thing employees have to do is go to the unemployment agency and fill out a form. The employees should take their Social Security card and identification with them. They will usually have to appear in person to file the initial claim. Employees should take the name and address of every employer that they have worked for during the last couple of years. To most unemployment agencies "fired" means "fired for misconduct"; so when they ask, do not say you were fired, say you were laid off.

The agency will contact the last employer to hear the other side of the story. Then the agency will make an initial determination. Once the initial determination has been made, the loser can ask for a hearing. It is your responsibility to find out what the deadlines are and follow them. If the notice says you have 12 days to appeal, that usually means 12 days from the time the agency mailed the notice, weekends included (calendar days, not workdays).

Both sides should consider getting an attorney to represent them. If the question is whether the employee quit or was fired, the burden is on the employer to prove that the employee quit. If the employee was fired, the burden is on the employer to prove that the employee was guilty of misconduct. If the employee quit, the burden is on the employee to prove he or she had a good reason to quit. Waiting too long after the good reason came up may cost the employee the case. If the employer waited too long to fire the employee after the misconduct, it may cost the employer the case (*Green #2*; *Curtis*; *Vernon*).

One reason for getting an attorney is that some states, such as Pennsylvania, will not allow hearsay evidence to be admitted at the hearing if it is objected to. Hearsay means *hear* and *say*. If someone is testifying to something someone else said, it is hearsay. The purpose of a hearing is to allow the hearing officer to see the witnesses and listen to the cross-examination. He or she cannot see someone who is not there, and there can be no cross-examination of an absent witness. Anytime the other side wants to admit a piece of paper as evidence, you should object. That is hearsay. A piece of paper cannot be cross-examined. We would like to have the person who wrote whatever is on the piece of paper at the hearing. There are all kinds of exceptions to the hearsay rule but you cannot be expected to learn them. Just object to anything that looks like hearsay.

The Pennsylvania courts are very strict about this rule. In one case the employer did not show up at the hearing; he sent a written statement instead. Because that was just hearsay, the employee won (*Vann*). In another case, a teacher had been fired for alleged improper conduct. The school board had held a hearing and wanted to submit the transcript of that hearing as evidence at the unemployment compensation hearing. The court said that the transcript could not be considered because it was hearsay and had been properly objected to by the employee's attorney (*Blue Mountain*). In Pennsylvania, even if the hearsay is admitted because it is not objected to, it must be corroborated by some other evidence. A decision cannot be based on hearsay alone (*Auddino*). Of course, this rule can work against the employee as well. In one case, Mrs. Woods testified that her husband had been transferred and that he had no control over the decision. She tried to introduce a written statement to that effect, but this was hearsay and was not admitted. She should have had both her husband and the husband's supervisor at the hearing so that they could testify in person (*Woods*).

Regular business records are usually going to be admitted into evidence under an exception to the rule that anything written on a piece of paper is hearsay. That means that letters of reprimand and employee evaluations will usually be allowed at the hearing. However, the person in charge of these records or the supervisor who created them will have to be there to testify that they are what they appear to be. Documentation is often the key to whether or not an employer wins an unemployment compensation case. The same applies to employees. Employees should keep a logbook of everything that happens at work. Sandra Bird kept a logbook and the Oregon Appeals Court allowed it into evidence (*Bird*). Every major incident at work and every outlandish thing the supervisor tells an employee to do should go into the logbook. It may or may not be admissible at the hearing, depending on the state, but even if it is not admitted into evidence, the employee can use it to refresh his or her memory. A witness who can recall details sounds much more convincing.

Employees seeking unemployment compensation should contact their nearest legal aid office as quickly as possible to see what assistance the office will give. In 1990, the Tennessee Supreme Court ruled that because the Tennessee Unemployment Agency had not told an unemployed worker about the possible availability of free or low-cost legal representation through legal aid, her right to a fair hearing had been violated (*Simmons*).

On Appeal

The losing side may appeal. First you will appeal to a review board or the employment commission itself, and then to the courts. Since you may have only 10 days to appeal (calendar days, not workdays), you need to act fast.

Generally you can appeal one of four things: (1) the proper procedure was not followed; (2) your constitutional rights were violated; (3) the statute or regulations were not interpreted correctly; and (4) the finding of the agency was not supported by substantial evidence (*Spencer*).

Collateral Estoppel

In 1986, the High Court of New York handed down a ruling that will cause problems for years to come. The New York court ruled that once the hearing officer makes findings of fact in an unemployment compensation case, both sides are stuck with those facts (*Guimarales*). This is called *collateral estoppel*. Collateral estoppel is a legal doctrine that says once the legal system determines a fact the parties involved are stuck with that fact. They cannot keep suing to try to change the legal system's mind. This doctrine makes sense when a case has been tried before a judge and jury. It does not make sense to give the factual findings of an unemployment compensation hearing the same weight. These hearings often last 15 minutes. Usually neither side has an attorney. The issues are very specialized and focus on the special terms of the unemployment compensation statute. Decisions in these cases should affect nothing except whether or not the worker gets unemployment compensation. To make them count for anything else is unfair to both employers and employees. In New York, some employees do not apply for unemployment compensation for fear the determination of the agency will keep them from winning a lawsuit later on. Employers may not challenge employees who apply for unemployment compensation for the same reason. If the employer does challenge the granting of compensation, then each side will probably need an attorney. The unemployment compensation hearing will become the most important hearing for both parties. Whoever wins at that hearing may well have won everything later on.

No other state supreme court has gone along with New York. The Colorado, Indiana, Illinois, Oregon, and South Dakota supreme courts have all rejected the idea that findings made at an unemployment compensation hearing have collateral effect (*Salida Sch.*; *McClanahan*; *Kolman*; *Mitchell*; *Heller*). The Missouri legislature amended the unemployment compensation statute in 1988 to make it clear that findings of fact and conclusions of law made in an unemployment compensation hearing have no collateral effect on any "separate or subsequent action." However, if an employer or employee has admitted something at the unemployment compensation hearing, or taken a position that something is indeed a fact, he or she may well be stuck, even in states other than New York (the law calls this an admission).

Employees thinking of suing their employer should consult an attorney before even filing for unemployment compensation. If they live in a state that agrees with New York, the attorney may want them either not to apply for unemployment compensation or to fight that case to the limit. And, of course, an employer living in New York, or in a state that agrees with New York, will want to consult an attorney before deciding whether to challenge an application for unemployment compensation.

The Future

We have an unemployment compensation system that ends at state borders. That may have been fine half a century ago but it is not fine today. During the 1980s, some states were in recession while others were booming. Under the present system, employers in boom states pay low unemployment taxes while employers in recession states pay very high unemployment taxes that they can ill afford. These increased taxes are just another factor preventing those states from recovering.

In an age of computers and closed-circuit television, most state unemployment agencies are still using the horse and buggy. These agencies can never do the job one big federal employment agency could do. An employer in Boston should be able to interview potential employees in Houston by closed-circuit television. Basic-skills tests should be performed once and the results beamed around the country. The answer seems simple. Turn the system back into what it was to begin with, a federal system. With economies of scale this should result in fewer bureaucrats and lower costs. It should also result in increased effectiveness.

In 1990, the Mississippi State Employment Service successfully defended itself against charges of race discrimination by proving that it was so overworked, undermanned, hamstrung by regulations, and inefficient that it was unreasonable to suppose that it could carry out any "policy," even a policy of racial discrimination (*Hill #3*). This was truly a red-letter day in the history of American unemployment compensation.

6

Wrongful Discharge and Contract Interference

Wrongful Discharge

Some employees think that they can sue their employer just because they have been fired. This is true if the employee has a term employment contract, a union contract, or a wonderful employee handbook. Most employees do not. They are at-will employees and can be fired for no reason at all.

Employees cannot be fired for an illegal reason. Throughout the twentieth century, Congress and state legislatures have passed laws making it illegal to fire employees for certain reasons. Employees who think they have been fired because of their union membership should turn to Chapter 15. Employees who think that they have been fired to keep them from getting their retirement or other company benefits should turn to Chapter 19. Employees fired because of their race, religion, sex, age, or handicap should turn to Chapters 7, 8, 9, and 10. Employees who have been fired for exercising their right of free speech should turn to Chapter 11. Employees fired because of a drug or lie-detector test should turn to Chapter 13.

Many judges feel these statutes have not been complete enough. Over time, cases have arisen in which the state supreme courts have felt that the law should protect an employee from discharge for "that reason" but no statute existed that afforded that protection. These courts invented the concept of *common-law wrongful discharge*. Most of these state supreme courts said that firing an employee for a particular reason violated the "public policy" of the state and was thus illegal. The landmark case came three decades ago in California. For many years this idea of common-law wrongful discharge remained just another strange idea of the California judges. During the 1980s, more and more state supreme courts came to believe that in some situations courts should declare a particular reason for firing someone to be illegal, even if the legislature had not gotten around to doing so.

Of course, not all state supreme courts feel this way. The Highest Court in New York has rejected this idea, and has said it is up to the New York legislature to add to the list of reasons employers cannot fire employees. Most pro-boss state supreme courts have refused to recognize the concept of common-law wrongful discharge. So far, Indiana, North Carolina, Ohio, and Pennsylvania are the only exceptions. In this chapter, we will discuss the major areas in which courts in most fair states will find a discharge to be illegal, even if the legislature has not gotten around to passing a statute to that effect.

Refusing to Commit an Illegal Act

The first common-law wrongful discharge case was the California case of *Petermann v. International Brotherhood of Teamsters*. In 1959, Petermann was told by his supervisors at the Teamsters Union to perjure himself before a legislative committee. When he refused, and told the committee the truth, the Teamsters Union fired him. The California Appeals Court found this to be contrary to the "public policy" of the state of California. The court said it would be "obnoxious to the interests of the state" to allow an employer to fire an employee for this reason. Over the years more and more states have come to accept the concept that employers cannot fire employees just because they refuse to commit an illegal act (*Tameny*; *Trombetta*).

The clearest case is when the employer tells an employee to do a clearly illegal thing. For example, the Texas Supreme Court had no trouble finding a case of wrongful discharge when a seaman was allegedly fired for refusing to pump the bilges of the ship into the water in violation of the federal environmental laws (*Sabine*).

The Massachusetts Supreme Court recognized the concept of wrongful discharge in a case involving a refusal to commit perjury, while the Indiana Supreme Court allowed a truck driver to sue because he was fired when he refused to drive an illegally overweight truck (*DeRose*; *McClanahan*). The Minnesota Supreme Court recognized this concept when it refused to allow a gas station attendant to be fired because he refused to put leaded gas in an unleaded engine in violation of federal law (*Phipps*).

Given these decisions, it is reasonable to expect that the supreme courts in most fair states would consider it wrongful discharge for an employer to fire an employee because the employee refused to commit an illegal act.

Whistleblowing

A number of state supreme courts have extended this concept of wrongful discharge to protect employees who were fired because they exposed the illegal activities of their fellow employees or supervisors.

First, there are the cases where the employees reveal illegal activity to the proper governmental authorities. In one case, a bank employee was fired for reporting violations of the banking laws to government officials. The West Virginia Supreme Court found this to be a wrongful discharge because it violated public policy (*Harless*).

Other courts have ruled the same way when faced with employees who were fired for reporting possible criminal activity to the local police or threatening to report patient abuse at a nursing home to state officials (*Palmateer;* *McQuary*).

Some courts have gone a step further and recognized wrongful discharge when the employee has been fired for reporting problems to someone in the company, not to the government. In one case, a quality-control inspector complained to his superiors that substandard raw materials in food products violated food and drug laws. The Connecticut Supreme Court found this discharge to be a violation of public policy and therefore wrongful (*Sheets*). The Supreme Court of Hawaii found it to be wrongful to fire the company comptroller because he discussed possible antitrust violations with the company attorney (*Parnar*).

While courts in most fair states appear to be willing to protect people who blow the whistle to a government official, there is some question about whether they should do the same when the employee has blown the whistle to higher management within the company. Is this something courts have any right to interfere with? Of course, if the courts protect only the employees who blow the whistle to governmental agencies, employees are not going to tell upper management first and those executives are not going to have a chance to correct the problem internally. In 1988, the Kansas Supreme Court said it did not matter; the employee would be protected if the report is made to either higher management or a government agency (*Palmer*).

If what the employee is complaining about is not a violation of law, the courts may not find it to be a violation of public policy to discharge him or her for exposing it. For example, in one case the employee complained to his superiors within the company about "questionable accounting practices" and was fired because of this complaint. The Michigan Supreme Court refused to find this to be a case of wrongful discharge. The employee was complaining about being forced to violate his professional code of ethics, which the Michigan Supreme Court did not feel was important enough to be protected by the concept of common-law wrongful discharge (*Suchodolski*).

If that employee could have cited a statutory provision, he might have had better luck. In an Illinois case, the chief financial officer of a company was allegedly opposed to certain accounting practices because he felt they violated federal securities law (*Johnson*). The Illinois Appeals Court found this to be a case of wrongful discharge, even though this employee complained only to other company officials. This court said the behavior complained of did not have to be illegal. What mattered was whether the employee believed in good faith that it was illegal.

The High Court of New York has refused to recognize any kind of common-law wrongful discharge for whistleblowing, a fact that led the New York legislature to pass a statute on the subject. A number of other states have passed similar statutes (see Table 6.1).

While a few of these statutes protect all employees, most protect only state or government employees from discharge. These statutes vary greatly. Some are very limited. For example, Rhode Island's statute protects only public employees who report violations of law. Delaware's statute protects only state employees and public school employees who blow the whistle to the Office of the State Auditor. Whistleblowing to anyone else or whistleblowing by any other kind of employee is not protected by the Delaware statute.

The New York whistleblower statute protects employees who disclose illegal activity either to their supervisor or a public body but the activity must present "a substantial and specific danger to the public health or safety." In 1990, the Highest Court in New York was faced with an employee who was fired for exposing a fraudulent billing scheme that cheated New York City out of thousands of dollars. The court ruled that because this fraudulent billing scheme did not pose a danger to "public health or safety," this employee was not protected by the law (*Remba*).

Any employee thinking of blowing the whistle should consult an attorney first. The statutes listed in Table 6.1 may change, and more may be added. Some of these statutes require the employee to blow the whistle in a very particular way (or to a particular agency) if he or she wants the protection of the statute. All things considered, it may not be worth it to blow the whistle in many states given the court decisions and statutes that apply.

Exercising a Legal Right or Performing a Legal Duty

In many states, the supreme court has decided an employee cannot be discharged for exercising a right created by statute or for performing a duty required by statute. The classic cases are: (1) being fired for filing a worker's compensation claim (exercising a legal right), or (2) being fired for having to serve on a jury (performing a legal duty). Some states have statutes that

Table 6.1   Whistleblower Statutes

Alaska 39.90.100 to 150	Protects public employees who report to a public body on a matter of public concern.
Arizona 38-531, 532	Protects public employees who report to a public agency on violations of law or regulations.
California Labor Code 1102.5	Protects all employees who report to a public agency on violations of law or regulations.
Colorado 24-50.5-101 to 107	Protects public employees who disclose truthful, nonconfidential information.
Connecticut 31-51m	Protects all employees who report to a public body on violations of law or regulations. Ninety days to sue; can collect attorney fees.
Delaware 29-5115	Protects state and public school employees who report to the Office of the State Auditor on violations of law or regulations. Ninety days to sue.
District of Columbia 1-616.2	Protects public employees who disclose information concerning illegal or unethical conduct that threatens the public health or safety or involves unlawful use of public funds, if such disclosure is not an invasion of privacy.
Florida 112.3187	Protects public employees who report to a public agency violations of law or regulations. Also protects employees of government contractors who report substantial dangers to public health, safety, or welfare. Also protects the reporting of malfeasance, waste, and neglect of duty by an agency.
Hawaii 378-61	Protects all employees who report a violation of law or rule. Ninety days to sue.
Illinois Tit. 127, 63b91	Protects state employees who report violations of law, mismanagement, gross waste of funds, abuse of authority or danger to health or safety.
Indiana 22-5-3-3	Protects employees of government contractors who report violations of law or misuse of public resources (must report to employer first).
Iowa 19A.19	Protects state employees who report to a public official on violations of law, mismanagement, gross abuse of funds, abuse of authority, or danger to public health or safety.
Kansas 75-2973	Protects state employees who report violations of law or regulations.
Kentucky 61.101 to 103	Protects public employees who report to a public agency on violations of law or regulations, waste, fraud, or danger. Ninety days to sue.
Maine 26-831 to 840	Protects all employees who report on violations of law or dangers to public health or safety, or who refuse to violate the law.

Table 6.1—*Continued*

Maryland Art. 64A, Sec. 12G	Protects state employees who report on violations of law, gross mismanagement, or danger to public health or safety.
Michigan 15.361 to .369	Protects all employees who report on violations of law or regulations. Ninety days to sue.
Minnesota 181.931 to .935	Protects all employees who report on violations of law or refuse to violate the law. Employees may collect attorney fees.
Nebraska 48-1114	Protects all employees who oppose or refuse to carry out any unlawful act.
New Hampshire 275E	Protects all employees who report on violations of law or refuse to violate the law.
New Jersey 34:19-1 to 19-8	Protects all employees who report on violations of law or refuse to violate the law. One year to sue; can get attorney fees.
New York Labor Sec. 740	Protects all employees who report on violations of law or refuse to violate the law. The activity reported must present a danger. Both employee and employer can collect attorney fees.
North Carolina 126-84 to 88	Protects state employees who report violations of law, fraud, misappropriation of resources, danger to public health, or safety.
Ohio 4113.51	Protects all employees who report on violations of law. Employee must notify the employer first. One hundred eighty days to sue.
Oregon 659.505 to 550	Protects public employees who report on violations of law, mismanagement, gross waste of funds, danger to health or safety, and private employees who report on violations of law.
Pennsylvania 43-1421 to 1428	Protects all employees who report waste or wrongdoing to employer or an appropriate authority.
Rhode Island 36-15	Protects public employees who report on violations of law or regulations.
South Carolina 8-27-10	Protects public employees who expose criminality, corruption, waste, fraud, gross negligence, mismanagement, or who testify at any trial or hearing.
Tennessee 50-1-304	Protects all employees who report on violations of law or refuse to violate the law.
Texas Art. 6252-16(a)	Protects public employees who report on violations of law. Ninety days to sue.
Utah 67-21	Protects public employees who report on violations of law or regulations or a waste of public funds. Ninety days to sue.
Washington 42.40	Protects state employees who report on improper activity.

Table 6.1—*Continued*

West Virginia 6C-1	Protects public employees who report on wrongdoing or waste to employer or an appropriate authority.
Wisconsin 230.80 to 89	Protects public employees who report. Sixty days to file complaint.

specifically protect people from discharge in these situations. Many state supreme courts have found these discharges to be wrongful even without a specific statutory provision.

In 1973, the Indiana Supreme Court was the first to hold, without a statute, that it was wrongful discharge to fire a worker simply because he or she filed a worker's compensation claim (*Frampton*). Since then, almost every state supreme court to rule on this issue has agreed. While the employee cannot be fired simply because he or she filed a worker's compensation claim, in most states they can still be fired if they are no longer able to do the work (*Clifford*). (The employee may have a handicapped-discrimination claim; see Chapter 10).

What if the employer thinks the employee is about to file for worker's compensation and fires him or her before he or she can file? In 1988, the Illinois and Kansas supreme courts said that was still wrongful discharge (*Hinthorn; Chrisman*).

In 1975, the Supreme Court of Oregon found that it was against public policy for employers to fire employees because they had to serve on a jury (*Nees*). Most other state supreme courts have agreed.

The interesting question becomes, What other legal rights or duties will the courts also protect in this way?

A New Jersey court held that it was wrongful to discharge a pharmacist who refused to leave the drug counter unsupervised. He had a duty under state law to ensure that the counter was supervised at all times (*Kalman*). A California Appeals Court held that it was wrong to discharge an employee because he was trying to achieve a reasonably smoke-free workplace for himself (*Hentzel*).

Exercising Private Rights

What if the employee is discharged not for exercising rights created by law but for exercising rights spelled out in company policy? We have already seen that the Massachusetts Supreme Court would not let NCR fire a salesman simply to deprive him of his commissions (*Fortune*). A Connecticut Appeals Court held that an employer may not fire someone simply to avoid paying bonuses (*Cook*). An Illinois Appeals Court ruled that a company may not discharge workers just to keep them from receiving disability payments pursuant to the employee handbook (*DeFosse*). A Pennsylvania Appeals Court ruled in 1988 that an employee cannot be fired just to keep pension rights from vesting (*Mudd*).

Many of these cases involve employees who feel that they have been discharged because they applied for benefits under the company benefit plan or filed a claim under group insurance plans. These cases are now controlled by the federal Employee Retirement Income Security Act (ERISA) discussed in Chapter 19. In other cases, it will depend on whether the state supreme court thinks employee handbooks are contracts. If they do, then these rights will probably be enforced.

Many employees are also shareholders. The Virginia Supreme Court has held that company executives may not discharge or threaten to discharge at-will employees in an effort to control the way they vote their stock as corporate shareholders (*Bowman*). An employee who works for a company that sells stock to the public should buy at least one share. As shareholders, employees have many rights, such as the right to examine the company records, that they do not have as employees.

Wrongful Discharge Statutes

More and more state legislatures have passed more and more statutes that specifically outlaw particular kinds of wrongful discharges. California has 24 such statutes at last count. Texas is more representative, with 7. It is a violation of Texas statutes to discharge someone because they filed a worker's compensation claim (Art. 8307c); because of their membership or nonmembership in a union (Art. 5207a, Sec. 2); because they had to serve on a jury (Prac. & Rem. Code Sec. 122.001(a)); because they were called up to active duty with the military (Gov't Code Sec. 431.006(a)); because of their race, color, handicap, religion, sex, national origin, or age (Art. 5221k, Sec. 5.01); because they are a public employee who blows the whistle (Art. 6252-16a, Sec. 2); or because they filed a complaint or exercised a right under the state Hazardous Materials Act (Art. 5182b, Sec. 15). Every state has at least one wrongful discharge act.

It is impossible to compile a complete list of all the federal wrongful discharge statutes, but a partial list would include:

- *The National Labor Relations Act* (29 U.S.C. Sec. 151).   Protects union members and union activity.
- *Title VII* (42 U.S.C. Sec. 2000e).   Protects against discharge because of race, color, religion, sex, or national origin.

- *Age Discrimination Act* (29 U.S.C. Sec. 621). Protects against discharge because of age.
- *Americans with Disabilities Act* (42 U.S.C. Sec. 12101). Protects against discharge because of handicap.
- *Occupational Safety and Health Act* (29 U.S.C. Sec. 651). Protects against discharge because employees file complaints concerning safety with the Occupational Safety and Health Administration.
- *Fair Labor Standards Act* (20 U.S.C. Sec. 201). Protects against discharge because employees file complaints with the Labor Department concerning minimum wage and overtime practices.
- *Jurors' Protection Act* (28 U.S.C. Sec. 1875). Protects against discharge because employees have to serve on a federal jury.
- *Judiciary and Judicial Procedure Act* (28 U.S.C. Sec. 1875). Protects against discharge because employees have to serve on a federal grand or petit jury.
- *Consumer Protection Act* (15 U.S.C. Sec. 1671). Protects against discharge because employees have had their wages garnished.
- *Bankruptcy Act* (11 U.S.C. Sec. 525). Protects against discharge because employees have had to file bankruptcy.
- *Employee Retirement Income Security Act* (29 U.S.C. Sec. 1140). Protects against discharge in an attempt to keep employees from vesting under a pension or benefit plan.
- *Energy Reorganization Act* (42 U.S.C. Sec. 5851). Protects against discharge because employees help in the enforcement of the Atomic Energy Act.
- *Clean Air Act* (42 U.S.C. Sec. 7622). Protects against discharge because employees help in the enforcement of the Act.
- *Water Pollution Control Act* (33 U.S.C. Sec. 1367). Protects against discharge because employees help in the enforcement of the Act.
- *Railroad Safety Act* (45 U.S.C. Sec. 441a). Protects against discharge because employees help in the enforcement of the Act or refuse to work because they reasonably believe the railroad is dangerous.
- *Mine Safety and Health Act* (30 U.S.C. Sec. 820). Protects against discharge because employees help in the enforcement of the Act or refuse to work because they reasonably believe the mine is dangerous.
- *Surface Transportation Assistance Act* (49 U.S.C. Sec. 2305). Protects against discharge because employees file safety complaints or refuse to operate unsafe equipment.
- *Veterans Reemployment Act* (38 U.S.C. Sec. 2021, 2028). Protects

reemployed veterans against discharge without cause for one year after reemployment.

- *Polygraph Protection Act* (29 U.S.C. Sec. 2001).   Protects against discharge because employees refuse to take a polygraph examination under most conditions.

An important question came up in the early 1990s. What if there is a state or federal wrongful discharge statute that makes it clear that discharge for a particular reason is against public policy but the statute grants employees little in the way of damages and is not a real incentive for them to sue to protect their rights? Can employees use the statute as a "statement of public policy" but sue for common-law wrongful discharge (and receive a jury trial and full damages in state court) instead of being stuck with the statutory procedures and statutory damages? In 1991, both the Nevada and Washington supreme courts said that employees could sue for common-law wrongful discharge. The Nevada case involved an employee who refused to work under unreasonably dangerous conditions, while the Washington case involved an employee who was fired for filing a worker's compensation claim (*D'Angelo*; *Wilmot*). Both of these employees had a limited statutory remedy. The supreme courts ruled that because the statutes did not provide a "comprehensive statutory remedy," the employees could sue for common-law wrongful discharge. (See Table 6.2 for a list of states whose supreme courts have accepted the concept of common-law wrongful discharge.)

Many employees would like to sue for race or sex discrimination under common-law wrongful discharge (and avoid the limits on damages and the rule that small employers are not covered by Title VII), but courts have generally found that these statutes do provide a comprehensive statutory remedy and have not allowed common-law wrongful discharge suits. In 1990, the California Supreme Court found a way around this rule. The case involved a victim of sex discrimination who wanted to sue for common-law wrongful discharge. The court said that because the California Constitution (Art. I, Sec. 8) provides that "a person may not be disqualified from entering or pursuing a business, profession, vocation, or employment because of sex, race, creed, color, or national or ethnic origin," this provided an independent statement of public policy and therefore the employee could sue under common-law wrongful discharge and was not "stuck" with the federal and state statutes on the subject (*Rojo*).

A number of states have recently passed much more comprehensive wrongful discharge statutes. For example, the Nevada statute makes it unlawful to discharge an employee because that employee uses a "lawful" product outside the employer's premises (Nev. 613.333). This would protect employees who smoke tobacco or drink alcohol away from work. The Colorado and North

Table 6.2 State Supreme Courts That Have Accepted the Concept of
Common-Law Wrongful Discharge

Alaska	*Knight*
Arizona	*Wagenseller; Wagner*
Arkansas	*Oxford; Cross; Wall-Mart*
California	*Petermann; Tameny; Foley; Gantt*
Colorado	*Lorenz*
Connecticut	*Sheets*
Dist. of Columbia	*Adams*
Hawaii	*Parnar*
Idaho	*Watson*
Illinois	*Palmateer; Kelsay; Hinthorn*
Indiana	*McClanahan; Frampton*
Iowa	*Springer*
Kansas	*Palmer; Anco; Chrisman*
Kentucky	*Firestone Textile*
Maryland	*Adler*
Massachusetts	*DeRose; Flesner; Wright*
Minnesota	*Phipps; Freidrichs; Brevik*
Montana	Has comprehensive wrongful discharge statute.
Nebraska	*Ambroz*
Nevada	*MGM; D'Angelo*
New Hampshire	*Monge; Cilley; Cloutier*
New Jersey	*Pierce; Velantzas*
New Mexico	*Vigil*
North Carolina	*Coman*
North Dakota	*Krein; Ressler*
Ohio	*Greeley*
Oklahoma	*Burk; Todd; Farmer's Coop.*
Oregon	*Nees; Delaney*
Pennsylvania	*Clay*
South Carolina	*Ludwick*
Tennessee	*Clanton; Harney*
Texas	*Sabine; Winters*
Utah	*Berube; Hodges*
Vermont	*Payne*
Virginia	*Bowman*
Washington	*Cagle*
West Virginia	*Harless; Wiggins*
Wisconsin	*Wandry*
Wyoming	*Griess*

Dakota statutes protect employees from discharge because they "participated
in a lawful activity off the employer's premises during nonworking hours"
(Colo. 24-34-402.5; N.D. 14-02.4-03).

There are so many wrongful discharge statutes that some have argued it
would make more sense to simply require employers to have "just cause"

before they could fire an employee. The United States is one of the last industrialized countries not to provide this kind of protection against arbitrary dismissal by all employers, public and private. In August 1991, the National Conference of Commissioners on Uniform State Laws adopted a Model Employment Termination Act. This act would protect all employees from dismissal without just cause after they had served a probationary period. So far, only Montana has adopted such a law (Mont. 39-2-901).

Will states adopt the Model Employment Termination Act? It is very unlikely because of what both employees and employers would have to give up and what they would get in return. Employees would give up the right to sue for common-law wrongful discharge and in return could be fired only for good cause; but the act's definition of good cause includes when an employer "thinks" it has good cause. This is not much protection. The employer would give up the right to fire employees at-will but could still face lawsuits for statutory wrongful discharge at both the state and federal level. The major problem with the present system is that both employers and employees can run the other side through a half dozen hearings and courts at great expense and with little to show for the effort at the end of the road. I firmly believe that at some point in the twenty-first century one federal department will handle everything discussed in this book from worker's compensation to Social Security, from unemployment compensation to wrongful discharge, and both employers and employees will be better off. Both sides will be able to go to one forum and resolve all of their disputes quickly and inexpensively. Both sides will benefit from a simple procedure. Employees will give up their right to receive millions in damages and employers will give up their right to fire employees at-will. Employers, having demonstrated that they had "real" (not imagined) good cause to dismiss a worker, will not then have to prove in half a dozen forums that they did not discharge the employee for a "wrongful" reason.

Interference with Contract

Pennzoil had a contract to buy Getty Oil. Texaco talked the owners of Getty Oil into selling out to Texaco instead of Pennzoil. The jury awarded Pennzoil $7.5 billion in compensatory damages (the money Pennzoil was out because they did not get the benefit of the contract) plus $3 billion in punitive damages. The Texas Appeals Court reduced the punitive damages to $2 billion (*Texaco*). The Texas Supreme Court upheld that decision.

The same principle applies to employment contracts. If a third party comes along and interferes with an employment contract, usually by talking the employer into firing the employee, the employee can sue the third party just as Pennzoil sued Texaco. Remember, every employee has an employment contract. Even if the employees are at-will, they can still sue anyone who talks the employer into firing them (*Eib*; *Deauville*; *Hooks*).

Take the case of Karen Lewis. Soon after she went to work for the Oregon Beauty Supply Company, she started dating the owner's son. When she told the owner's son she wanted to see other men, he harassed her at work until she quit. The Oregon Appeals Court found this to be a case of interference with a contract (the court called it interference with an economic relationship). It did not matter that Lewis was an at-will employee; she still had a contract with her employer that was interfered with by the employer's son. The court upheld an award of punitive damages against the son (*Oregon Beauty*).

The law understands if one of the two parties to a contract has to break the contract. The law does not understand when some third party comes along and talks one of the parties into breaking the contract.

The law also does not like people who interfere with other important relationships, such as a person's relationship with government. In one case, the employer told the Maryland Unemployment Compensation Agency that Julianna Ellett had quit, which would make her ineligible for unemployment compensation. This turned out to be a lie. The Maryland Appeals Court found this to be interference with a government relationship (the court called it interference with perspective advantage) and allowed Ellett to sue the employer (*Ellett*).

In another case, the employer got a government agency to revoke the employee's license to work. That also qualified as interference with a government relationship and the employer was held liable (the court called this interference with an advantageous relationship) (*Willis*).

What if the employer is a corporation and the person who interferes (by firing the employee) is the employee's own supervisor? Can the employee sue the supervisor? Yes, but to win, the employee has to prove that the supervisor fired the employee for personal reasons. A supervisor has every right to fire an employee for business reasons.

In a Vermont case, several Bennington College administrators talked Bennington College into firing Professor Lyon (*Lyon*). The Vermont Supreme Court held that Professor Lyon could sue Bennington College for breach of contract and the administrators for interference with contract. The Vermont Supreme Court said that if the administrators made their recommendation for business reasons, fine; if they did it for personal reasons, then they would be held liable. It would be up to the jury to decide.

Other courts have said that employees may sue their supervisors for contract interference if they can prove the supervisors acted with "malice or contrary to the corporation's interests" or that the interference was "intentional and improper" (*Helmi*; *Hunter*; *Intermountain*; *Batt*; *Sorrells*). Still others have said that the supervisor has a "privilege" to interfere with the employee's contract as long as the supervisor is acting for business not personal reasons (*Chapman*).

Many employees find that it is not their supervisor but their fellow employees who are conspiring to get them fired to further their own personal goals. These employees can be sued for contract interference. In a recent Texas case, the jury found that the fellow employees acted out of malice (they disliked the employee and were jealous of that employee's success). The jury awarded punitive damages against the interfering employees (*Flach*).

In some cases, it is one member of a board or commission who talks the other members into firing an employee for what are really personal reasons. These people can be sued for contract interference. The employment contract is with the organization, not the individual board members. Take the case of George Mouchette. He was fired from his job as benefits director with the Oakland School District in California at the age of 61. Mouchette alleged that one member of the school board, James Norwood, wanted him fired for refusing to give district legal business to his friends. The jury awarded Mouchette $348,000 in compensatory damages, $125,000 in emotional distress damages, and $25,000 in punitive damages; the California Appeals Court upheld that verdict (*Mouchette*). In a similar case from Florida, a county commissioner got a county employee fired because that employee had run unsuccessfully against him for the office of county commissioner. The Florida jury awarded $1 million in punitive damages, and the Florida Appeals Court upheld that verdict (*Gandy*).

While a few courts have ruled that at-will employees may not sue for contract interference because they do not have a contract to be interfered with, that is not the opinion of most state supreme courts. Both the Texas and North Carolina supreme courts have ruled recently that at-will employees do have contracts and can sue for contract interference (*Sterner*; *Hooks*).

7

Work and Religion

The First Amendment of the U.S. Constitution states that "Congress shall make no law respecting an establishment of religion, or prohibiting the free exercise thereof." This provision provides two separate mandates to separate the church from the state. The first requires that government not engage in "establishing" religion. The second requires that government not interfere with the "free exercise" of religion. The difficulty over the past two centuries has been in deciding what constitutes establishing a religion and what kinds of activities religious people are free to engage in.

The meaning of "religious freedom" was first put to the test in Utah when a Mormon was arrested in the 1870s for violating the law against bigamy. The accused argued that because his behavior did not adversely affect anyone else he should be allowed to engage in it for religious purposes. A unanimous Supreme Court disagreed (*Reynolds #3*). The Court held that a religious belief was not a justification for committing an overt act that violated the criminal law. The justices believed that to rule otherwise would be to set up a system whereby one set of laws applied to the religious and another applied to everyone else.

Several general principles were laid down during the 1960s and 1970s that impact all cases concerned with religion and the First Amendment, including those related to employment issues. During the 1960s, in cases involving people who wished exemption from compulsory military service on the grounds of "conscientious objection," the Court laid down the principle that someone did not have to belong to an organized sect to take advantage of the exemption but did have to have a "sincere and meaningful" religious belief (*Seeger*). The Court felt that to require membership in an organized sect would constitute an establishment of religion in violation of the First Amendment. In 1969, in a dispute over which faction in a church would own the church building, the Court ruled that if the church is part of a larger church organization (a hierarchical church organization), then the dispute would be decided by the supreme body of that larger organization (*Blue Hull*). The Court had ruled in the nineteenth century that, in most cases, decisions in an independent church would be made by majority rule unless some other principle was set out in the church charter (*Bouldin*). The Court also laid down the principle that judges may not interpret religious doctrine or make decisions concerning ecclesiastical issues and must apply only neutral principles of law in deciding these types of disputes (*Wolf*).

Employment Regulation

The U.S. Supreme Court has ruled on several occasions that the dictates of religion generally do not excuse the religious from the application of neutral laws designed to regulate employment. In 1944, a Jehovah's Witness was convicted of violating the child labor laws when she allowed her nine-year-old daughter to sell the *Watchtower*. The Court upheld the conviction, finding that the state had the power to protect children from labor, even the labor of selling religious publications (*Prince*). In 1982, a member of the Amish sect sued to get back Social Security taxes he had paid for his employees and himself, arguing that paying such taxes and receiving Social Security payments was against his religion. The U.S. Supreme Court ruled that he had to pay the taxes (*Lee #2*). In 1985, the U.S. Supreme Court ruled that the Fair Labor Standards Act applied to a religious foundation that operated a number of commercial businesses, such as a motel, gas station, and grocery store, to provide food, shelter, and clothing to more than 300 recovering drug addicts. None of the drug-addict employees received money for their work at the foundation-owned enterprises. The Court ruled that requiring the foundation to comply with the minimum wage and overtime provisions of the Fair Labor Standards Act did not violate the free exercise clause of the First Amendment (*Alamo Foundation*).

Recently federal circuit courts have ruled that the Equal Pay Act and the Fair Labor Standards Act apply to lay faculty at religious schools but not to ministers and priests who also teach at these schools (*Shenandoah Baptist*; *Dearment*). They have also ruled that religious organizations must pay worker's compensation fees for employees (other than ministers) and are subject to federal immigration laws and regulations concerning the hiring of illegal immigrants (*South Ridge Baptist*; *Intercommunity*).

Hiring and Firing Ministers

It is not always easy to tell when a court should apply "neutral principles of law" to resolve a dispute, and when the court should stay out of the matter altogether because any involvement would mean interfering with ecclesiastical decisions. This is particularly true in the area of hiring and firing ministers.

In 1972, the Fifth Circuit Court ruled that when it comes to hiring and firing ministers and priests, civil rights laws do not apply. The case involved Mrs. Billie McClure, an ordained minister of the Salvation Army. Mrs. McClure filed a complaint with the Equal Employment Opportunity Commission (EEOC) because she believed that she was receiving less salary and fewer benefits than were male ministers with similar duties. The court ruled that to allow the EEOC to look into these charges would be to unreasonably interfere with the workings of a religion in violation of the First Amendment. The court also ruled that questions involving the assignment, salary, and duties of a minister were "ecclesiastical" in nature and beyond the power of the courts (*McClure*). The Fifth Circuit reaffirmed that decision two years later, ruling that a pastor who alleged he was the victim of racial discrimination could not sue the church (*Simpson #3*). In 1985, the Fourth Circuit came to the same conclusion concerning a woman who alleged racial and sexual discrimination when she was not hired as an associate pastor (*Rayburn*).

Who is a minister? Federal circuit courts have ruled that employees at a nonprofit religious publishing house and lay faculty and support staff at a religious school are not ministers and are protected by the civil rights laws (*Pacific Press*; *Southwestern Baptist*). On the other hand, courts have recently ruled that priests, ministers, and chaplains at nonprofit religious hospitals are ministers and, therefore, cannot sue for wrongful termination, defamation, civil rights violations, or intentional infliction of emotional distress growing out of their terminations (*O'Conor*; *Higgins #2*; *Scharon*).

Two cases from Michigan illustrate the line courts appear to be drawing. In one, a 61-year-old white man sued when he was fired from his job as church organist because the church wanted to hire a "younger black organist." The court ruled that the organist was like a minister and could not sue. On the other hand, when a teacher at a private Christian school sued when she was fired for having a child in violation of school rules, which did not allow women with preschool children to work at the school, the court said she could sue for sex discrimination (*Assemany*; *McLeod*).

The Kansas Supreme Court ruled in 1991 that the employees of a nonprofit religious nursing home were protected by the law, in this case the law enforcing the terms of employment handbooks. The court said it was up to the jury to determine what it means when an employment handbook says employees will be treated in a "Christian" way (*United Methodist*).

Unemployment Compensation

The relationship between religious beliefs and the paying or withholding of unemployment compensation has been another difficult area for the courts. Five decisions by the U.S. Supreme Court provide the basis for the law in this area. The first decision, handed down in 1963, involved an employee who was fired when she refused, as a member of the Seventh-Day Adventist Church, to work on Saturday, her Sabbath. She was then unable to find another job because of her unwillingness to work on Saturday, so she filed for unemployment compensation. The state of South Carolina denied her claim because she was refusing to accept suitable work when it was offered. The U.S. Supreme Court ruled that withholding unemployment compensation in this situation unreasonably interfered with the employee's right to freely exercise her religious beliefs (*Sherbert*).

In 1981, the Court was faced with a Jehovah's Witness who was initially hired to work in a foundry fabricating sheet steel for a variety of civilian uses. When that section of the foundry was closed, the employee was transferred to the division that made turrets for military tanks. The employee quit rather than violate his religious beliefs concerning the making of weapons. Indiana refused to grant him unemployment compensation because this was not a case of "quitting with good cause." The U.S. Supreme Court overruled and granted the compensation. It also said that it did not matter that not every member of the sect held these beliefs or that this particular individual was "struggling" with his own personal beliefs. The only question was, Did he so believe? If he did, then he was entitled to unemployment compensation (*Thomas #2*). Chief Justice Burger said that religious beliefs need not be "acceptable, logical, consistant, or comprehensible to others in order to merit First Amendment protection." The Court felt that to rule otherwise would put religious workers in the position of having to give up their religious beliefs to receive a governmental benefit.

In 1987, the Court was faced with an employee, Paula Hobbie, who worked for over two years and then became a member of the Seventh-Day Adventist Church. Because she could no longer work on Saturday, she was fired. Florida ruled that she had been fired for "misconduct" and refused to grant Hobbie unemployment compensation. The U.S. Supreme Court overturned this decision and granted her compensation. The Court again felt that this unreasonably burdened her right to freely exercise her religious beliefs (*Hobbie*). In 1989, William Frazee refused to work on Sunday, and

Illinois refused to grant him unemployment compensation because he did not belong to a particular religious sect. The U.S. Supreme Court said it did not matter, as long as he held a sincere religious belief, and ordered compensation (*Frazee*).

It is not unreasonable, given what had come before, that the most important decision by the U.S. Supreme Court concerning the meaning of the "free exercise of religion" clause of the First Amendment should occur in an unemployment compensation case. The case involved two drug rehabilitation counselors who were fired when they ingested peyote for sacramental purposes at a ceremony of a Native American Church. When they applied for unemployment compensation from the state of Oregon, it was denied because the state ruled that they had engaged in "misconduct." The Oregon Supreme Court overruled this decision, finding that it unconstitutionally infringed on the right to freely exercise religion. The Oregon Supreme Court also determined that to the extent that this use of peyote was a criminal offense under Oregon law, that law was also unconstitutional. The U.S. Supreme Court reversed, holding that the right to "freely exercise" one's religion did not include the right to violate criminal laws, even laws involving so-called victimless crimes. The Court reaffirmed what it had said over a century before, that to rule otherwise would create one law for the religious and another for everyone else. The Court did suggest that states could make exceptions, as some have, for the use of peyote by members of the Native American Church. The Court did not address whether this kind of exception would violate the "no establishment of religion" clause of the First Amendment (*Smith #2*).

Most states allow churches and religious organizations the option of not paying unemployment compensation taxes and thus not having employees covered by the system. In 1991, a hospital operated by the Roman Catholic Church applied for exemption from the tax. The Arkansas Supreme Court ruled that the exemption applied only to organizations operated primarily for religious purposes; because the major function of the hospital was healing, not religion, the exemption was denied (*Terwilliger*). Whether or not religiously affiliated schools qualify for this exemption is a difficult question. Most states grant them an exemption. In one recent case from Pennsylvania, a teacher at St. James Catholic School sued when she was denied unemployment compensation because her employer had never paid into the system. The Pennsylvania Appeals Court ruled that her right to "equal protection" under the law had not been violated and she was not entitled to unemployment compensation (*Thomas*).

Another difficult question comes when a teacher at a religious school is fired for violating rules that would not apply to them if they worked for a nonreligious school. Courts have been unable to come up with a consistent way of dealing with this problem. For example, one teacher found that her contract to teach at a Catholic school was not renewed because she had announced her plans to marry outside of the Roman Catholic Church. The state of Rhode Island granted her unemployment compensation and the Catholic school appealed. The Supreme Court of Rhode Island ruled that marrying outside of the church was not "misconduct." The court felt that while the school had the option of not being a part of the unemployment compensation system, if it chose to join it had to live by the general rules of that system, including the definition of misconduct (*St. Pius*). On the other hand, a Pennsylvania Appeals Court ruled (four to three) that a teacher at a Roman Catholic school who had announced her plans to marry a divorced man in violation of school policy had engaged in "willful misconduct" and would not receive unemployment compensation (*Bishop Leonard*).

One of the most difficult unemployment compensation questions for many states concerns spouses who quit to move with their wife or husband, making it impossible to continue to work at their old job. Most states have ruled that this is not "good cause" for quitting. Barbara Austin tried to get around this general rule by arguing that her religion required her to live with her husband; she said she could not do that and continue to work at her old job when her husband moved 150 miles from her job site. She quit, but the state of Virginia refused to grant her unemployment compensation. The Fourth Circuit Court, after much deliberation, ruled that this denial of compensation did not infringe on her right to freely exercise her religion (*Austin*). In June 1992, the U.S. Supreme Court affirmed this decision.

Religious Discrimination

In general, a suit for religious discrimination is similar to a suit for racial discrimination, and the general rules set down in Chapter 8 also apply to cases involving religious discrimination. Employees must prove either that their religion was a motivating factor behind the employer's decision not to hire them or to fire them, or that they were qualified for the job but someone of another religion was hired instead. For example, Stephen Soffer, a Jewish employee, objected to Bible verses printed on the face of the payroll checks and asked that they be deleted from his. He also objected to the religious content of the company newspaper. Soffer was ultimately fired despite a history of high ratings from supervisors. The Pennsylvania Appeals Court upheld a finding by the state Human Relations Commission that Soffer had been the victim of religious discrimination and ordered him to receive back pay, punitive damages, compensatory damages, and to be reinstated to the job (*Brown Trans.*).

While suits for religious discrimination are essentially similar to suits for racial discrimination, there are two special provisions that apply to religious discrimination claims that do not apply to racial discrimination claims. First, federal civil rights law, and many state civil rights laws, require employers to reasonably accommodate the dictates of an employee's religion if that "reasonable accommodation" will not cause "undue hardship" for the employer. Second, federal law, and many state laws, specifically allow religious entities to discriminate on the basis of religion. The U.S. Supreme Court has handed down one decision in each area.

Mr. Hardison began studying the religion known as the Worldwide Church of God. This religion requires its adherents not to work from sunset on Friday until sunset on Saturday. TWA accommodated him at first by transferring him to the 11 P.M. to 7 A.M. shift. Then Mr. Hardison bid for and received a transfer to a different building. Here he went on a different seniority list (he was now second from the bottom), and he could no longer use his seniority to maintain a work schedule that allowed him to observe his Sabbath. The union refused to violate the seniority rules of the collective-bargaining contract, and TWA refused to allow Hardison not to work on Saturday without a replacement. Hardison was fired for refusing to work on Saturday. The Eighth Circuit Court ruled that TWA had failed to provide reasonable accommodation because it could have provided Hardison with a four-day workweek, filled his Saturday shift with another employee (paying overtime pay), or arranged a swap between Hardison and other employees so that each could have his Sabbath day off. The U.S. Supreme Court reversed, finding that all three of these options would have amounted to "undue hardship" to TWA. The Court ruled that employers and unions do not have to violate seniority rules to accommodate religious employees (*TWA #3*).

As to the question of allowing religious organizations to discriminate on the basis of religious belief, the U.S. Supreme Court faced this issue in 1987 in a case involving the Morman Church. The Deseret Gymnasium in Salt Lake City, Utah, was a nonprofit facility, open to the public, and run by the Mormon Church. An employee of 16 years was fired when he could no longer provide a certificate that he was a member in good standing of the Mormon Church. He argued that the "religious" exception should not apply to nonreligious jobs such as building engineer. The Supreme Court disagreed. Because this was a nonprofit operation adjunct to a church (many churches provide recreational facilities), the church was free to discriminate on the basis of religion. The Court specifically did not rule on whether this exception would be allowed if a church engaged in for-profit activities and imposed a religious qualification on its employees (*Amos*).

These two principles raise a number of questions that the lower courts are struggling to answer. In one case, a 56-year-old teacher at a religious school was fired supposedly because she no longer met the religious test for employment. The Wisconsin Appeals Court said that while she could not sue for religious discrimination, she could sue for age discrimination; a court or administrative agency could then investigate to see if the religious reason was simply a pretext for illegal age discrimination (*Sacred Heart*). In another case, a member of the Church of God was told when he was hired that he would not have to work on Sunday. Later, as the employer needed to work extra shifts, the employee was fired for refusing to work on Sunday. The Fourth Circuit Court ruled that this amounted to religious discrimination. Other employees testified that they would have been willing to work in this employee's place (*Ithaca Ind.*). The Massachusetts Supreme Court found it to be discrimination when an employer refused to allow a religious employee to have a week off for religious observance. The court felt that the employer could have shifted other employees around to cover for this employee and that this would not have been an "undue hardship" on this employer (*MCAO*). The Ninth Circuit Court has ruled that while employers may hold religious services at work, they must excuse employees who do not wish to attend (*Townley*).

In 1991, the Third Circuit Court was faced with a non-Catholic lay teacher who was fired by the St. Mary Magdalene Parish schools because she remarried in violation of church teaching. The court ruled that because Title VII allows religious schools to discriminate on the basis of religion, they may also discriminate against employees whose behavior does not conform to their religious teaching (*Little*).

A special rule applies to public school teachers because of the need to prevent a public school from appearing to support a particular religion. Public school teachers can be fired for appearing to promote a particular religion to their pupils. For example, when Janet Cooper, a special education teacher in the Eugene, Oregon, public schools, became a Sikh, she donned white clothes and a white turban and wore them to school. This was a violation of Oregon law, which prevents public school teachers from wearing "religious dress" while teaching. Janet Cooper was suspended and her teaching certificate was revoked by the state. The Oregon Supreme Court upheld these actions because of the need for public schools to maintain religious neutrality and to avoid giving children the impression that the school approves or shares in a particular religious belief (*Cooper*). A Pennsylvania Appeals Court ruled the same way when faced with a public school teacher who continually talked about devils, demons, and God in front of the schoolchildren despite warnings to refrain from these discussions (*Rhodes*). What if such a teacher has been fired and applies for unemployment compensation? In 1990, the Mississippi Supreme Court ruled (five to four) that a public school teacher fired for wearing a head-wrap to school was nevertheless entitled to receive unemployment compensation and that to rule otherwise would interfere with her right of religious freedom (*McGlothin*).

Negligent Hiring and Supervision

One area in which courts have usually applied a different standard to churches is in the area of vicarious liability. Courts have been reluctant to hold churches liable for the intentional torts of their employees under the theory of *respondeat superior* (the master is liable for injuries caused by the servant). In recent years, plaintiffs have begun to get around this reluctance by suing the church directly for negligent hiring and negligent supervision. These doctrines say that anyone injured by an employee can sue the employer if the employer should have known when the employee was hired, or at some point after the employee began work, that the employee was likely to commit the wrong involved in the case. Three state supreme courts have recently ruled that churches can be sued under these doctrines when their employees commit intentional harm.

In the Virginia case, a mother alleged that her 10-year-old daughter was repeatedly raped by a church employee and that the church was negligent in hiring this employee because an investigation would have revealed that he had been convicted of aggravated sexual assault on a young girl and that a condition of his probation was that he not be involved with children. The lower court threw the case out and the mother appealed. The Virginia Supreme Court ruled that she could sue the church for negligent hiring and that this was an exception to the usual immunity from lawsuits that religious organizations enjoy in Virginia (*Victory Tabernacle*). In Colorado, a divorced husband sued the Roman Catholic diocese, alleging that the priest who acted as a marriage counselor for him and his now former wife only created additional marital problems when he engaged in sexual relations with the wife. The Colorado Supreme Court ruled that he could sue the Catholic Church for failing to properly supervise the priest who performed the marriage counseling. The court said he would have to prove the church either knew, or should have known, that this employee subjected people to an unreasonable risk of harm (*Destafano*). Finally, in a 1991 case from Alaska, a mother alleged that the woman in charge of the church nursery where she left her three-year-old daughter sexually assaulted the child. The Alaska Supreme Court held that the mother could sue the church for negligent hiring and negligent supervision of the woman in charge of the "tiny tots" room (*Broderick*).

PART THREE

CIVIL RIGHTS

8

Racial Discrimination

The only way to make sense out of the civil rights laws of the United States is to see their development as a debate between the Supreme Court and Congress over two centuries. When the Constitution was written, the drafters of that document decided not to decide the slavery issue. The problem did not become acute until the second decade of the nineteenth century, when Missouri wanted to enter the Union as a slave state. The Senate agreed to admit Missouri, while the House, dominated by northern congressmen, refused. The deadlock was broken when it was agreed to admit Missouri as a slave state and Maine as a free state. It was also agreed in the Missouri Compromise of 1820 that the Louisiana Territory south of Missouri would be slave while the rest of the territory would be free. This compromise held until 1857, when the U.S. Supreme Court declared it unconstitutional in *Dred Scott v. Sandford*.

Dred Scott

Dred Scott was a slave who had been taken through the free state of Illinois and the part of the Louisiana Purchase territory that had been declared "free" by the Missouri Compromise. A number of courts in other countries had decided that once a slave entered free territory, he or she automatically became free. Dred Scott sued his owner and lost. There were eight different opinions, which makes it difficult to say what "the" Court decided, except that the Missouri Compromise was held to be unconstitutional and void.

Chief Justice Taney reasoned in his opinion that slaves are "property," not people, and the Constitution did not give Congress the power to interfere with people's property. The Missouri Compromise was therefore invalid because it deprived slave owners of their property without due process of law. He argued that the Constitution granted citizenship to all people who were free at the time of the Revolution and to their descendants, and that it gave Congress the power to provide for immigration and naturalization. However, the chief justice believed that this power to grant citizenship applied only to people who were born in foreign counties; it did not give Congress the power to "raise to the rank of a citizen anyone born in the United States, who, from birth or parentage, by the laws of the country, belongs to an inferior and subordinate class." In other words, the only way Congress could turn former slaves into citizens would be through a constitutional amendment, but the possibility of getting one approved was nonexistent, short of civil war. Abraham Lincoln was elected president in 1860, and Fort Sumter was shelled on April 12, 1861. Lincoln signed the Emancipation Proclamation on January 1, 1863. Robert E. Lee surrendered on April 9, 1865, and President Lincoln was assassinated six days later. The period of Reconstruction left us with three constitutional amendments and the Reconstruction civil rights acts.

The Thirteenth, Fourteenth, and Fifteenth Amendments

The Thirteenth Amendment says "neither slavery nor involuntary servitude, except as a punishment for crime whereof the party shall have been duly convicted, shall exist within the United States, or any place subject to their jurisdiction." It was this amendment that officially freed the slaves. Some Southern states tried to deal with the new freedmen by arresting them and leasing them out to their former masters who would pay their fine. The Supreme Court declared this to be a violation of the Thirteenth Amendment in 1914 (*Reynolds*).

The Fourteenth Amendment begins by saying, "All persons born or naturalized in the United States, and subject to the jurisdiction thereof, are citizens of the United States and of the State wherein they reside." With that, Chief Justice Taney's decision in *Dred Scott* was overturned. The Amendment goes on to say:

> no State shall make or enforce any law which shall abridge the privileges or immunities of citizens of the United States; nor shall any State deprive any person of life, liberty or property without due process of law; nor deny to any person within its jurisdiction the equal protection of the laws.

Over the years, the Supreme Court decided that this amendment made the Bill of Rights of the U.S. Constitution applicable to state and local governments. That meant that government employers could not fire employees for exercising their right of free speech, invade their privacy, or deny them due process of law (see Chapters 11, 12, 13). It also meant that governments had to treat people equally. For example, in 1978, the U.S. Supreme Court struck down an Alaska statute that required companies using state oil leases to hire residents of Alaska before hiring residents of other states. This law denied the citizens of other states the "equal protection" of the law (*Hicklin*).

The Fifteenth Amendment says that "the right of citizens of the United States to vote shall not be denied or abridged by the United States or by any State on account of race, color or previous condition of servitude." Some states required voters to own property, pay poll taxes, and pass literacy tests. The Supreme Court declared the property ownership and poll tax requirements to be unconstitutional in the 1960s (*Reynolds #2; Hill; Harper*). In 1970, Congress passed the Voting Rights Act outlawing literacy tests as a requirement for voting, and the Supreme Court upheld the statute (*Oregon*).

The Reconstruction Civil Rights Acts

Congress passed a series of civil rights acts after the Civil War that were all but forgotten by the end of the 1870s. The Reconstruction civil rights acts were rediscovered and declared valid by the Supreme Court in 1968 (*Jones*). The most relevant part, Section 1981, says "all persons" shall have the same right to "make and enforce contracts" as "white citizens" (42 U.S.C. sec. 1981). In 1975, the Supreme Court ruled that this included the right to make employment contracts and that this statute could be used to sue both private and government employers for racial discrimination (*Railway Express*). The next year, the Court said that this section also prevented discrimination against whites and, in 1987, the Court made it clear that Section 1981 outlawed all intentional racial discrimination, even discrimination against Arabs and Hispanics (*McDonald; St. Francis*).

Historically, suing under the Reconstruction civil rights acts had several advantages over suing under Title VII. Under Title VII, damages were limited. Generally, employees got up to two years' back pay and their job back. They could not get emotional distress damages, punitive damages, or a jury trial. In one case tried under the Reconstruction acts, the jury awarded $123,000 for emotional distress, $176,000 for lost wages, and $300,000 for punitive damages (*Rowlett*). This right to a jury trial and almost unlimited damages was a major incentive for people to use the Reconstruction civil rights acts whenever possible. However, early on the Supreme Court limited its scope to cases involving intentional racial discrimination.

Title VII of the 1964 Civil Rights Act

President Kennedy proposed a Civil Rights Act in 1963. It was passed in 1964 and became effective in July 1965. The section concerned with employment discrimination is Title VII, which says:

(*a*) It shall be an unlawful employment practice for an employer:

(1) to fail or refuse to hire or to discharge any individual, or otherwise to discriminate against any individual with respect to his compensation, terms, conditions, or privileges of employment, because of such individual's race, color, religion, sex or national origin, or

(2) to limit, segregate, or classify his employees or applicants for employment in any way which would deprive or tend to deprive any individual of employment opportunities or otherwise adversely affect his status as an employee because of such individual's race, color, religion, sex or national origin (42 U.S.C. sec. 2000e-2).

The 1964 Act created the Equal Employment Opportunity Commission (EEOC). This agency writes regulations interpreting the act, investigates charges of discrimination, attempts to negotiate settlements when charges are filed and, in a few cases, files lawsuits to stop discrimination.

The basic procedure under Title VII requires the employee to file a complaint (called a "charge") with the EEOC within 180 calendar days after the discriminatory act. If there is a state humans rights commission and the employee files a complaint with that commission, the deadline for filing with the EEOC is extended to 300 days (*Com. Office Prod.*). The EEOC has 180 days to try to negotiate a settlement or file a lawsuit. If the EEOC decides not to sue (it almost never does), it will issue a "right to sue letter" to the employee who then has 90 days to file a lawsuit in federal court (*Stebbins; Lynn*). If an employee misses these deadlines, he or she may still be able to sue in state court under the state civil rights act, or in federal court under the Reconstruction civil rights acts.

Title VII covers businesses if they have at least 15 employees during at least 20 weeks in a year and if their business "affects commerce." Almost every business *affects commerce* as that term has been defined. It covers religious and educational organizations but allows religious organizations and schools affiliated with religious denominations to discriminate on the basis of religion. Title VII applies to state and local governments as well as to the federal government itself (employees of the federal government must follow a special procedure). It also applies to employment agencies, labor unions, and licensing agencies such as state bar associations and medical boards (*Tyler*).

Title VII specifically allows discrimination if it is the result of a bona fide seniority or merit system (42 U.S.C. sec. 2000e-2(h)). This is true even if the seniority system perpetuates past discrimination (*Teamsters*). Title VII also allows discrimination if sex, religion, or national origin are "bona fide occupational qualifications" (BFOQ) reasonably necessary to the normal operation of the business. To qualify as a BFOQ, the favored sex or religion must possess a quality essential to the job. Just because customers prefer one sex over the other is not good enough. The airlines argued that customers preferred female stewardesses over male stewards but that was not a BFOQ (*Diaz*).

Types of Discrimination

The key question soon became: What types of behavior does Title VII outlaw and how do people who believe that they have been the victims of discrimination go about proving it in court? Title VII (and the Reconstruction civil rights acts) clearly outlawed open, obvious, intentional discrimination. This kind of discrimination was proven by presenting witnesses who heard the employer say things like, "I'm not going to hire any blacks around here." By the 1970s, most employers no longer made such statements.

Some employers tried to get around the law with sex-plus and race-plus rules. For example, one company refused to hire women with preschool-aged children (*Phillips #2*). The U.S. Supreme Court said that this was illegal. While an employer may refuse to hire "anyone with children," it cannot refuse to hire "women" or "blacks" with children. While employers can say "employees cannot be married" (unless a state law forbids this), they cannot say female employees cannot be married (*TWA; Sprogis; Airline Stewards*).

Next, employers tried to discriminate by harassing minority employees until they quit. The courts reacted by creating the idea of "constructive discharge." If someone is treated so badly that they are literally forced to quit, it will be viewed as equivalent to an actual firing. Courts also allowed employees who had been the victim of racial harassment to sue for an injunction to stop the harassment because Title VII says employers may not discriminate with respect to the "conditions" of employment.

Over time, the U.S. Supreme Court developed the idea that there were two types of discrimination: disparate treatment and disparate impact.

In 1973, the Supreme Court explained how someone proved that they were the victim of disparate treatment in *McDonnell Douglas*. First, the employee had to prove that he or she: (1) was within a protected class; (2) applied for the job or promotion; (3) was qualified for the job or promotion; (4) was not hired or promoted (or was fired); and (5) that the employer hired someone of a different race, color, religion, sex, or national origin.

Once the employee has made out this prima facie case, then the employer had to present a "legitimate reason" why the employee was not hired or promoted. Then it was up to the judge to decide if this reason was legitimate or merely a pretext for discrimination (*Sweeney*).

Cases in the 1970s were easy. Two white employees were dismissed while a black employee accused of the same theft was not. The Supreme Court found this to be a clear case of race discrimination (*McDonald*). In another case, a group of black police officers were fired while white police officers accused of the same bribe-taking were not. Again, the judge found the bribe-taking to be a mere pretext for race discrimination (*Corley*).

However, the *McDonnell Douglas* "disparate treatment" decision raised many questions. If the employee can simply make out a case by being qualified and a member of a protected class, what about white men? If they are covered by the law as well, and the Supreme Court said that they were, then can they do the same thing? And, if they can, then do employers face a lawsuit every time they make a personnel decision? Federal courts dealt with this problem for a time by making an exception for cases involving white men. They had to prove something extra, something more that would lead the court to believe that they were the victim of race discrimination.

For example, in one case, a white man was fired from a black-oriented radio station in Houston because he did not have the right "voice." The judge said that this was just a pretext for race discrimination (*Chaline*).

Finally, the U.S. Supreme Court said that while an employee could make out a disparate treatment case by proving the five aspects of the prima facie case, if employers are able to present any legitimate reason for their decision the burden is still on the employee to ultimately prove discriminatory intent on the part of the employer.

If the employee cannot prove intentional discrimination, there is another way to prove discrimination under Title VII: disparate impact. The landmark case in this area is *Griggs v. Duke Power Co.*, handed down by the U.S. Supreme Court in 1971. The Duke Power Company required a high school diploma and passing scores on two intelligence tests before it would consider an applicant for a job, any job. These requirements had a "disparate impact" on black job applicants. The federal district judge ruled in favor of Duke Power because there was no evidence of an intent to discriminate. The U.S. Supreme Court overruled this decision, saying "the act proscribes not only overt discrimination, but also practices that are fair in form but discriminatory in operation." While Title VII specifically allows employers to use tests, it requires that the tests not be "intended, designed or used" to discriminate.

It is important to realize that this case required the employee to prove that the job requirement or test prevents a greater percentage of a particular group from meeting the qualifications. Just because a test or requirement makes no sense does not make it illegal. For example, if an employer was willing to hire only people whose favorite color was blue, and 40 percent of all men, 40 percent of all women, and 40 percent of each minority group had the favorite color blue, this requirement would not have a disparate impact. In *Griggs*, statistics showed that 12 percent of blacks had a high school diploma in North Carolina compared with 34 percent of whites.

Once the employee proves disparate impact (the fact of discrimination), the burden shifts to the employer to prove there is good reason to impose this particular requirement. In some cases, the courts have ruled that the requirement is "obviously" job related. For example, one court felt a high school diploma was an obvious requirement for being a police officer (*Castro*). However, courts do not always agree on what is obvious. The California Supreme Court felt that the ability to pass an agility test was obviously related to being a police officer, but the Ninth Circuit Court did not agree (*Hardy*; *Blake #2*).

Watson v. Ft. Worth Bank & Trust

In June 1988, the Supreme Court handed down a decision in the case of *Watson v. Ft. Worth Bank & Trust*. That decision began a chain of events that ultimately resulted in the passage of the 1991 Civil Rights Act. The case involved Clara Watson, a black woman, hired by Ft. Worth Bank & Trust in 1973 (*Watson #2*). In 1976, she was promoted to teller. During the 1980s, she applied for four different promotions, but in each case they were given to white men. The bank did not have any formal, explicit criteria for these jobs but instead relied on the subjective judgment of supervisors acquainted with the candidates for promotion. The executives making the promotion decisions were all white men. The federal district court found that Watson had not met her burden under "disparate treatment" analysis because she had not been able to prove that the "legitimate and nondiscriminatory reasons" for the promotion decisions presented by the bank were merely a pretext for racial discrimination. Watson asked the district court to also consider her case using "disparate impact" analysis, but the district court refused.

Justice O'Connor began her decision for the Supreme Court by pointing out that in "disparate treatment" cases the employee ultimately has the burden of proving that the employer had a "discriminatory intent or motive." The order of proof in these cases begins with the employee establishing a simple prima facie case (discussed above). Then the employer must produce "some evidence" that it had a legitimate, nondiscriminatory reason for the decision. The employee must then prove that this is simply a pretext for discrimination.

Justice O'Connor then turned to the issue of proving "disparate impact."

In these cases, what appears on its face to be a race-neutral rule has a "dispro-portionate" adverse impact on a particular group. While these cases had generally involved the use of tests and specific requirements such as the high school diploma requirement in *Griggs*, this did not have to be the case. Disparate impact analysis can be used in cases such as Ms. Watson's in which the allegation is made that subjective criteria are having a disparate impact on a particular racial group. It would certainly be ironic to decide otherwise and use a law designed to end race discrimination to force out objective job criteria and replace them with subjective criteria even more susceptible to discrimination.

Ms. Watson had statistical evidence that showed that these subjective criteria, over a four-year period, had resulted in 16.7 percent of white appli-cants receiving jobs or promotions compared with 4.2 percent of black appli-cants. An expert testified that the odds of this happening by chance were ten thousand to one.

A unanimous Court (Justice Kennedy did not take part in the decision) agreed that disparate impact analysis could be used in this type of case. The difficult question then became, How would an employer "prove" that its subjective criteria were reasonably related to expected job performance? When objective criteria such as diplomas or tests are involved, this is done either by showing that the test measures a skill needed on the job or by conducting a scientific validation study to show that the test actually predicts job perfor-mance. How would employers do this for subjective criteria? This is where the Court divided. The four most conservative justices (Justices O'Connor, White, Scalia, and Chief Justice Rehnquist) answered this by saying, first of all, that the employee would have to identify a "specific employment practice" or selection criterion and prove that this had a disparate impact on a particular group. This group of four justices also argued that employers would not have to present "validation studies" to prove "business necessity" or "job relatedness." Instead, they would simply have to show a "manifest relationship to the employment in question." The three more liberal justices (Justices Blackmun, Brennan, and Marshall) argued to the contrary, that the employer would still have the burden of "proving" that its criteria were job related or served a business purpose. They believed the fact that subjective criteria would not always be amenable to proof by "validation studies" did not relieve employers from the responsibility of proving that their "subjective" job crite-ria were job related.

Watson was handed down in June 1988. During the year that followed, it is fair to conclude that many members of the Court came to the conclusion that they had taken Title VII as far as they could without further guidance from Congress. After all, it was the Supreme Court that decided that Section 1981 of the Reconstruction civil rights acts applied to employment discrimination, not the specific wording of the statute. It was the Supreme Court that decided that Title VII outlawed not just intentional discrimination but also unintentional discrimination. It was the Supreme Court that developed the order of proof and set the burden of proof, not the statute. Having decided that it was time for Congress to get back into the act, the Supreme Court, in May and June 1989, handed down five decisions that would ultimately force Congress to pass the Civil Rights Act of 1991.

The Five Supreme Court Decisions of 1989

On May 1, 1989, the Court handed down a decision in *Price Waterhouse v. Hopkins*. This case involved a woman, Ann Hopkins, who was a senior manager for the accounting firm of Price Waterhouse and was turned down for promotion to partner (*Hopkins*). As part of the selection process, partners were asked to submit statements suggesting why candidates should or should not be promoted. She was the only woman even proposed for partner status that year. While many partners praised her, others felt she was too "macho" and did not "walk" the way women are supposed to walk. The Court felt that these statements proved that Hopkins was the victim of "sex stereotyping" but that other legitimate factors also played a roll in the decision. The Court divided into three groups over the question of what to do with a "mixed motive" case. Justice Brennan, joined by three other justices, stated that the employee need only prove that an unlawful consideration played "some" motivating roll in the decision. Justices O'Connor and White believed the employee should have to prove that the illegitimate consideration was a "substantial factor" in the decision, while the other three justices argued that discrimination exists only if the illegitimate factor "makes a difference" in the decision. If the employer would have come to the same conclusion anyway, then there was no illegal discrimination. Some people call this the "but for" test because the employee must prove that "but for" the illegitimate factor they would still have a job. With this decision, what had been clear to civil rights attorneys for many years became clear to everyone, namely, that the key is who has the burden to prove what. Ultimately, Ms. Hopkins received her partnership by order of a federal judge (*Hopkins #2*).

On June 5, 1989, the Court decided *Wards Cove Packing Co. v. Atonio*. This case involved an Alaska salmon cannery with two types of jobs, unskilled canning jobs filled mainly by nonwhites, and white-collar jobs filled mainly by whites (*Wards Cove*). The nonwhite workers sued, arguing that this statistical disparity (disparate impact) was the result of hiring practices that had the effect of racial discrimination. The circuit court ruled that the plaintiffs had proven disparate impact simply by showing the statistical divergence between the two work groups and did not have to prove that a particular job-selection criterion had a disparate impact. The circuit court also ruled that once disparate impact had been shown, the burden fell on employers to prove their hiring criteria were job related.

A majority of the U.S. Supreme Court overruled both aspects of the circuit court decision. First, the Supreme Court said a case of disparate impact cannot be made simply by showing that nonwhites fill most of one type of job and whites most of another. There would have to be some showing that nonwhites had applied for and were basically qualified for the jobs in question. The issue is the percentage of qualified nonwhite applicants hired compared with the percentage of qualified white applicants hired. A majority of the Court felt that to allow lawsuits to proceed simply because a large percentage of those holding a particular job were white would put every employer at risk and force the adoption of race quotas as the only defense. To avoid this, employees would be required to prove that one or more particular hiring practices or criteria resulted in a significant disparate impact on the minority group. The Court argued that this would not be difficult to do because most employers fall within the Uniform Guidelines on Employee Selection Procedures of the EEOC, which require employers to keep records disclosing the impact of tests and selection procedures on different races, sexes, and ethnic groups. Second, once the employees have proven that a selection procedure has a disparate impact, they must also prove that the procedure or criteria are "not" job related.

This second aspect of the case, that employees bear the burden of proving that a test, job criterion, or procedure is "not" job-related, was a clear break with past decisions by the Court. While it may be difficult for employers to prove that their selection criteria "are" job-related, it would, in most cases, be impossible for employees to "prove" that these factors "are not" job-related. This is why the law almost never requires someone to prove a "negative." Try proving that you "did not" murder someone!

On June 12, 1989, the Court decided *Martin v. Wilkes*. This case involved a lawsuit that had been brought by black employees against the city of Birmingham, Alabama, alleging racial discrimination in hiring and promotions (*Wilkes*). Ultimately both sides agreed to a negotiated court order (called a consent decree) that would set goals for the hiring and promotion of black firefighters. This consent decree was then challenged by white firefighters who felt that they were the victims of intentional racial discrimination. These white firefighters had never been an actual party to the original lawsuit. The issue was whether they would be allowed to sue after the consent decree had been handed down or would they, and others in their position, be forced to intervene when the original case was being handled or forever hold their peace. The Supreme Court held that these white firefighters were not precluded from suing. They had not been a party to the original lawsuit and, therefore, were not bound by the decision.

On June 12, 1989, the Court decided *Lorance v. AT&T*. This case involved a union contract that in 1979 changed the way seniority was calculated for "testers" (*Lorance*). This change said that no longer would employees who became testers be able to bring their seniority with them. The only relevant seniority would be that earned as a tester. This change put women at a disadvantage so they sued, arguing that the change violated Title VII. The women believed that this change had been made in the union contract to protect male testers who had more seniority as testers but did not have as much overall seniority as some of the women who were now becoming testers. A majority of the Supreme Court ruled against the women. They pointed to the specific language of Title VII, which allows seniority systems to have a discriminatory impact unless it can be proven that discrimination was the intended result of the change. The women would have to prove an intent to discriminate. However, the women in this case did not even get a chance to prove that because the Court said they waited too long to file their complaint with the EEOC. They waited until they were actually demoted, but the Court said they should have filed their complaint when the change was made in the union contract. Because they waited too long, they were out of luck.

On June 15, 1989, the Court decided *Patterson v. McLean Credit Union*. In this case, Brenda Patterson, a black woman, alleged that her employer harassed her because of her race (*Patterson*). The issue was whether she could sue under Section 1981 of the Reconstruction civil rights acts and receive full damages and a jury trial, or was she stuck with Title VII? The district court ruled that Section 1981 did not reach a charge of racial harassment. The Supreme Court had many options when the case came before it. It could have overruled two decades of decisions and decided that Section 1981 was not intended to cover racial discrimination in employment after all. It did not. It could have decided that if Section 1981 covers hiring and firing (making and breaking employment contracts), then it also covers racial harassment because harassment is generally viewed as simply a way to force employees to quit so the employer does not have to actually "fire" them. Instead, the Court looked to the specific language of Section 1981 and compared it with the specific language of Title VII. Section 1981 speaks only of "contracts." Title VII specifically outlaws discrimination concerning the "terms, conditions, or privileges of employment." While this language could clearly be interpreted to outlaw racial harassment, the language of Section 1981 could not. This decision was not totally bad for employees, however. The Court also said that the "disparate treatment" system of proof would apply to Section 1981 cases as well. This means that to recover under Section 1981, the employee needs to prove only that he or she is qualified for the position, was rejected, and the employer continued to search or filled the position with a person of a different race (remember Section 1981 deals only with race). This creates an inference of discrimination, which the employer can overcome by "articulating" a legitimate, nondiscriminatory reason for its actions. The employee then must prove that this is mere pretext and that the real reason was intentional racial discrimination.

Federal circuit courts followed the Supreme Court's lead in *Patterson* and ruled that because Section 1981 only speaks of "making" contracts, it only outlaws discrimination in hiring, not firing (*McKnight*; *Prather*). The Supreme Court refused to review these decisions.

These five decisions brought the main problem into sharp focus. The Supreme Court had been asked for over two decades to reconcile two civil rights laws, passed into law a century apart, without any guidance from Congress. The Court also had come to the realization in *Watson* of just how potentially far-reaching its decisions could be. Was it really the intent of Congress to force employers to justify every job criterion and hiring practice that had a negative impact on a particular group, or had the Court gone too far in *Watson*? A good argument could be made that a majority of the representatives and senators who voted for the Civil Rights Acts of 1866 and 1964 would be surprised to learn how far the Court had taken those laws without further guidance from Congress.

Congressional leaders spent the next two years trying to come up with a new civil rights law that either a majority of Congress and the president could agree on or two-thirds of each house of Congress could agree on. Finally, in November 1991, it looked as if a compromise had been reached that two-thirds of both houses of Congress might be willing to accept. At that point, President George Bush stepped in and agreed to sign the Civil Rights Act of 1991.

The Civil Rights Act of 1991

The act begins by saying that its main purpose is to overturn the *Wards Cove* decision, to provide guidance in disparate impact cases, and to respond to several "recent" Supreme Court decisions. The act amended Section 1981 of the Reconstruction civil rights acts to read that the term *make and enforce contracts* includes "the making, performance, modification, and termination of contracts, and the enjoyment of all benefits, privileges, terms, and conditions of the contractual relationship," and that the section applies to "impairment by nongovernmental discrimination" as well as "impairment under color of State law." This took care of the argument that Section 1981 did not apply to racial harassment or firing that was made in *Patterson v. McLean Credit Union* and the cases that followed it.

The act also addressed another discrepancy. Section 1981 had allowed victims of intentional racial discrimination to sue for full compensatory and punitive damages while people suing under Title VII for sex, religious, national origin, or handicap (under the new Americans with Disabilities Act) discrimination were stuck with a little back pay. The 1991 Act says that these people may sue for compensatory damages if they can prove intentional discrimination, and punitive damages if they can prove the employer "engaged in a discriminatory practice . . . with malice or with reckless indifference to the federally protected rights of an aggrieved individual." They may not sue government employers for punitive damages under this new law.

The act then limited the amount of that part of the compensatory damage award that is intended to compensate for "future pecuniary losses, emotional pain, suffering, inconvenience, mental anguish, loss of enjoyment of life, and other nonpecuniary losses" plus punitive damages to $50,000 for employers with more than 14 and less than 101 employees, $100,000 for employers with more than 100 and less than 201 employees, $200,000 for employers with more than 200 and less than 501 employees, and $300,000 for employers with more than 500 employees. It is important to realize that these limits do not apply to other compensatory damages such as actual out-of-pocket expenses and back pay caused by the discriminatory act. Also, these limits do not apply to people suing for intentional racial discrimination under Section 1981.

What about the question of a jury? The act says that anyone suing for compensatory or punitive damages can have a jury.

The 1991 Act then turned to *Wards Cove* and the question of how to handle "disparate impact" cases. The act says the employee must prove a "particular employment practice" causes a disparate impact. While the employee must, in most cases, prove that a particular practice has a disparate impact, if the employee "can demonstrate to the court that the elements of a respondent's decisionmaking process are not capable of separation for analysis, the decisionmaking process may be analyzed as one employment practice." The burden of proof then shifts to the employer to prove that the employment practice is "job related for the position in question and consistent with business necessity." If the employer can prove that the particular practice does not have a disparate impact, the employer does not have to prove that it is required by business necessity. In other words, the first issue is: Does the practice or practices in question have a disparate impact on a particular group? If the answer is no, then it does not matter whether the practice is related to the job. If it does have a disparate impact, then the employer must prove that the job requires this particular qualification or skill. The only way to prove that for criteria that are not "obviously" job related will be with validation studies that most employers will not be able or willing to perform. The act also says that the fact that an employment practice is required by business necessity may not be used as a defense against a claim of intentional discrimination.

If the employer proves that the challenged practice is job-related and consistent with business necessity, the act says the employee can nevertheless establish an unlawful employment practice by demonstrating that a "less discriminatory alternative practice" that would serve the employer's legitimate interests is available and that the employer refuses to adopt that practice.

One of the ways many employers tried to deal with the problem of tests that had a disparate impact on a particular group was to increase the score of that particular group. To understand this requires a step back into history. The early intelligence tests consisted of a series of tests measuring different aspects of what we might call intelligence. It took several hours to conduct the full test. Over time, this procedure was thought to be too expensive and time-consuming, so it was decided to use just one of the many subtests to give an approximate score. The question was, Which of the subtests had the best correlation with the overall score? The answer was the vocabulary subtest. The vocabulary subtest became the standard "quick and dirty" intelligence test. While that might be fair for many people, it was not fair for people who grew up in an environment in which something other than standard English was spoken. These people, as a group, came up with predictably lower scores. The test makers could have dealt with this problem by developing other "quick and dirty" tests that did not have this result, but instead it was decided to simply add to the scores of the affected group to make up for the difference in test results. During the 1980s, many women felt that this practice discriminated against them because they would come up with a high score on a standard test only to have a minority male candidate beat them once the minority add-on was applied. There was also resentment because it was assumed that all Hispanics or blacks suffered from the same deprivation, which is a silly assumption. The 1991 Civil Rights Act makes it illegal "to adjust scores of, use different cutoff scores for, or otherwise alter the results of, employment related tests on the basis of race, color, religion, sex or national origin." It is important to realize that this means that many tests used in the past will not be used in the future because they will have a disparate impact.

What about the decision in *Price Waterhouse v. Hopkins* that stated that even if the employee could prove that race, sex, religion, or national origin was a factor in making the hiring decision, the employer would be given the chance to prove that a similar decision would have resulted even if this discrimination had not been a factor in the decision? The 1991 Act says that the employer is guilty of discrimination once it is proven that race, color, religion, sex, or national origin was a "motivating factor . . . even though other factors also motivated the practice." In other words, as Justice Brennan said in *Hopkins*, if an illegal consideration played any part in the decision, it is illegal. However, if the employer can prove that the same decision would have been reached without the illegal factor being considered, the court may grant only "declaratory relief," "injunctive relief," and "attorney's fees and costs." The court may not award any "admission, reinstatment, hiring, promotion, or payment."

What about the decision in *Martin v. Wilkes* that deals with whether people other than those directly involved in the lawsuit can intervene to protect themselves from what they perceive to be discrimination caused by a federal court decision? The 1991 Act says that a "litigated or consent judgment or order" may not be challenged by anyone who was given notice that the decision was about to be made and an opportunity to object to the decision. Also, the decision may not be objected to by anyone whose "interests were adequately represented by another person who had previously challenged the judgment or order on the same legal grounds and with a similar factual situation, unless there has been an intervening change in law or fact." Presumably this means that if a group of whites have already attacked an order, another group of whites, hired later and finding themselves the victims of the order, cannot file another lawsuit to challenge the order unless something has happened to make their allegations different from those of the group who had sued over the same issue before.

The 1991 Act also dealt with what had become a difficult question, namely, the extent to which U.S. companies doing business outside the country were bound to follow the dictates of the U.S. Civil Rights Act. The act says that American citizens working for U.S. companies or their foreign subsidiaries are protected in foreign countries, but those U.S. companies doing business in foreign countries may defend themselves by showing that they were only obeying the laws of the particular foreign country. This overturned the 1991 Supreme Court decision in *EEOC v. Arabian American Oil Co.*, which held that American civil rights laws did not reach beyond the borders of the United States (*Arabian American*).

What about the seniority system problem of *Lorance v. AT&T*? The 1991 Act says that "an unlawful employment practice occurs, with respect to a seniority system that has been adopted for an intentionally discriminatory purpose in violation of this title . . . when the seniority system is adopted, when an individual becomes subject to the seniority system, or when a person aggrieved is injured by the application of the seniority system." That means people in a position similar to the women in the *Lorance* case may sue.

The act allows judges to award expert witness fees and interest on judgments. The act also puts congressional employees, presidential appointees, and higher level state-appointed officials under the federal civil rights laws.

The Quota Question

Throughout much of the debate over the 1991 Civil Rights Act, the issue of quotas came up time and again. What was lost in this discussion was the fact that there is no government agency capable of telling employers for each job position how many women or minorities (or handicapped people or over-40 people) there are in the relevant labor pool for that position. While some federal judges have ordered quotas, that has been in situations in which only one race was involved and only after extensive testimony from experts about how many of that race are available in a limited labor pool (the state of Alabama, for example).

What will employers do now that the 1991 Civil Rights Act is law? They will stop using job criteria that they cannot justify in a court if those criteria have a negative impact on women or a minority group. They will continue to use criteria that are obviously job related, such as high school diplomas for police and an ability to read, write, and use a computer for secretaries. What if an employer has used obviously acceptable criteria and still has a 100 applicants for 10 positions? If there is no valid way to rank those applicants (and for most jobs there will not be), then the only fair way will be to put the names in a hat and draw out 10.

What if an employer said, "Enough. Tell me how many of each sex, race, and group to have and I will comply if you will promise me I will be free from civil rights lawsuits as a result." Under the current federal law, there is no way the EEOC or any other agency could make that promise. Many federal laws have what is called a "safe harbor" that simply says if you "do it this way," you cannot be sued. Should the civil rights laws provide employers with some kind of safe harbor if they actually have a balanced work force?

The Future of Disparate Impact

The major purpose of the 1991 Civil Rights Act was to legislatively legitimate the concept of disparate impact. Several circuit court decisions handed down in 1990 and 1991 suggest what the future may hold in this area.

In one case, a section of the United States Army had very few blacks above the GS-11 level. The black employees proved that this was the result of using "performance awards" as a major criterion in making promotion decisions. These performance awards were given out based on the subjective judgment of supervisors. The army failed to prove that people who received performance awards actually performed better in the higher ranks. The court ruled that performance awards may no longer be used as a criterion for promotion in this section of the army (*Emanuel*). A private employer used subjective decisions by supervisors to make promotion decisions and almost no black employees were promoted. The employer failed to show why objective criteria could not be used and failed to justify the use of subjective decisions. The court ruled that subjective decisions may no longer by used in making promotions (*Mozee*). In another case, applicant flow data demonstrated that the job interview had a disparate impact on black applicants, and the employer failed to show any justification for using job interview performance to make hiring decisions. Interviews can no longer by used by this employer (*Green*).

The city of Jacksonville, Florida, used a written test to make promotion decisions in its fire department. The test was passed by 15 percent of black applicants and 57 percent of white applicants. The city admitted that the test had no relationship to the jobs in question because the higher level jobs required supervisory skills and the test did not measure these skills. The test may no longer be used (*Nash*). The city of Bridgeport, Connecticut, used a written test for promotion in its police department that had a disparate impact on black and Hispanic candidates. The court ruled that the test may be used to decide who "passed" but not to rank candidates. Also, black and Hispanic police officers from outside the state will now sit on the review board that makes promotion decisions in the future (*Bridgeport*). The town of Harrison, New Jersey, had a rule that only city residents could apply for city jobs. This had a disparate impact on blacks who made up a large percentage of the local labor pool but a small percentage of the city's residents. This criterion may no longer be used (*Newark NAACP*).

In 1991, the Seventh Circuit Court was faced with a Chicago manufacturer who never advertised job openings but simply waited for people to walk in and apply. This resulted in very few black employees because the factory was located in a Hispanic and Asian section of the city, and most of the employees who might tell others about job openings were Hispanic and Asian. Hispanics and Asians made up 80 percent of the work force. The court ruled that using only "word of mouth" to attract job candidates is illegal if it has a disparate impact on a minority group. It sent the case back for further fact-finding (*Chicago Miniature*).

These decisions suggest that many employers in both the private and public sector are in for a rude awakening now that the 1991 Civil Rights Act has legitimated these decisions.

Affirmative Action

It is almost funny that the 1991 Civil Rights Act says it does not affect affirmative action that is in "accordance with the law," because there is no federal statute on the subject of affirmative action. The only mention of affirmative action in the 1964 Civil Rights Act is a command that federal judges not use affirmative action to correct an imbalance between the percentage of minority members working for a particular employer and the percentage of qualified minority members in the work force (42 U.S.C. sec. 2000e-2j). Affirmative action is even more an invention of the U.S. Supreme Court than is disparate impact analysis. Many decisions in favor of affirmative action were decided by a five-to-four vote with Justices Brennan, Marshall, and Powell being three of the five winning votes. All three of these justices have since been replaced by justices who are believed not to favor affirmative action. Given that fact, what are the current rules on affirmative action?

It is important to distinguish between four types of possible affirmative action plans. Type One Plans simply say that an employer will do more to seek out and encourage minorities and women to apply for jobs. This is not what lawyers mean by the term *affirmative action*. Type Two Plans say that if two candidates are essentially equal in qualifications, then the job will go to the woman or minority candidate if women or minorities are underrepresented in the company or agency at that position. While this does result in discrimination, it seems acceptable to many people. Type Three Plans require that women or minorities get the job if they meet the minimum qualifications, even if there are clearly more qualified white male candidates. This type is more objectionable to many people. Type Four Plans say that women or minorities will get the job and the search will continue until acceptable women or minority candidates can be found regardless of whether a white male is currently available and qualified. This is the most objectionable type of affirmative action plan to many people.

Three rules of affirmative action are probably still in force after the change in the makeup of the Court: the O'Connor Rule, the White Rule, and the Powell Rule.

Mississippi Women's University was founded in 1884 as the Mississippi Industrial Institute and College for the Education of White Girls. A century later, Joe Hogan wanted to attend Mississippi Women's University to study nursing, but the school refused to accept him because he was a man. Justice O'Connor, writing for a majority of the Court, held that this violated the equal protection clause of the Fourteenth Amendment. Mississippi argued that its single-sex admission policy was an affirmative action plan designed to compensate for past discrimination against women. Justice O'Connor did not buy this given that 98 percent of all nurses are women. The O'Connor Rule says you cannot have an affirmative action plan that protects the majority (*Hogan*).

Because of a budget crisis, the city of Memphis, Tennessee, was faced with having to lay off firefighters. It became obvious that if the city laid off on the basis of seniority, most of those cut would be newly hired blacks. The federal district judge ordered the city to forget seniority and lay off more whites than blacks. Justice White, writing for a majority of the Court, said this violated Title VII, which specifically allows the use of bona fide seniority systems (*Stotts*). In 1986, the Court was faced with an agreement between the Jackson School Board and the Jackson Teacher's Union that would have protected minority teachers from layoffs. Justice White was the swing vote and again he ruled that this plan was illegal because it resulted in the laying off of white teachers who would not have otherwise been laid off (*Wygant*). The White Rule says there is a fundamental difference between not being hired and being fired. An affirmative action plan can prevent some whites from being hired but it cannot cause whites to be fired.

The *Bakke* case involved a white man who was turned down for admission to the University of California at Davis Medical School because of his race. The school had set aside a fixed number of positions for minority applicants even though the school had no history of intentional discrimination. The school was simply trying to correct what it perceived to be an imbalance in the medical profession. Four justices liked the plan and four did not. Justice Powell was the swing vote and wrote his own opinion. The Powell Rule rejects strict quotas unless there is a history of intentional discrimination at the institution. In this case, there was no such history so the quotas would have to go. These rules can be applied to two types of affirmative action plans—those required by a federal judge and voluntary plans.

Until recently, federal judges were allowed to use affirmative action plans if they met the above three rules and followed what might be called the Powell criteria. This is illustrated by a 1986 case involving a union that had engaged in "egregious" intentional racial discrimination (*Local 28*). The federal judge ordered an affirmative action plan that would be in place until the level of nonwhite members in the union had reached 29 percent (the percentage of nonwhites in the relevant labor pool—New York City). Justices Brennan, Marshall, Stevens, and Blackmun found the plan acceptable. Justice Powell wrote his own opinion approving this plan because it met his own personal list of criteria:

1. There were really no alternative remedies.
2. The plan would last a short length of time.
3. The plan was related to the percentage of minorities in the relevant labor pool.
4. The plan allowed the judge to waive the quota if in good faith the quotas could not be met.
5. The plan did not result in the firing of whites.

Because the plan satisfied all of these criteria, he allowed it.

In 1987, the Supreme Court was faced with a federal district judge who found the Alabama Department of Public Safety guilty of egregious intentional racial discrimination (*Paradise*). The judge ordered the department to promote one black officer for each white officer promoted until 25 percent of the corporals were black. Again Justice Powell was the swing vote and again he allowed the plan because it met his personal list of criteria. Justices Brennan, Marshall, and Powell are no longer on the Supreme Court, so what the current rules are for court-ordered affirmative action plans is anybody's guess.

What are the current rules on voluntary affirmative action plans? It seems clear that Type One Plans are allowed. Everyone is in favor of reaching out to women and minorities and trying to get them to apply for jobs or promotions that they may not be aware of. On the other hand, no Type Four Plan has ever been approved by a federal circuit court. The case of Dennis Walters provides an example (*Walters*). He applied twice for the job of Cyclorama director with the city of Atlanta. The Cyclorama is a giant painting, 50 feet high and 350 feet in circumference, that depicts the Civil War battle of Atlanta. Dennis Walters decided at the age of six that he wanted to be the director of the Cyclorama when he grew up. In 1981, the position became open and the city established a list (called a register) of eligible applicants for the position. Seven people were on the list, all white. Three were recommended to the parks commissioner, who refused to hire any and asked for a new register. At that point Dennis Walters sued under the Reconstruction civil rights acts for intentional race discrimination. In 1982, a new register was established and Walters was again one of the three finalists for the position. The position was given to a black man who was not one of the three finalists. This gentleman was fired the next year for violating city regulations. The jury found that Walters was the victim of intentional racial discrimination. He was awarded back pay and given the job. Because he had sued under the Reconstruction civil rights acts he also received $150,000 for mental anguish and $7,000 for punitive damages.

What about Type Two Plans that allow women or minorities to get the job if they are essentially equally qualified? In 1987, the Supreme Court decided the case of *Johnson v. Santa Clara County, California* (*Johnson #2*). The case involved the job of road dispatcher for the county. When the job came open, none of the 238 people holding jobs in the skilled-craft category was a woman. A panel conducted interviews, and seven applicants scored above 70 on the interview. Paul Johnson, a white man, scored 75 while Diane Joyce, a white woman, scored 73. Joyce got the promotion under the county affirmative action plan, and Johnson sued. Justices Brennan, Marshall, Blackmun, Stevens, and Powell approved the plan because of the gross underrepresentation of women in a "traditionally segregated job category." Justice O'Connor agreed, finding this to be a clear case in which a voluntary affirmative action plan could be used even though there was no evidence of past intentional discrimination. It seems that a Type Two Plan may be allowed to increase female or minority representation in a "traditionally segregated job category."

What about Type Three Plans that set up quotas? In 1979, the Court allowed a voluntary affirmative action plan agreed to between a union and an employer that required half of all people admitted into the employer's training program to be black until the percentage of blacks in the plant was equal to the percentage of blacks in the local labor pool (*Steelworkers*). In 1986, six justices approved a similar plan worked out between the city of Cleveland and the firefighter's union (*Local 93*). The Court liked these plans because they were temporary, did not lay off white workers, and allowed some whites to continue to enter the training programs. However, three of the justices that voted in favor of these plans no longer sit on the U.S. Supreme Court. These kinds of plans seem the most vulnerable to future Supreme Court action.

Type Three Plans have led to a great deal of resentment in American society, whether they are voluntary or the result of a court order. To see why, we have only to examine one such plan. In 1989, the Supreme Court declared a plan by the city of Richmond, Virginia, to be a violation of the equal protection clause of the Fourteenth Amendment (*Richmond*). The plan required contractors with the city to hire 30 percent of their subcontractors from businesses at least 51 percent owned by blacks, Spanish-speakers, Orientals, Native Americans, Eskimos, or Aleuts. The Court was appalled that this plan favored Spanish-speakers, Orientals, Native Americans, Eskimos, and Aleuts when there was no reason to think these groups had ever been the victim of discrimination in Richmond, Virginia (has an Aleut ever set foot in Richmond?). Justice Stevens was very unhappy because this plan benefited people who could not possibly have ever been the victims of past discrimination. Justice O'Connor was unhappy because this plan allowed minority firms from all over the country to come to Richmond and receive a special privilege even though the plan was supposed to make up for past discrimination inside Richmond.

It is anticipated that, at some point in the 1990s, the current Supreme Court will do to affirmative action plans what it did to civil rights law in general in May and June of 1989. It will then be up to Congress to reach a compromise on which types of affirmative action plans are allowed under what circumstances. That will be even more difficult than writing the Civil Rights Act of 1991.

Discrimination by Treaty

It often comes as a shock to many American workers that the foreign companies they work for can legally discriminate against them because they are Americans. This is because the United States has signed treaties with many foreign countries that allow American companies to discriminate in favor of Americans in those countries and foreign companies to do the same in the United States. That doesn't mean that these companies can discriminate on any other basis. For example, one executive sued Korean Air claiming age discrimination when he was replaced by a younger Korean. The Third Circuit Court ruled that the Korean company had a right to discriminate against the American on the basis of nationality under the treaty but did not have a right to discriminate on the basis of age. It sent the case back for the district court to determine if age played a part in the decision (*Korean Air*). In 1991, the Seventh Circuit Court came to the same conclusion in a similar case involving a Japanese company (*Quasar*).

State Laws

Table 8.1 provides a summary of the state civil rights statutes and constitutional provisions. Many state laws protect much more than just "race, color, religion, sex, or national origin." A number of states prohibit discrimination based on marital status or parenthood. Others prohibit discrimination based on mental disorder or mental retardation. Still others prohibit discrimination based on sexual orientation, personal appearance, or political affiliation.

Employees cannot sue under Title VII unless their employer has 15 employees. Employees cannot sue under the Reconstruction civil rights acts unless they are the victims of intentional racial discrimination. In many states, employees can sue under the state civil rights statute even if they work for smaller companies, and they may receive full damages and a jury trial. For example, in Minnesota, an employee may be awarded up to three times the compensatory damages along with mental anguish damages, punitive damages, and attorney fees (*Cooper #2; Kolstad*). In Iowa, employees can receive mental anguish damages, back pay, front pay, and attorney fees (*Hy-Vee; Lynch*). In many states it is still not clear whether the employee gets a jury trial under the state civil rights law. Everyone in Iowa assumed that they did until the Iowa Supreme Court decided in 1990 (with a five-to-four decision) that they did not (*ADM*).

The legislators of at least one state, Michigan, became so unhappy with the way affirmative action plans were being created and enforced in their state that they amended the state civil rights law to require that all such plans be

Table 8.1   State Civil Rights Statutes

Alaska 18.80.220	Race, color, religion, sex, national origin, age, handicap, marital status, change in marital status, pregnancy, parenthood.
Const., Art. 1, sec. 3	Const. protects against race, color, creed, sex, or national-origin discrimination by government.
Arizona 41-1461, 1463	Race, color, religion, sex, national origin, age, handicap (boss must have 15 employees).
23-340, 341	Equal pay for women.
Const., Art. 2, sec. 13	Const. guarantees equal protection for all.
Arkansas 11-4-601 to 612	Equal pay for women.
21-3-201 to 205	No age discrimination in public employment.
Const., Art. 2, sec. 3.18	Const. guarantees equality under the law.
California Gov't Code 12940 to 12945	Race, color, religion, sex, national origin, ancestry, age, handicap, marital status, pregnancy, medical condition (boss must have 5 employees).
Const.	Const. guarantees equality under the law.
Art. 1, sec. 7 Art. 1, sec. 8	Const. protects against race, sex, creed, color, or ethnic-origin discrimination.
Colorado 24-34-402	Race, color, creed, sex, national origin, ancestry, age, handicap. Employers with over 24 employees may not prevent their employees from being married to each other.
8-5-102	Equal pay for women.
Const., Art. 2, sec. 29	Const. protects against sex discrimination by government.
Connecticut 46a-60, 70	Race, color, religious creed, sex, national origin, age, ancestry, sexual orientation, mental disorder, mental retardation, marital status, physical disability (boss must have 3 employees).
31-75	Equal pay for women.
Const.	Const. guarantees equal rights.
Art. 1, sec. 1 Art. 1, sec. 20	Const. protects against race, color, religion, ancestry, or national-origin discrimination by government.
Delaware 19-710 to 718	Race, color, religion, sex, national origin, marital status, age (boss must have 4 employees).
19-720 to 728	Employers with over 19 employees may not discriminate against the handicapped.
19-1107A	Equal pay for women.
District of Columbia 1-2512, 1-2505	Race, color, religion, sex, national origin, age, handicap, marital status, personal appearance, sexual orientation, family responsibilities, matriculation, political affiliation, pregnancy, childbirth.

Table 8.1—*Continued*

Florida	Race, color, religion, sex, national origin, age, handicap,
760.10	marital status (boss must have 15 employees).
448.07	Equal pay for women.
Georgia	Handicap (boss must have 15 employees).
34-6A-1 to 6	
34-5-1 to 7	Equal pay for women.
Const., Art. 1, sec. 1	Const. guarantees equal protection of the law.
Hawaii	Race, color, religion, sex, ancestry, age, physical handicap,
378-2	sexual orientation, marital status, arrest record.
Const.	Const. guarantees equal rights.
Art. 1, sec. 2,	Const. protects against sex, race, religion, or ancestry
Art. 1, sec. 3.5	discrimination by government.
Idaho	Race, color, religion, sex, national origin, age, handicap
67-5909	(boss must have 5 employees).
44-1701 to 1704	Equal pay for women.
56-707	Government may not discriminate against handicapped.
Const., Art. 1, sec. 2	Const. guarantees equality under the law.
Illinois	Race, color, religion, sex, national origin, ancestry, age,
Ch. 68 sec. 1-101	handicap, marital status, unfavorable military
to 9-102	discharge (boss must have 15 employees).
	Handicap (boss must have 1 employee).
Const., Art. 1, sec.	Const. protects against discrimination because of race,
17, 18, 19	color, creed, national ancestry, sex, or handicap by
	private employers or government.
Indiana	Race, color, religion, sex, national origin, ancestry,
22-9-1-1 to	handicap (boss must have 6 employees).
22-9-2-11	Age (boss must have 1 employee).
22-2-2-4	Equal pay for women.
Const., Art. 1, sec. 23	Const. guarantees equal privileges for all.
Iowa	Race, color, religion, creed, sex, national origin,
601A.6	handicap, age (18 or over), pregnancy, childbirth
	(boss must have 4 employees).
19A.18	The state will not discriminate because of political
	opinion, religion, race, national origin, sex, or age.
Const., Art. 1, sec. 6	Const. guarantees equal privileges for all.
Kansas	Race, color, religion, sex, national origin, ancestry, age,
44-1009	physical handicap (boss must have 4 employees).
44-1113	
Const., Bill of Rt.,	Const. guarantees equal rights.
sec. 1	
Kentucky	Race, color, religion, sex, national origin, age, handicap,
344.040	smokers (boss must have 8 employees).
207.150	
337.420	Equal pay for women.
Const., Bill of Rt.,	Const. guarantees equality under the law.
sec. 3	

Table 8.1—*Continued*

Louisiana 23:1006	Race, color, religion, sex, national origin (boss must have 15 employees).
23:972	Age (boss must have 20 employees).
23:1002	Sickle-cell trait (boss must have 20 employees).
Maine 5-4572	Race, color, religion, sex, national origin, ancestry, age, whistleblowers, people who assert worker's compensation claims, handicap.
26-628	Equal pay for women.
Const., Art. 1, sec. 6-A	Const. guarantees equal protection of the law.
Maryland Art. 49B, sec. 16, 17	Race, color, religion, sex, national origin, age, physical or mental handicap, marital status, pregnancy, childbirth (boss must have 15 employees).
Labor Code 3-304	Equal pay for women.
Const., Dec. of Rt., art. 46	Const. protects against sex discrimination by government.
Massachusetts Ch. 151B, sec. 4	Race, color, religion, sex, national origin, ancestry, age, sexual orientation, handicap (boss must have 6 employees).
Ch. 149, sec. 24A	Age (boss must have 1 employee).
Ch. 149, sec. 105A	Equal pay for women.
Michigan 37.2202	Race, color, religion, sex, national origin, age, height, weight, marital status.
37.1202	Handicap (boss must have 4 employees).
408.397	Equal pay for women.
Const., Art. 1, sec. 2	Const. guarantees equal protection of the law. Const. protects against religion, race, color, or national- origin discrimination by government.
Minnesota 363.03 181.81	Race, color, religion, sex, national origin, age, disability, marital status, status with regard to public assistance.
181.67	Equal pay for women.
Const., Art. 1, sec. 2	Const. guarantees equal protection of the law.
Mississippi 25-9-149	The state as employer may not discriminate because of race, color, religion, sex, national origin, age, or handicap.
79-1-9	A corporation may not interfere with the social, civil, or political rights of its employees.
Missouri 213.010 to .126	Race, color, religion, sex, national origin, ancestry, age, handicap (boss must have 6 employees).
290.400 to .460	Equal pay for women.
Const., Art. 1, sec. 2	Const. guarantees equal rights under the law.
Montana 49-1-101 to 49-4-511	Race, color, religion, sex, national origin, age, handicap, marital status.
39-3-104	Equal pay for women.

Table 8.1—*Continued*

Nebraska	Race, color, religion, sex, national origin, marital status,
48-1104	disability (boss must have 15 employees).
48-1001	Age (boss must have 25 employees).
48-1219 to 1227.01	Equal pay for women.
Nevada	Race, color, religion, sex, national origin, age, handicap
613.330	(boss must have 15 employees).
608.017	Equal pay for women.
New Hampshire	Race, color, religion, sex, national origin, age, handicap,
354-A:8	marital status (boss must have 6 employees).
275:37	Equal pay for women.
Const.	Const. guarantees equality under the law.
Pt. 1, Art. 1	Const. protects against race, creed, color, sex, or
Pt. 1, Art. 2	national-origin discrimination by government.
New Jersey	Race, color, creed, sex, national origin, ancestry, age,
10:5-12 to 29.1	handicap, marital status, dishonorable discharge,
	atypical hereditary cell, or blood type.
Const., Art. 1, sec. 5	Const. protects against religion, race, color, ancestry, or
	national-origin discrimination by government.
New Mexico	Race, religion, creed, sex, national origin, ancestry, age,
28-1-7	handicap (boss must have 4 employees).
Const., Art. 1, sec. 18	Const. protects against sex discrimination by
	government.
New York	Race, color, creed, sex, national origin, age, disability,
Exec. sec. 296	marital status (boss must have 4 employees).
Labor sec. 194	Equal pay for women.
Const., Art. 1, sec. 11	Const. protects against race, color, creed, or religious
	discrimination by government.
North Carolina	Race, color, religion, sex, national origin, age, handicap
143-422.2	(boss must have 15 employees).
95-28.1	Sickle-cell or hemoglobin C trait (boss must have 1
	employee).
Const., Art. 1, sec. 1	All people are created equal.
North Dakota	Race, color, religion, sex, national origin, handicap, age,
14-02.4-01 to 21	marital status, public assistance status, participating in
34-01-17	lawful activities during nonworking hours (boss must
	have 1 employee).
34-06.1	Equal pay for women.
Ohio	Race, color, religion, sex, national origin, ancestry, age,
4112.02; 4101.17	handicap (boss must have 4 employees).
Oklahoma	Race, color, religion, sex, national origin, age, handicap
Tit. 25, sec. 1302	(boss must have 15 employees).
Oregon	Race, color, religion, sex, national origin, age (18 or
Ch. 659	over), handicap, marital status, expunged juvenile
	record.

Table 8.1—*Continued*

Pennsylvania Tit. 43, sec. 955	Race, color, religion, sex, national origin, ancestry, age, handicap (boss must have 4 employees).
Tit. 43, sec. 336.1	Equal pay for women.
Const., Art. 1, sec. 26	Const. protects against discrimination by government.
Rhode Island 28-5-7	Race, color, religion, sex, ancestry, age, handicap (boss must have 4 employees).
28-6-1 to 21	Equal pay for women.
South Carolina 1-13-80	Race, color, religion, sex, national origin, age (boss must have 15 employees).
South Dakota 20-13-10	Race, color, religion, sex, national origin, ancestry, disability.
60-12-15, 16	Equal pay for women.
Const., Art. VI, sec. 18	Const. guarantees everyone equal privileges and immunities.
Tennessee 4-21-401	Race, color, religion, creed, sex, national origin, age (boss must have 8 employees).
8-50-103	Handicap (boss must have 1 employee).
50-2-202	Equal pay for women.
Texas 5221K	Race, color, religion, sex, national origin, age, handicap (boss must have 15 employees).
Const., Art. 1, sec. 3a	Const. protects against race, color, sex, creed, or national-origin discrimination by government.
Utah 34-35-6	Race, color, religion, sex, national origin, age, handicap (boss must have 15 employees).
Const., Art. 1, sec. 2	Const. guarantees equal protection of the law.
Vermont Tit. 21, sec. 495	Race, color, religion, sex, national origin, ancestry, age, handicap, place of birth.
Virginia 40.1-28.6	Equal pay for women.
Const., Art. 1, sec. 11	Const. protects against race, religion, color, sex, or national-origin discrimination by government.
Washington 49.60.180	Race, color, creed, sex, national origin, age, handicap, marital status (boss must have 8 employees).
49.12.175	Equal pay for women.
Const., Art. 1, sec. 12	Const. guarantees equal privileges for all.
West Virginia 21-5C-7(b)	Race, color, religion, sex, national origin, ancestry, age, handicap (boss must have 6 to 12 employees,
5-11-9	depending on provision).
21-5B	Equal pay for women.
Wisconsin 111.31 to 34	Race, color, creed, sex, national origin, ancestry, age, handicap, marital status, sexual orientation, arrest record, conviction record, National Guard membership.

Table 8.1—*Continued*

Wyoming	Race, color, creed, sex, national origin, ancestry, age,
27-9	handicap (boss must have 2 employees).
27-21-301	Equal pay for women.
Const., Art. 1, sec. 3	Const. protects against race, color, sex, or individual
	circumstances discrimination by government.

Note: The law is always changing. Consult an attorney about your situation.

approved by the state Civil Rights Commission (M.C.L. 37.2210). In one 1990 case, Richard Victorson scored "highly qualified" on a written exam and received the highest score on the oral interview when he applied for the position of Auditor IX at the Michigan Department of the Treasury. A woman scored "qualified" on the written exam but was given the job under an agency affirmative action plan. Richard Victorson sued for discrimination and won. Because the agency had not received permission from the state Civil Rights Commission to institute its affirmative action plan, it could not be used as a defense to the charge of discrimination (*Victorson*).

At the end of 1990, the Supreme Court of California handed down a very important decision (*Rojo*). For years employees had tried to argue that they should be able to sue for "common-law wrongful discharge" when they sue for discrimination. This would guarantee them a jury trial and full damages without regard to the number of persons employed by the employer. State supreme courts rejected this idea. In a 1990 case, the California Supreme Court was faced with a woman suing for sex discrimination who argued that Article I, Section 8, of the California Constitution provided the necessary statement of public policy. That provision says: "A person may not be disqualified from entering or pursuing a business, profession, vocation or employment because of sex, race, creed, color, or national or ethnic origin." The California Supreme Court agreed that this provided an independent statement of public policy and allowed her to sue for common-law wrongful discharge. Whether other state supreme courts will interpret similar provisions in their state constitutions similarly remains to be seen.

People who are the victim of discrimination or harassment should also consider suing under state common law for assault, battery, or intentional infliction of emotional distress. In several cases, state courts have found the use of racial epithets in the workplace to be outrageous and have allowed the victims to sue for intentional infliction of emotional distress (*Alcorn; Agarwal; Franklin*).

9

Sex Discrimination

Equal Protection

The Fourteenth Amendment guarantees to "any person" the "equal protection of the laws." A century passed before women were included in the definition of "person."

This changed in 1971, when a unanimous U.S. Supreme Court struck down an Oregon statute that said "males must be preferred to females" in choosing the administrator of an estate (*Reed*). The Court said this violated the equal-protection clause of the Fourteenth Amendment because it discriminated against women. In 1973, the Court struck down a rule that allowed male members of the armed forces to have their wives receive dependent benefits automatically while female military personnel had to prove their husbands were actually dependent on them for support (*Frontiero*).

In 1975 and 1977, the Court struck down provisions in the Social Security Act that allowed widows to receive benefits denied to widowers (*Weinberger; Califano*).

Today it is clear that governments cannot discriminate against people because of their sex.

The Equal Pay Act

In 1963, Congress passed the Equal Pay Act (29 U.S.C. Sec. 206(d)) as an amendment to the Fair Labor Standards Act originally passed in 1938 and discussed in Chapter 14. Because the law covers almost every employer, it will include some employers that are too small to be covered by Title VII. The Equal Pay Act prohibits the employer from discriminating between employees on the basis of sex by paying wages to employees in such establishment at a rate less than the rate at which he pays wages to employees of the opposite sex . . . for equal work on jobs the performance of which requires equal skill, effort, and responsibility, and which are performed under similar working conditions, except where such payment is made pursuant to (i) a seniority system; (ii) a merit system; (iii) a system which measures earnings by quantity or quality of production; or (iv) a differential based on any other factor other than sex. (29 U.S.C. sec. 206(d)(1))

The Equal Pay Act allows an employer to have different pay scales in different facilities (called "establishments"). However, a federal judge may treat these different facilities as one "establishment" if he or she feels that is necessary to achieve the purposes of the Equal Pay Act (*Goose Creek*).

While the act requires equal pay for equal work, that does not mean the work must be identical. When jobs are "substantially equal," equal pay must be provided (*Shultz*). Judges have decided that the work of male tailors is equal to that of female seamstresses and that the work of male barbers is equal to that of female beauticians (*City Stores; Usery*).

In theory, to prove a violation of the Equal Pay Act, an employee must prove that four things are substantially equal: (1) skill, (2) effort, (3) responsibility, and (4) working conditions. Federal judges have refused to get bogged down in these factors. The real test is, Do the jobs look basically alike?

If male employees perform "extra" duties, federal judges will allow them to be paid more if the extra duties are (1) real; (2) regularly performed; (3) substantial; and (4) a type of work that justifies higher wages (*Shultz; American Can; Fairmont*).

The employer can justify unequal pay for equal work with any one of four reasons (the act calls them defenses): (1) a seniority system; (2) a merit system; (3) the quantity or quality of production; or (4) "any factor other than sex."

The justification must be legitimate. For example, two banks paid men more than women for clerical work. At one bank the men were part of a bona fide training program. The federal judge allowed the bank to pay the male trainees more (*First Victoria*). Another bank argued that it also had a training program, a secret, informal training program open only to men. The judge did not allow that bank to pay men more for the same work (*Security*).

An employee who has been the victim of unequal pay can skip the Equal Employment Opportunity Commission and file a lawsuit directly in federal court. If she wins she gets the difference between what she was paid and what she should have been paid for the previous two years, attorney's fees, and a federal court order forcing the employer to pay women equally in the future. In some cases, women suing under the Equal Pay Act have also received punitive and emotional distress damages in federal court (*Soto*).

More than half the states also have equal pay acts. In those states, a victim has a choice of suing under either the federal or the state statute (see Table 8.1 on pages 111–116).

Title VII

In 1964, when it looked as if the Civil Rights Act was going to pass, a group of congressmen decided that they had a surefire way to stop it. They added "sex" to the list that already included "race, color, religion, and national origin." The act passed anyway.

These opponents then added the "Bennett Amendment." This amendment says: "It shall not be an unlawful employment practice . . . to differentiate on the basis of sex in determining . . . wages . . . if such differentiation is authorized by" the Equal Pay Act (42 U.S.C. sec. 2000e-2(h)).

Both acts allow discrimination based on seniority and merit. While the Equal Pay Act allows "factors other than sex" to justify discrimination, the U.S. Supreme Court has said that these must be legitimate factors and cannot be just an excuse for discriminating against women (*Gunther*). With this interpretation, the Bennett Amendment has not been much of an obstacle to women suing under Title VII.

Everything said in Chapter 8 about Title VII applies to women. The complaint must be filed with the Equal Employment Opportunity Commission (EEOC) within the time limit, and the employee receives two years' back pay, reinstatement, and attorney fees if she wins. Generally, women who are being discriminated against on the basis of pay will want to proceed under both the Equal Pay Act and Title VII. This means going to the EEOC before suing in federal court. When the employee ultimately gets her right-to-sue letter and sues, the judge can figure out which law applies and proceed accordingly. Of course, a woman can sue under Title VII for everything any other minority group member can sue for: not being hired, being fired, being segregated, and being harassed.

The 1991 Civil Rights Act

As you saw in Chapter 8, prior to 1991 people suing for racial discrimination could also sue under the Reconstruction civil rights acts and receive compensatory and punitive damages and a jury trial; however, people suing for sex discrimination were stuck with limited damages and no jury trial under Title VII. The 1991 Civil Rights Act has changed that. It allows the victims of sex discrimination to sue for compensatory damages and to receive a jury trial if they can show that the employer "engaged in unlawful intentional discrimination." They can also sue for punitive damages if they can show the employer (other than a government employer) "engaged in a discriminatory practice . . . with malice or with reckless indifference to the federally protected rights." The limits on damage awards discussed in Chapter 8 apply to sex discrimination and sex harassment cases filed under Title VII.

The Legend of Comparable Worth

Once upon a time a group of female government employees realized that they were performing high-skill jobs for low wages while some male government employees were performing low-skill jobs for high wages. These female employees convinced a number of cities and states to hire consultants to study the "comparable worth" of these jobs. The consultants found that when they compared male-dominated jobs with female-dominated jobs for skill, effort, and responsibility, the women were doing high-skill work for low pay. As a result, a number of cities and states raised the wage scales for female-dominated jobs. Many did not.

Some of the factors that the consultants looked at were the same as those listed in the Equal Pay Act (skill, effort, responsibility). Some female government employees decided that if the states would not implement the findings of these comparable-worth studies, they would ask federal judges to force them to do so under the provisions of the Equal Pay Act. They took this idea to several circuit courts in the 1970s and lost (*Columbia; Angelo; Christensen; Lemons*). The judges said that they would not compare apples with oranges (secretaries with janitors). If the jobs did not look alike, the judges would not order equal pay.

In 1981, the U.S. Supreme Court breathed new life into the comparable-worth concept with the *Gunther* case. The case involved female jail guards who were paid 70 percent of what the male jail guards were paid. A consultant told the county that the women's jobs were "worth" 95 percent of what the men's jobs were "worth" but the county refused to raise the women's pay scale. These jobs looked very similar. The U.S. Supreme Court said this was not a "comparable worth" case but a case of intentional sex discrimination and sent it back to the lower court for further proceedings. No one was sure what the *Gunther* decision meant, but some women hoped it meant that comparable worth was a legitimate concept under the Equal Pay Act. The American Federation of State, County, and Municipal Employees (AFSCME) brought a comparable-worth lawsuit against the state of Washington in the Ninth Circuit Court in 1985 and lost (*AFSCME*). The judges said what they had said in the 1970s: they would not compare apples with oranges. The case did not reach the U.S. Supreme Court because the state settled out of court, agreeing to raise women's salaries by almost half a billion dollars between 1986 and 1992 (female secretaries will eventually make as much as male janitors).

Sexual Harassment

Federal judges arrived at the concept of sexual harassment in two ways. First, the judges said that if an employer made an employee's life so miserable that the employee could not take it any longer and quit, the judges would consider that the equivalent of being fired (constructive discharge). Second, Title VII says employers cannot discriminate with respect to the "conditions" of employment. The judges decided sexual harassment constituted a condition of employment that penalized women.

In 1977, three different federal circuit courts ruled that sexual harassment violated Title VII. Each case involved a woman who had been fired because she refused the sexual advances of her male supervisor. The courts asked if these women would have been fired if they had not been women. The answer was no, so the firings violated Title VII (*Tomkins; Barnes; Garber*).

In 1980 the EEOC defined sexual harassment:

> Unwelcome sexual advances, requests for sexual favors, and other verbal or physical conduct of a sexual nature constitute sexual harassment when (1) submission to such conduct is made either explicitly or implicitly a term or condition of an individual's employment, (2) submission to or rejection of such conduct by an individual is used as a basis for employment decisions affecting such individual, or (3) such conduct has the purpose or effect of unreasonably interfering with an individual's work performance or creating an intimidating, hostile, or offensive working environment. (29 C.F.R. sec. 1604.11(a))

Parts (1) and (2) of this definition outlaw what has come to be known as "quid pro quo" sexual harassment. Part (3) of the regulation outlaws conduct that interferes with a person's work performance or creates a hostile working environment. This has come to be called "hostile environment" sexual harassment. Through the 1980s circuit court after circuit court agreed that creating a hostile working environment for women constituted sexual harassment and violated Title VII.

When Sandra Bundy was subjected to repeated sexual advances by her supervisors, she complained to their supervisor, who said, "Any man in his right mind would want to rape you." The District of Columbia Circuit Court ruled that this was sexual harassment (*Bundy*).

Barbara Henson, a police dispatcher, finally resigned after two years of sexual harassment by the police chief. The court said this was constructive discharge and a violation of Title VII (*Henson*).

Deborah Katz, an air-traffic controller, had to undergo vulgar sexual epithets at work. She complained to a supervisor, who did nothing about it. The court found this to be a case of "hostile environment" sexual harassment (*Katz #2*).

With sexual harassment firmly established as something women could sue for under Title VII, two questions have occupied the judges: What exactly constitutes sexual harassment, and when can the company be held liable for the acts of its employees and supervisors?

It is easy to define quid pro quo sexual harassment. Defining "hostile environment" sexual harassment has not been easy. Federal judges have ruled that the following is not "hostile environment" sexual harassment:

1. A supervisor who flirts (*Bouchet*)
2. A supervisor who asks for a kiss (*Jackson*)
3. A supervisor who calls the employee the Dolly Parton of the office (*Downes*)
4. A supervisor who calls female employees "honey, babe, and tiger" (*Volk*)

Federal judges have ruled that the following is "hostile environment" sexual harassment:

1. Being forced to wear revealing clothes (*Sage Realty*)
2. Being rubbed up against by the supervisor and having to listen to him talk about sex all the time (*Bohen*)
3. Having the male supervisor peer over the bathroom stall while the female employee is going to the bathroom (*Mays*)
4. Having to listen to abusive language and having sexually oriented drawings posted at work (*Zabkowicz*)
5. Having the supervisor keep track of the female employee's menstrual cycle on his office calendar and being asked by the supervisor when the employee was "going to do something nice" for him (*Coley*)

The Reasonable Woman Standard

In 1991, several events suggested that the definition of sexual harassment may be changing and that behavior not believed to be harassment in the 1980s may now be harassment.

In January 1991, the Ninth Circuit Court ruled that the new test in sexual harassment cases should be the "reasonable woman" standard. That means that the activity should be viewed not from the perspective of men, but from the perspective of women, particularly the perspective of the particular woman in the case. In this case, the female employee received two notes from a male employee that shocked and frightened her. The notes expressed love and said that the male employee was "watching" her. While many people might not have been frightened by these notes, this woman was, and it was not unreasonable from a woman's perspective for her to be frightened. Because her employer, the Internal Revenue Service, did not reprimand the male employee, it was guilty of sexual harassment (*Ellison*).

In July 1991, a Michigan Appeals Court came to the same conclusion. The woman worked for a veterinarian who, at one point, sat down beside her on the couch, put his arms around her, and tried to kiss her. The court said this one incident was enough to make out a case of sexual harassment. While courts in the 1980s talked about the need for a "severe" and "pervasive" hostile environment and generally did not believe a single incident could constitute such a hostile environment, this court said that it can. The judges said the situation must be viewed from the point of view of a "reasonable woman" and that it was not reasonable to expect her to have to subject herself to more of this kind of activity before complaining and taking legal action (*Radtke*).

In October 1991, the nation listened to the confirmation hearings of Justice Clarence Thomas and the charges of sexual harassment brought by Professor Anita Hill. The focus of the hearings was whether or not the events she alleged actually happened. Everyone seemed to accept the fact that what she charged him with constituted sexual harassment. She accused him of telling her about an obscene movie, telling her about his sexual prowess, and making some strange comments about pubic hair and a Coke can. These comments were made over a period of years. She never said that he touched her in any way. Most judges in the 1980s would not have found these allegations to come up to the level of sexual harassment (not severe or pervasive enough). In a very real sense, because of the national outcry in this case, the definition of what is and what is not hostile environment sexual harassment has probably changed and cases that come in the 1990s will use the "reasonable woman" standard to bring that change into the law.

Collecting from the Company

The issue in many sexual-harassment cases has been whether the company can be held liable for harassment carried out by supervisors or employees without company approval. The Eleventh Circuit Court held that the company can be held liable for sexual harassment only if "higher management knew or should have known of the sexual harassment and failed to take remedial action" (*Henson*). They require this even if a supervisor is the harasser. On the other hand, the Third Circuit Court has decided that if a supervisor takes part in the harassment that is enough to hold the company liable (*Craig*).

In 1986, the U.S. Supreme Court handed down its first decision in a sexual-harassment case (*Meritor*). In a decision written by Chief Justice Rehnquist, the High Court acknowledged that "hostile environment" is a kind of sexual harassment forbidden by Title VII. In this case, the D.C. Circuit Court (their opinion was under review) had agreed with the Third Circuit Court that a woman who is being harassed by her supervisor did not have to complain to higher management before the company could be held liable. Chief Justice Rehnquist's decision is confusing on this issue. The opinion says that the D.C. Circuit Court "erred in concluding that employers are always automatically liable for sexual harassment by their supervisors." However, he went on to point out that this company did not have a policy against sexual harassment and the company grievance procedure required the employee to file a grievance with the very supervisor who was sexually harassing her. This was too much for Chief Justice Rehnquist, who held the company liable for the harassment.

Chief Justice Rehnquist's opinion holds out the possibility that if a company has a policy against sexual harassment, and a grievance procedure that allows the harassed employee to go directly to higher management, the company might not be held liable for the damages. In a special concurring opinion, Justice Marshall (joined by Justices Brennan, Blackmun, and Stevens) said that a company is always liable for sexual harassment by supervisors. However, he also said if an employee "without good reason bypassed an internal complaint procedure she knew to be effective, a court may be reluctant to find constructive termination and thus to award reinstatement or back pay." In other words, if the company has a legitimate grievance procedure, the sexually harassed employee should try to solve her problems inside the company before going to the EEOC. Also, both opinions suggest that if an employee is being harassed by co-workers instead of her supervisor, she should tell the supervisor before making a federal case out of it.

Taking Concerted Action

There is more than one way to deal with sexual harassment. In one case, the company hired a new supervisor, David Jamison, on September 13, 1976. "By Monday, September 20, 1976, Jamison had requested the sexual favors of six female employees" (*Downslope*). On Wednesday morning, September

22, 1976, several women refused to start work until Mr. Lane, the plant manager, agreed to listen to their complaints. When Lane arrived at the factory, he told the women either to work for Jamison or to "hit the clock." Jamison left town. The women complained to the National Labor Relations Board, which ordered the company to give them back their jobs. The NLRB ruled that these women had a right under federal labor law to "engage in concerted action" for their "mutual aid and protection" (see Chapter 15).

Collecting Real Damages

In many cases, the victims of sexual harassment have not been satisfied with the limited damages they might receive under federal law. Even with the passage of the 1991 Civil Rights Act, many victims of harassment will still find their damages limited. During the 1980s, more and more women combined their civil rights lawsuits with a suit under the state common law for things such as assault, battery, invasion of privacy, and intentional infliction of emotional distress. In many cases, this resulted in an award of significant damages that would not have been available under either the federal or state civil rights laws alone.

In one case, Ray Smalley fired Brenda Phillips because she refused to have sex with him (*Phillips*). The federal judge awarded her $2,666 in back pay. She also sued under Alabama state law for invasion of privacy. Smalley had asked her how often she and her husband had sex, what positions they used, and if she engaged in oral sex. The federal circuit court asked the Alabama Supreme Court if this was something people can sue for under Albama common law. The Alabama Supreme Court said it was. Phillips was awarded an additional $25,000 to compensate her for the invasion of her privacy and for mental anguish.

Evelyn Priest, a waitress, sued under Title VII and under California common law for intentional infliction of emotional distress, false imprisonment, invasion of privacy, and battery (unwanted touching). The federal district judge found that her employer

> touched intimate parts of her body, tried to kiss her, rubbed his body on hers, picked her up and carried her across the bar room, made sexually suggestive comments to and about her in the presence of others which violated her right to privacy, exposed his genitals to her, and subjected other female waitresses to similar treatment. . . .

The judge awarded $12,563 for back pay under Title VII, along with $95,000 compensatory damages and $15,000 punitive damages for the violation of California common law (*Priest*).

The Tenth Circuit Court ruled in 1990 that once an employee tells higher management about the harassment and the harassment continues, the employee may sue the company for intentional infliction of emotional distress. Not taking action to stop harassment is outrageous conduct for which the company can be held directly liable (*Baker*).

Suing under State Civil Rights Laws

During the 1980s, many attorneys decided to take sex-discrimination and sexual-harassment cases to state rather than federal court. Many state statutes provide more damages than does Title VII. Washington state's civil rights act allows women to sue for mental anguish as well as back pay (*Cagle*). In a 1986 sexual harassment case filed under Michigan's civil rights act, the court awarded $240,000 in compensatory damages and $32,000 in punitive damages (*Eide*).

The Massachusetts Supreme Court and an Illinois Appeals Court have both ruled that victims of sexual harassment by supervisors do not have to complain to higher management in order to sue the company under the state civil rights acts (*College-Town; Green Hills*).

In 1991, the Highest Court in New York upheld an award by the state human rights commissioner of $450,000 in damages for mental anguish under the New York Civil Rights Act. In this case, the employer, who routinely allowed male employees who asked for restricted duty because of health problems to have a light work load, refused the same privilege to a female employee who was pregnant and feared the possibility of a miscarriage. When she had the miscarriage and got pregnant again, the employer would not allow her to work at all. This was too much, even for the Highest Court in New York, which affirmed the award of almost half a million dollars for mental anguish damages (*NYC Transit*).

Pregnancy and Parenting

In 1976, the U.S. Supreme Court ruled than an employer could provide disability and sick-leave benefits and at the same time exclude pregnancy (*Gilbert*). Congress then amended Title VII to make it clear that discrimination based on pregnancy is sex discrimination (42 U.S.C. sec. 2000e(k)). In 1983, the U.S. Supreme Court acknowledged that Congress had overruled the *Gilbert* decision (*Newport*). This case involved a company that allowed its female employees to have pregnancy benefits under the health-insurance plan but gave lesser benefits to the wives of male employees. The U.S. Supreme

Court said this was sex discrimination against the male employees and a violation of Title VII.

In 1991, the U.S. Supreme Court handed down its decision in *Johnson Controls*. This case involved a company that made batteries and refused to allow women who either were pregnant, or might become pregnant, to work in the assembly area where they would be exposed to lead. The company justified this policy, which kept many women out of the higher paying jobs, by arguing that it feared harm might come to future children of these female employees. The Supreme Court found this to be a clear case of sex discrimination. The question then became whether the employer had a bona fide occupational qualification (BFOQ) that justified the discrimination. The Court ruled that it did not, finding that this question was controlled by the amendment to Title VII which says that women may not be discriminated against because they are pregnant (or might become pregnant) unless their condition actually prevents them from doing the work. There was no question that women could do the work in this case. The Court said that "fertile women, as far as appears in the record, participate in the manufacture of batteries as efficiently as anyone else," and, because of this, Title VII does "not allow a woman's dismissal because of her failure to submit to sterilization."

In 1991, the Third Circuit Court ruled that an employer who did not count pregnancy leave as time worked toward early retirement had violated federal law. The employer counted disability leave for this purpose, and the court felt that the employer could not discriminate against pregnancy leave (*Pallas*).

Marital-Status Discrimination

As can be seen from looking at Table 8.1, many states outlaw discrimination based on marital status. This means that employers may not hire or fire employees because they are, or are not, married. The difficult question has been whether employers may fire, or refuse to hire, because of the particular person an employee is married to? This problem is illustrated by a 1991 case from Hawaii. A man and woman lived together and worked for a hotel. When they got married, the man was fired because the hotel had a policy which kept "relatives" from working in the same department. The Hawaii Supreme Court reviewed the decisions from other states and found that in Washington, Minnesota, and Montana this would be considered a violation of the law, while in New Jersey, New York, and Michigan it would not. The Hawaii Supreme Court ruled that this action did violate the Hawaiian law against marital-status discrimination because here the employee was put in the position of either getting a divorce or losing his job. The court was particularly struck by the fact that as long as these two employees "lived in sin" it was all right in the eyes of the hotel. It was only when they got married that the hotel felt obliged to take action (*Ross*).

Family and Medical Leave

During the 1980s and 1990s, more and more states have felt it necessary to pass laws protecting employees who must take extended leaves because of the birth of a child or the illness of a child or family member. These laws generally require the employer to reinstate the employee to a comparable position after the leave and to continue the employee's health insurance during the leave. Some laws require employees to provide advance notice when possible. See Table 9.1 for a summary of these state statutes.

Courts are only beginning to interpret these statutes. For example, Dawn Schimmel had to go to the emergency room because of an attack of bronchitis. Later she had to go to the emergency room because her son had been injured, and then she was required to stay with her daughter who was in the hospital with a high fever. The Wisconsin Family and Medical Leave Act allows up to two weeks of unpaid leave in a year if the employee has a serious health condition and up to two weeks of unpaid leave in a year if a child, spouse, or parent has a serious health condition. The court ruled that her bronchitis was not "serious," so her trip to the emergency room for herself was not covered by the law. Her trips to the hospital because of her son and daughter were protected by the act (*MPI*).

In 1991, courts in Wisconsin and Minnesota were faced with employees who were demoted upon their return from maternity leave. The Wisconsin court found that because the employee was receiving the same pay and benefits, the maternity leave statute had not been violated even though her responsibility had been reduced (*Kelley*). The Minnesota court ruled that a similar employee had good grounds to quit and was entitled to receive unemployment compensation rather than work in the lower position (*Polley*).

In 1990, the Third Circuit Court ruled that a union contract that granted maternity leave to female employees but not to male employees violated Title VII (*Schafer #2*). In states that require maternity leave for female employees, employers may have to grant the same leave privileges to male employees to avoid violating federal law.

Table 9.1   State Family and Medical Leave Statutes

California Gov. Code 12945	Female employees get up to 4 months of unpaid leave for pregnancy and childbirth.
Gov. Code 12945.2	Employees get up to 4 months of unpaid leave every 2 years because of the birth or adoption of a child or the serious illness of a child, spouse, or parent (boss with 50 or more employees).
Colorado 19-5-211	Employers who grant leave to biological parents must give adoptive parents the same privilege.
Connecticut 31-51aa to 51gg	Employees get up to 16 weeks of unpaid leave every 2 years for the birth or adoption of a child or the serious illness of a child, spouse, or parent or because of their own serious illness (boss with 75 or more employees).
Dist. of Columbia 36-1302	Employees get up to 16 weeks of unpaid leave every 2 years for the birth or adoption of a child or the serious illness of a child or family member.
Hawaii 398-1 to 10	Employees get up to 4 weeks of unpaid leave each year for the birth or adoption of a child or the serious illness of a child, spouse, or parent (boss with 100 or more employees).
Iowa 601A.6	Female employees disabled by pregnancy, childbirth, or related medical conditions must be granted up to 8 weeks of unpaid leave.
Louisiana 23:1008	Female employees get up to 4 months of unpaid leave for pregnancy or childbirth.
Maine 26-843 to 848	Employees get up to 10 weeks of unpaid leave every 2 years for the birth or adoption of a child or the serious illness of a child, spouse, or parent or because of their own serious illness (boss with 25 or more employees).
Massachusetts Ch. 149, Sec. 105D	Female employees get up to 8 weeks of unpaid leave for the birth or adoption of a child.
Minnesota 181.941	Employees get up to 6 weeks of unpaid leave for the birth or adoption of a child (boss with 21 or more employees).
Montana 49-2-310	Female employees get a reasonable unpaid leave for pregnancy.
New Jersey 34:11B	Employees get up to 12 weeks of unpaid leave every 2 years for the birth or adoption of a child or the serious illness of a child, spouse, or parent (boss with 50 or more employees).
Oregon 659.360, 565–570	Employees get up to 12 weeks of unpaid leave for the birth or adoption of a child or the serious illness of a child, spouse, or parent (boss with 50 or more employees).

Table 9.1—*Continued*

Rhode Island 28-48-1 to 10	Employees get up to 13 weeks of unpaid leave every 2 years for the birth or adoption of a child or the serious illness of a child, spouse, or parent or because of their own illness (boss with 50 or more employees).
Tennessee 4-21-408	Female employees get up to 4 months of unpaid leave for pregnancy or childbirth.
Vermont 21-472	Female employees get up to 12 weeks of unpaid leave for pregnancy or childbirth.
Washington 49.78	Employees get up to 12 weeks of unpaid leave every 2 years for the birth or adoption of a child or to care for a terminally ill child (boss with 100 or more employees).
West Virginia 21-5D	Employees of the state or county boards of education must get up to 12 weeks of unpaid leave every 12 months for the birth or adoption of a child or the serious illness of a child, spouse, or parent.
Wisconsin 103.10	Employees get up to 6 weeks of unpaid leave every 12 months for the birth or adoption of a child; up to 2 weeks every 12 months for the serious illness of a child, spouse, or parent; up to 2 weeks every 12 months for their own serious illness (boss with 50 or more employees).

10

Age and Handicap Discrimination

Age Discrimination

In 1967, Congress passed the Age Discrimination in Employment Act (ADEA). It was amended in 1974 to include government employees at the state, local, and federal levels. The act originally protected people between the ages of 40 and 65. In 1978, the upper age was raised to 70 and, in 1987, the upper age was eliminated. Today an employer cannot discriminate against anyone 40 years of age or older because of age (29 U.S.C. sec. 631). Many states also have laws that protect against age discrimination, but most protect only people between the ages of 40 and 65 or 70. The federal law applies only to employers with 20 or more employees. Most state statutes apply to employers with many fewer employees (see Table 8.1 in Chapter 8).

The ADEA protects only people 40 years of age or older. If an employer fires a 39-year-old and hires an 18-year-old, that is not a violation of the federal act, even if the employer fires the 39-year-old simply because of age. The same is true in most states. Statutes in Iowa, Kansas, and Oregon protect anyone 18 years of age or older from age discrimination.

It is a violation of the ADEA and most state civil rights statutes to discriminate because of age not only in hiring and firing but also in wages, hours, and working conditions. Employers cannot retaliate against workers who file charges against them, testify against them, or oppose age discrimination in the workplace (29 U.S.C. sec. 623(d)).

Defenses

The ADEA provides the employer with a number of defenses. First, employers can discriminate if age is a "bona fide occupational qualification reasonably necessary to the normal operation of the particular business" (29 U.S.C. sec. 623(f)(1)). The federal regulations acknowledge two legitimate BFOQs: when a federal law or regulation requires age discrimination (airline pilots), or when an actor of a particular age is needed to play a part (29 C.F.R. sec. 860.102(d)). The U.S. Supreme Court and federal circuit courts have struck down mandatory retirement policies for police, firefighters, and airline flight engineers (*EEOC; Johnson #5; Western Airlines*). The ADEA does allow mandatory retirement of executives who are at least 65 years old and who will receive a pension of at least $44,000 a year (29 U.S.C. sec. 631(c)(1)).

It is not a BFOQ just because it would cost more to train older employees or because the employer has some stereotyped belief about older employees (they cannot lift things). Even if most older employees would not be able to do the work, each employee has to be given a chance to prove he or she is capable of doing the work (29 C.F.R. sec. 860.103(d)(f)). The ADEA allows age discrimination in apprenticeship programs if the programs meet federal guidelines.

The ADEA allows employers to discriminate as part of a "bona fide employee benefit plan" (29 U.S.C. sec. 623(f)(2)). It is easier to explain what that means by first explaining what it does not mean. It does not mean that employers can use an employee benefit plan as an excuse not to hire someone because of age ("If I hired you, my insurance premiums would go up"). It also does not mean that employers can use an employee benefit plan as an excuse to fire someone ("Your higher age caused my insurance premiums to go up").

It does mean that employers may reduce benefits because of age if the reduction is justified because providing benefits to older employees cost more. However, employers may not require older employees to make larger contributions to employee benefit plans because they cost more (29 C.F.R. sec. 120(d)(4)(i)). For example, employers who provide life insurance can reduce the amount of life insurance for older employees so that the premiums stay the same, but they cannot keep the amount of insurance the same and force the older employees to pay the higher premiums.

The ADEA allows employers to discriminate because of a "bona fide seniority system" or because of "reasonable factors other than age" (29 U.S.C. sec. 632(f)(1)).

Procedure

A victim of age discrimination must file a complaint with the Equal Employment Opportunity Commission (EEOC) within 180 days of the incident and wait 60 days while the EEOC tries to negotiate a settlement. Generally victims should also file a complaint with the state human rights commission at the same time (*Cahoon*; *Sullivan*). The Civil Rights Act of 1991 requires victims of age discrimination to get a right-to-sue letter just like other discrimination victims and requires age discrimination victims to sue within 90 days of the receipt of that letter. Generally, victims of age discrimination should discuss the proper procedure with their own attorney before doing anything. Unlike Title VII cases, victims of age discrimination get a jury trial in federal court.

Proving Age Discrimination

There are two ways to prove age discrimination. First, the employee can prove the employer intentionally discriminated because of age. Generally, the employer does not send a letter saying, "Because of your age I am letting you go," but there is other evidence of intent. In one case, the employer refused to let the older employee bump less-senior employees during the reduction in force and then hired younger workers when new jobs opened up. The Seventh Circuit Court said that was proof of intentional age discrimination (*Ayala*).

In most cases, employees prove age discrimination the same way they prove race discrimination: (1) they are a member of the protected group (over 39), (2) they were qualified for the job when they applied (or doing a good job when they were fired), (3) they were fired or not hired, and (4) they were replaced by a younger worker (*Loeb*). Then the employer has a chance to prove that there was a legitimate reason to fire or not hire this employee, and the employee has a chance to prove that this reason is just a pretext for age discrimination.

In many cases, employers try to hide age discrimination by reorganizing the work force in such a way that the older workers lose out. Generally, they have not gotten away with this. In one case, a golf course split the work between two supervisors so that it could hire a younger supervisor and then "reorganized" the work back into one unit, leaving the older worker (the original supervisor) without a job. The total reorganization resulted in the firing of five workers over the age of 40. The jury found that to be "willful" age discrimination and awarded double damages (*Lakeway*). In another case, the employer fired the three oldest workers and everyone left was under the age of 42. The court said that the jury could consider as evidence of age discrimination the fact that the employer had changed the reason for these discharges over time (*Estes*).

Damages

The ADEA allows the judge to grant "such legal or equitable relief as may be appropriate" (29 U.S.C. sec. 626(b)). The usual damages are back pay, reinstatement, and attorney's fees. The judges can award double the amount of back pay if they decide the employer acted "willfully" (*Laffey*; *Coston*).

Some courts have awarded money to compensate for pain, suffering, and mental anguish, and some have even awarded punitive damages (*Kennedy*).

Some judges have awarded "front pay" instead of reinstatement. In one case, the judge decided reinstatement would be inappropriate because the employer-employee relationship had been irreversibly damaged by the animosity growing out of the lawsuit. Instead, the judge ordered the employer to pay back and front pay (what the employee would have earned in the future) totaling $242,659 (*Whittlesey*).

Benefits, Waivers, and Arbitration Agreements

In 1989, the U.S. Supreme Court decided the case of June Betts (*Betts*). Ms. Betts was covered by the Ohio Public Employees Retirement System. This system had a rule that if employees became disabled before reaching the age of 60, they would receive at least 30 percent of their final average salary upon retirement. Someone who became disabled after reaching the age of 60 would not benefit from this rule. Betts became disabled at the age of 61 and received a monthly payment of $158.50. If she had been disabled prior to the age of 60, her monthly payment would have been $355.02. She sued under the federal Age Discrimination Act. The U.S. Supreme Court ruled that even though the only reason June Betts received less money every month was because of her age, she was not the victim of age discrimination. In 1990, Congress passed the Older Workers Benefit Protection Act to overturn this decision. With this law Congress tried once again to make it clear that the only justification for providing different benefits based on age was the higher cost of providing those benefits to older workers. Rules like the one in the *Betts* case, which simply provide higher benefits to younger workers, are illegal. In 1991, the Ninth Circuit Court ruled that an employer who provided a different profit-sharing plan for employees who were over 65 violated federal law (*AARP*).

The Older Workers Benefit Protection Act also dealt with what had become a major problem for many older workers: being asked to sign a waiver when accepting early retirement benefits. A waiver is an agreement not to sue for age discrimination or anything else. In many cases, the employee was given a few minutes to either accept the early retirement package and sign the waiver or pass up the opportunity to receive those benefits. The new federal law requires employers to give employees at least 21 days to decide whether or not to sign a waiver (45 days if the waiver is given to a group of employees), and the employee must have 7 days to revoke the waiver after signing it. The waiver must be written in plain English; it may not cover claims that arise after the date on which the waiver is signed; the employer must provide something of value in exchange for the waiver; the employer must advise the employee in writing to consult with an attorney prior to signing the waiver; and the waiver must specifically refer to the federal age discrimination law if it is to effectively waive rights granted by that law. A waiver may effectively waive the right to sue, but the employee still has a right to file a complaint with the EEOC, and the EEOC still has the right to investigate and file a lawsuit on its own. If a waiver is requested in connection with an "exit incentive" (such as early retirement) or a termination program offered to a group of employees, those employees must be told how it was decided who would be in the group receiving the offer, the job titles and ages of the employees selected for the program, and the ages of the employees in the same job class or unit who were not selected. In a dispute over the waiver, the employer has the burden of proving that the waiver was signed voluntarily and by employees who knew what they were doing.

In May 1991, the Supreme Court ruled that employees who sign agreements to arbitrate "controversies arising out of employment or termination" must submit any claim of age discrimination to arbitration (*Gilmer*). Until that decision, most people assumed that these agreements did not include claims for age discrimination. This finding was not overruled by the Civil Rights Act of 1991. The *Gilmer* decision may force Congress to face this issue and provide guidelines for when employees may agree to arbitrate such claims, just as they have done with waiver agreements. It will not be too soon. The current federal Arbitration Act was passed in 1925.

Suing under State Law

As seen in other chapters of this book, there are many times when employees are better off suing under state civil rights law or under state common law for things such as assault or intentional infliction of emotional distress.

Mr. Wilson was a 60-year-old, college-educated executive who had been with the company for 30 years when the new, 42-year-old chairman of Monarch Paper Company circulated a memorandum that he wanted "new blood" in the company. Wilson was given three choices: accept a sales job at half his current salary; be terminated with three months' severance pay; or accept a position as a warehouse supervisor at the same salary but with reduced benefits. Wilson accepted the position as warehouse supervisor. He was given no one to help run the warehouse, which meant he ended up sweeping the floors and cleaning the cafeteria by himself. He felt ashamed and depressed and was ultimately hospitalized for a manic-depressive illness that continued for two years. The jury awarded $300,000 for age discrimination and $3.1 million for intentional infliction of emotional distress. In 1991, the Fifth Circuit Court upheld this verdict, finding the company's actions toward Wilson to be so outrageous as to be beyond the bounds of what "civilized society" should have to tolerate (*Monarch Paper*).

Handicap Discrimination

The history of efforts to end discrimination against people with handicaps is a history of both state and federal legislation. The Social Security Act of 1935 provided handicapped people with financial assistance. The LaFollette-Barden Act of 1943 provided funds for rehabilitation. The Urban Mass Transportation Act of 1970 required local transit systems to be accessible to the handicapped and, in 1975, Congress passed the Education for All Handicapped Children Act. The federal Rehabilitation Act of 1973 required federal agencies and federal contractors to implement affirmative action plans to hire and promote handicapped employees. It also outlawed discrimination against handicapped people in programs that received federal funds. During the 1970s and 1980s, state after state passed laws that prohibited discrimination against handicapped people in employment until by the end of the 1980s most workers were covered by some kind of state handicapped-discrimination law (see Table 8.1). Finally, in 1990, Congress passed the Americans with Disabilities Act, providing protection for all Americans against handicap discrimination.

Americans with Disabilities Act of 1990

The Americans with Disabilities Act of 1990 goes into effect in July 1992 for employers with 25 or more employees and in July 1994 for employers with 15 or more employees. The law outlaws discrimination against handicapped people who can perform the "essential functions" of the job. Employers who before advertising a job prepare a written job description that spells out what the essential functions of the job are will be allowed to place that job description into evidence at a trial. The act also says the employer's judgment concerning what are or are not essential functions will be given "due consideration."

The act requires employers to provide "reasonable accommodation" in order to make the job available to handicapped people. This may mean making physical changes to the workplace or restructuring the job and modifying work schedules. The employer does not have to make any accommodation that would cause "undue hardship." Undue hardship usually means that it costs too much money. In deciding whether it costs too much, the courts are instructed by the act to consider both the size of the employer and the employer's financial resources.

The act outlaws preemployment medical examinations until the job has been offered to a particular individual. Then the employer may require a medical examination if it requires all newly hired employees to take such an examination and if it keeps the results of the examination private. Managers may be told of the examination's results to the extent that they need to know to make necessary accommodations for the employee. First aid and safety personnel may also be informed if the disability might require emergency treatment. Employers may also conduct voluntary medical examinations as part of an employee health program. Generally, employers may not inquire about mental or physical handicaps except as these might affect the employee's ability to perform job-related functions.

President Bush stated that one purpose of the new law was to prevent discrimination against people with acquired immunodeficiency syndrome (AIDS) and other diseases that are not transmitted through casual contact. The act requires the secretary of health and human services to publish a list of communicable diseases and allows employers to refuse to hire people with those diseases if the employees will be handling food and the employee's disease cannot be reasonably accommodated.

The act does not protect people who are currently engaging in the illegal use of drugs. It does protect people who are currently in a supervised drug rehabilitation program or who have successfully completed such a program and are no longer using illegal drugs. A test to discover the illegal use of drugs is not a "medical examination" and is not prohibited by the act.

The 1991 Civil Rights Act allows handicapped employees to sue for compensatory and punitive damages just like employees who are the victims of sex discrimination. This means that they must prove "intentional discrimination" to recover compensatory damages and "malice or reckless indifference" to recover punitive damages. Also, the damage amounts are limited, as discussed in Chapter 8. Handicapped employees may not recover these kinds of damages if the employer, in consultation with the handicapped employee, has made a good-faith effort to provide reasonable accommodation.

The Americans with Disabilities Act defines a handicapped person as someone who has a physical or mental impairment that "substantially limits one or more major life activities," has a record of "such impairment," or is "regarded as having such an impairment." That is the same definition contained in the federal Rehabilitation Act of 1973, so we already have two decades of federal court decisions on who is and who is not covered by that very broad definition. Regulations published under the Rehabilitation Act made it clear that people with diseases such as cancer and epilepsy were considered handicapped along with people suffering from mental retardation, emotional disorders, and learning disabilities. Even obesity is covered.

Suing under State Law

Most employees in the United States will be covered by both the federal law and a state law that also outlaws handicapped discrimination. This means that employees may choose to sue under one or both laws, depending on the procedures that apply and the damages sought. It is important to note that the definition of handicapped under the federal law and many states laws includes people whom the employer "thinks" is handicapped, whether they really are or not. In one Illinois case, the employee had a heart attack. The court decided that because the employer "perceived" the employee to be handicapped, the employee was protected by the Illinois handicapped discrimination law (*Kenall*).

Some states have more restrictive definitions than the federal act or the statutes have been interpreted by state courts to be very limited. For example, in 1990, the West Virginia Supreme Court ruled that testing positive for the human immunodeficiency virus (HIV) qualifies for protection under the West Virginia statute while the North Carolina Supreme Court came to the opposite conclusion (*Benjamin*; *Burgess*). In 1991, the Pennsylvania Supreme Court ruled that obesity is not a handicap under the Pennsylvania law while a New Jersey Appeals Court came to the opposite conclusion when interpreting New Jersey law (*Civil Service #2*; *Gimello*). The federal definition includes "mental impairment," which many state definitions do not.

The federal law requires reasonable accommodation, but federal courts have generally been reluctant to require much in this regard. Many state courts have been much more accommodating to handicapped employees. For example, a Pennsylvania court ruled that if an employer could accommodate an employee by buying a mechanical device, the employer had to buy the mechanical device (*Jenks*). The Colorado Supreme Court ruled that under Colorado's handicapped-discrimination act, the burden was on the employer to prove that no reasonable accommodation is possible (*Fire Protection*).

Laws against handicapped discrimination may force some employers to reexamine their standard policies and procedures. For example, one employer had an "off-duty accident rule" that prevented employees from returning to work after an off-duty accident until they had fully recovered. In 1991, a

Minnesota Appeals Court ruled that this constituted handicap discrimination and that this employer was required by state law to provide "reasonable accommodation" to make it possible for such employees to return to work as quickly as possible (*LaMott*). Many employers provide different levels of health insurance coverage for employees with handicaps or employees with a high risk of future loss, such as those who test HIV positive. This kind of "benefit discrimination" will be a violation of federal law once the Americans with Disabilities Act goes into effect.

Alcoholics, Drug Addicts, and Cigarette Smokers

The Americans with Disabilities Act of 1990 specifically excludes from its protection people who use illegal drugs. It also allows employers to hold people who use illegal drugs and alcoholics to the same job performance and behavior standards that they require other employees to meet. While the Texas handicapped-discrimination law specifically excludes people addicted to illegal drugs from the protection of the law, most state laws do not. This means that drug addicts and alcoholics are going to be protected under some state handicapped-discrimination laws. However, before they are protected, they are going to have to prove that they really are drug addicts or alcoholics. In 1988, the New Jersey Supreme Court ruled that the employee did not prove he was a "real alcoholic" and, therefore, was not protected by the law (*Clowes*).

If an employee is a "real" alcoholic or drug addict, then the next question is, Does his or her addiction affect job performance? If it does not, then it may be handicapped discrimination to fire the employee. If it does affect job performance, some state courts have ruled that the employer must give the alcoholic or drug addict a chance to complete a treatment program before discharging the employee (*Greater Cleveland*; *Cahill*).

During the 1980s, more than a dozen states passed laws specifically out-lawing discrimination against people who smoked tobacco during nonwork-ing hours. These laws were probably unnecessary. Such people will be protected by both state handicapped-discrimination laws and the Americans with Disabilities Act. That does not mean that they will be allowed to smoke at work and thereby endanger the health of their fellow employees.

Homosexual Discrimination

On January 19, 1992, New Jersey Governor Jim Florio signed into law a bill prohibiting discrimination in employment, housing, public accommodation, and credit based on sexual orientation. New Jersey became the fifth state to outlaw sexual-orientation discrimination after Connecticut, Hawaii, Massachusetts, and Wisconsin. The District of Columbia also has laws against this kind of discrimination.

Recent medical research suggests that some people are homosexual because of the abnormally small size of a gland near the brain. If this is true, then homosexuals could argue that they are handicapped under both federal and state laws that prohibit handicapped discrimination. The argument could also be made that some employers view homosexuals as potential HIV carriers, which may also qualify them for protection under the handicapped-discrimination laws.

In 1992, a Washington Appeals Court ruled that a transsexual who was fired for refusing to stop wearing a pink pearl necklace was the victim of handicapped discrimination. The court felt that this handicap could easily be accommodated by the employer (*Boeing*).

PART
FOUR

CONSTITUTIONAL RIGHTS

11

The Right of Free Speech

Free Speech for Public Employees

The Basic Free Speech Right

In 1968, the U.S. Supreme Court handed down the first decision holding that governments could not fire or take any other adverse action against their employees simply because the government employer did not like something the employee said (*Pickering*). The case involved a teacher who was fired for sending a letter to the local newspaper criticizing the school board. In deciding that the school board had violated the teacher's constitutional rights, the U.S. Supreme Court said:

> Free and open debate is vital to informed decision-making by the electorate. Teachers are, as a class, the members of a community most likely to have informed and definite opinions as to how funds allotted to the operation of the school should be spent. Accordingly, it is essential that they be able to speak out freely on such questions without fear of retaliatory dismissal.

The Supreme Court ruled that a government employer cannot fire an employee in retaliation for the employee's exercise of the right of free speech.

At the same time, the Supreme Court recognized that a balance would have to be struck between the right of employees to speak out on "matters of public concern" and government's need to conduct business in an efficient manner. The Court said that if the things said had interfered with the employee's ability to teach or get along with co-workers, the decision might have been different.

In 1972, the Supreme Court reaffirmed this principle in a case involving

Professor Perry from Odessa Junior College (*Perry*). As president of the Texas Junior College Teachers Association, Perry often testified before the Texas legislature. The Board of Regents of Odessa Junior College did not like what Perry was saying to the legislature, so they fired him (technically they did not renew his contract for another year). Their main disagreement was over whether Odessa Junior College should become a four-year college. Perry supported this change while the board of regents opposed it. The U.S. Supreme Court held that the board of regents could not fire Perry as "a reprisal for the exercise of constitutionally protected rights."

After these decisions, some judges feared that public employees who felt that they were about to be fired would run to the newspaper to criticize their supervisors, hoping to be able to sue for a free-speech violation if they were actually fired. In 1977, the Supreme Court addressed this problem in the *Mt. Healthy* case. A teacher called a radio station to criticize the teacher dress code. These comments were broadcast over the air, and this teacher's contract was not renewed for the coming school year. The school district said that it had good reasons to fire this teacher, which included fighting with other teachers and using obscene gestures with students. The Supreme Court imposed what has come to be called the Mt. Healthy procedure. First, the dismissed employee must prove that he or she was fired for exercising the right of free speech. Then the employer has a chance to prove that it would have fired the employee anyway, even if the employee had not exercised his or her right of free speech. Then the employee can come back and try to prove that these "good reasons" are only pretext.

Comments on "matters of public concern" do not have to be made in "public." In a 1979 case, a teacher was fired after she criticized the school's lack of racial integration in a private discussion with the school principal (*Givhan*). The Supreme Court said that even her "private expression" of opinion was protected.

However, only speech about "matters of public concern" is protected by the U.S. Constitution. A 1983 U.S. Supreme Court case involved an assistant district attorney who circulated a questionnaire among her co-workers. The questionnaire dealt with transfer policies, office morale, and the need for an employee grievance committee. The district attorney fired her for insubordination and the Supreme Court refused to reinstate her. The Court said that

> when a public employee speaks not as a citizen upon matters of public concern, but instead as an employee upon matters only of personal interest, absent the most unusual circumstances, a federal court is not the appropriate forum in which to review the wisdom of a personnel decision taken by a public agency allegedly in reaction to the employee's behavior.

The Court did not feel the questionnaire dealt with "matters of public concern" but only with "matters of personal interest" (*Connick*).

Adverse Action

A government employer is not supposed to take any "adverse action" against a public employee because of something the employee says. Of course, that means the employee cannot be fired. What else can a government employer not do in retaliation for an employee's exercise of free speech? One teacher was transferred to another school while another teacher was reassigned to different teaching duties. In each case, the federal judge ordered the school district to put the teacher back where she had been before she exercised her right of free speech (*Bernasconi; Childers*). In other cases, just placing a letter of reprimand in the employee's file was enough to bring in a federal judge with a court order to remove the letter of reprimand (*Swilley, Aebisher; Columbus Ed. Assoc.*). In other words, a government employer is not supposed to do anything to retaliate against an employee who has exercised his or her right of free speech.

While employers clearly could not take adverse action against an employee for the exercise of the right of free speech, the question remained as to whether public employers could refuse to hire employees for this reason. In 1991, the District of Columbia Circuit Court answered this question in the negative. The case involved a former member of the District of Columbia police force who had spoken out about drug use by members of Congress and their staffs and was not hired by the Environmental Protection Agency (EPA) as a result. The court said that this refusal to hire him violated his right of free speech (*Hubbard*).

Matters of Public Concern

If government employees have a constitutional right to speak out on "matters of public concern" but not on "matters of personal interest," whether the topic of their conversation qualifies as a "matter of public concern" becomes of special importance. In one case, a teacher felt that students were being placed in classes for the mentally retarded because they were being tested in English rather than Spanish, the language they grew up with. When the teacher advised parents to seek legal advice, she was transferred to another school. The Ninth Circuit Court ruled that she could not be transferred for speaking to the parents about a matter of public concern (*Bernasconi*).

In another case, a teacher in Mississippi appeared on television and criticized the school superintendent, saying, "We'll either have to discipline the superintendent or put him back on one of those long midnight trains to Georgia" (*Jordan*). The federal judges found this to be a statement on a matter of public concern.

Several cases involved government employees who have been fired or mistreated because of their union activity. The courts have ruled that the right of free speech includes the right to engage in union activity as long as it is not disruptive (*Durango, Childers*).

Other comments that have been found to be comments on "matters of public concern" include: editorials critical of school-district policies broadcast from the school district's own radio station; picketing by teachers to protest the layoff of fellow teachers; comments to newspapers about being assaulted at work; and comments by teachers about how the school's funds were being spent (*Trotman; Aebisher; Glanville*).

One case involved a coach who was relieved of his coaching duties because he wrote a letter to the school board making suggestions on how the athletic program could be improved (*Central Point*). The superintendent was particularly upset because the coach had not followed the "channel rule," which required advance notice to the superintendent of any communication with the school board. The federal judge said the "channel rule" was unconstitutional. The coach had a right to communicate with his elected representatives on the school board, and the superintendent could not require him to report to the superintendent first. In a 1987 case, a group of Arkansas teachers wrote a letter to the state department of education complaining about the way programs for handicapped children were being run in their school district. The Eighth Circuit Court said that the firing of these teachers was clearly a violation of their First Amendment rights, and these teachers could not be required to follow a similar "channel rule" (*Southside*).

Government employees do not have a right to make a nuisance of themselves over matters of personal interest. For example, one college professor kept complaining about his individual salary and his position on the organizational chart (*Mahaffey*). The judge said these were "private concerns," not "public concerns," and therefore not protected. In general, if the speech is about the individual employee's working conditions, it is not protected by the First Amendment (*Ballard; Renfroe; Callaway*).

Harmony among Co-Workers

The right of government employees to speak out, even on matters of public concern, may be limited if the speech interferes with the efficient operation of government. This problem was explored in an early decision handed down by the Seventh Circuit Court (*Donahue*). The case involved a chaplain at a state mental hospital who was fired for criticizing the hospital's policies in the local newspaper. The circuit court ruled that a government employer might be justified in taking action against an employee if the statements:

1. Interfered with harmony among co-workers
2. Interfered with the need for confidentiality
3. Interfered with the employee's ability to perform his or her duties
4. Were totally untrue, and the statement suggested that the employee was totally incompetent
5. Interfered with a close working relationship between the employee and the supervisor in a situation that called for personal loyalty and confidence

Because the judges did not feel that the chaplain's situation fit any of these situations, the chaplain got his job back.

In a few cases, the animosity among co-workers has been so great it outweighed the right of the individual employee to make comments about matters of public concern. In one case, a teacher made a speech at the annual teacher's association dinner in which she insulted many of her fellow teachers (*Moore*). The judge refused to reinstate her. In another case, a teacher made false charges against the principal and distributed leaflets inciting the students to violence (*Gilbertson*). The need to run an efficient school outweighed the free-speech right of this teacher.

Employees who occupy confidential or administrative positions do not have the same right to speak out on matters of public concern that other employees have. Phyllis Hamm was hired to assist the university administration in investigating charges of employment discrimination (*Hamm*). In several cases, Hamm released information to the newspaper before she had even reported to the administration. The judges felt that, because Hamm had been placed in a confidential position, the "interests of discipline and harmony outweighed the rights of the employee."

The right of free speech is not a license to be abusive. The speech of a junior college administrator in Arkansas was not protected because it was accompanied by "abuse and threats" (*Russ*).

While a government employee has a right to speak out, a government employer has a right to run an efficient operation and avoid disruption. It is often difficult to see where the line should be drawn between these two worthwhile goals. In 1987, the U.S. Supreme Court handed down a five-to-four decision. The case involved a 19-year-old black woman who performed data entry in the constable's office in Harris County, Texas. On March 30,

1981, when she heard a radio announcement of the attempted assassination of President Reagan, she turned to a co-worker and said, "If they go for him again, I hope they get him." She was fired on the spot. The Supreme Court ruled that this was a comment on a matter of public concern and that it did not impair discipline in the office. Justice Powell, who cast the deciding vote, said, "The risk that a single, off-hand comment directed to only one other worker will lower morale, disrupt the work force, or otherwise undermine the mission of the office borders on the fanciful" (*Rankin*).

Whistleblower Laws

Congress and many state legislatures have passed whistleblower laws to protect civil servants. The federal law is part of the Civil Service Reform Act of 1978 (5 U.S.C. sec. 2302(b)(8)(A)). The act protects federal employees from adverse action if they disclose information regarding a violation of law or mismanagement, unless national security requires that the illegal activity or mismanagement be kept secret.

A number of states have passed similar laws. In some states, the manager who wrongly fires a civil servant may even go to jail (see Chapter 6).

A government employee fired for whistleblowing should discuss with an attorney whether to sue in federal court for violations of the First Amendment or follow the whistleblowing statute.

Hatch Acts: The Right to Engage in Political Activity

Hatch acts are laws that limit the kind of political activity that government employees can engage in. These laws usually prevent government employees from campaigning for the people who will ultimately be their bosses. For example, federal employees can engage in local politics but not national. City employees can engage in national politics but not local.

Some people wonder how to reconcile the fact that public employees have the right to speak out about matters of public concern with the fact that they do not have the right to speak out about the matter of most public concern— who should be elected to public office. To understand how these laws came about and why they are constitutional requires a brief look at history.

Until the twentieth century, the federal bureaucracy was small in comparison with state and local bureaucracies. That began to change in the 1930s, as New Deal programs required civil servants to make them a reality. There was a fear that Franklin D. Roosevelt would turn the federal bureaucracy into a giant Democratic Party machine, like the big-city machines that held power in cities throughout America.

In 1940, Congress passed the federal Hatch Act. The act prevents federal civil servants from taking an active part in partisan political activities. Today there are two types of federal laws: criminal laws that make some kinds of political activities a crime (18 U.S.C. ch. 29) and other laws that result in dismissal (5 U.S.C. ch. 73).

The criminal laws carry fines of up to $10,000 and jail terms of up to five years. It is a crime for military officers to station troops near polling places or to interfere with the voting in any way. It is even a crime to take a public-opinion poll of members of the armed forces, asking them how they voted or if they voted. The law also prohibits using threats or coercion to try to influence the way people vote in federal elections.

Candidates for federal office are not allowed to promise jobs or other benefits in exchange for political activity or to threaten to take jobs away if someone does not engage in political activity. It is also a crime if candidates for federal office solicit campaign contributions from federal employees or for federal employees to make campaign contributions to federal candidates.

The noncriminal laws basically outlaw taking an active part in political campaigns. The law does allow federal civil servants to participate in nonpartisan politics as well as local politics in and around Washington D.C.

In 1947, the U.S. Supreme Court declared the federal Hatch Act to be constitutional (*United Public*). The vote was four justices for, three against, with two abstentions. The four justices who voted for the act felt that Congress had a right to control the excesses of machine politics and to prevent a "one-party system." The three dissenters felt that the act was too vague. This question of vagueness came up again in 1973, and again the law was upheld (*Civil Service*).

Many states and large cities have their own Hatch acts, which generally have been found to be constitutional (*Broadrick; Wachsman*). In a few cases, the laws have been struck down because of vagueness (*Barrett*).

Some state and local laws have run into trouble because of the need to allow union activity on the one hand and prevent political activity on the other hand. For example, in one case, the president of the St. Louis Firefighters Union criticized the vote of the city council and suggested that people should not vote for a particular city councilman in the next election (*Blackwell*). He was suspended for a month without pay for violating the city's Hatch act. The Missouri Appeals Court overturned the suspension, holding that he was speaking as a union president, not a city employee, and therefore his speech was protected by the First Amendment and did not violate the city Hatch act.

While a government employee has a constitutional right to speak out on matters of public concern, he or she does not have a constitutional right to engage in political campaign activity if that activity is outlawed by statute.

The Right to Belong to a Political Party

Do government employees have the right to belong to the political party of their choice? That seems like a simple question, but it is one of the most difficult questions ever asked. Is belonging to a political party like speaking out on matters of public concern—in which case it is protected by the Constitution—or is it like engaging in political activity—in which case it is not protected?

Until June 1976, the answer seemed simple. Government employees were divided into two groups: those protected by civil service laws who could not be fired because of their political-party affiliation because that was not "good cause" for dismissal; and the rest, at-will employees (often political appointees) who could be fired for any reason, including their political-party affiliation.

In June 1976, the U.S. Supreme Court handed down its decision in the *Elrod* case and everything changed. When Sheriff Elrod, a Democrat, was elected sheriff of Cook County, Illinois, in 1970, he fired all the non-civil-service employees, who were Republicans, and replaced them with Democrats. These fired Republicans sued, arguing that they could not be fired simply because of their political-party affiliation.

The case raised the most difficult kind of problem the Supreme Court has ever had to face. The United States political system is based on two fundamental beliefs: a belief in democracy and a belief in individual rights. The greatest legal problems come about when these two fundamental beliefs conflict. In this case, they were in conflict because, it could be argued, our democratic system depends for its very survival on patronage (appointing members of the winning political party to positions of power). If candidates cannot hold out the possibility of jobs to campaign volunteers, there would be no campaign volunteers. On the other hand, surely people have a right to belong to whatever political party they want to without interference from government.

Justice Brennan, in a decision joined by Justices Marshall and White, recognized this dilemma. He felt that policy-making employees could be replaced because of their political-party affiliation. Justice Brennan recognized that when the people elect a president or a sheriff, they expect new policies to be carried out. These elected officials could not do that without the help of trusted assistants who were politically and personally loyal to them. However, he felt that this power to replace because of political-party affiliation should not extend to low-level employees who perform routine tasks. Brennan believed their right to belong to the political party of their choice is protected by the First Amendment.

Justices Stewart and Blackmun agreed with Brennan's decision, but they wrote their own opinion to emphasize that both confidential and policy-making employees can be fired because of their political-party affiliation.

Justice Powell wrote an impassioned dissent. He pointed out that the patronage system is basic to the American political system because the patronage system is the backbone of the political-party system. The political-party system makes elected officials accountable to the voters, and without accountability there is no democracy. With patronage, a candidate who is not rich still has a chance. Without patronage, only the rich would be able to buy the campaign workers and campaign advertisements that are necessary to win political campaigns in America.

The Supreme Court dealt with this problem again in 1980 (*Branti*). A newly appointed public defender in Rockland County, New York, fired the Republican assistant public defenders and replaced them with Democrats. A majority of the Supreme Court felt that this violated the Constitution. Justice Stevens wrote the opinion for a majority that included Chief Justice Burger. Justice Stevens said that the question is, Is party affiliation an appropriate requirement for the effective performance of the office? In this case, he did not think it was.

Federal judges, some of whom became federal judges through the political patronage system, have had great difficulty making decisions that apply the standards laid out in *Elrod* and *Branti*.

What jobs can be a part of the patronage system? The city attorney and his or her assistants can be patronage appointments because they give legal advice to elected officials (*Ness*). Assistant district attorneys can also be replaced because of their political-party affiliation (*Mummau; Livas*). Confidential secretaries for elected officials and high-level administrators can also be patronage appointments (*Hodge; Shakman*).

Jobs that are obviously protected from patronage politics are low-level road workers (*Bever*), administrative assistants (*Gannon*), city clerks (*Visser*), and town bookkeepers (*Grossart*).

While it is clear that employees who occupy policy-making or confidential positions can be fired for patronage reasons, it is less clear whether administrators who do not have any input into policy making can be fired. For example, Donald Tomczak held the second highest post in the Chicago Water Department. The district judge ruled that he could not be fired because he did not have any input into policy making. The Seventh Circuit Court disagreed, finding that Tomczak occupied a position "where his political affiliation could affect the ability of a new administration to implement new policies" (*Tomczak*).

In another case, a court bailiff in Gary, Indiana, was fired. He did not occupy a "confidential" or "policy-making" position, but he did work closely with elected officials. The Seventh Circuit Court upheld his dismissal. The court felt that it would "strain credulity to read the First Amendment or *Elrod* to require an elected official to work in constant direct contact with a person viewed as a political enemy" (*Meeks*). While the Seventh Circuit Court has ruled that employees who occupy administrative positions, or have jobs in which they must work closely with elected officials, can be fired because of their party affiliation, other circuit courts do not agree.

Throughout the 1980s, the federal circuit courts debated whether or not this principle would apply to things other than dismissal. What if the employee was harassed into quitting or simply was not hired in the first place because of his or her political-party affiliation? Many federal courts came to the conclusion that these situations were not covered by the principles of *Elrod* and *Branti*. They said that the action taken against the employee had to be "substantially equivalent to a dismissal" before the employee would be protected. The U.S. Supreme Court overturned these decisions in 1990. The Court said the rule applied to any action from hiring to dismissal and included transfers and promotions (*Rutan*).

In the 1980s, Mississippi passed a statute to prevent political affiliation from being a factor in the hiring and firing of most state employees. When Jesse Gill was hired as a game warden and fired a few weeks later, he took his case to the Mississippi Supreme Court. It seems that several powerful legislators had someone else in mind for that job. Was this enough to bring him under the protection of the new law? The Mississippi Supreme Court said that it was. It said if political affiliation is protected, then a lack of political affiliation is also protected. Mr. Gill would not be punished because he had not taken the time to cultivate political friends at the state capitol (*Gill*).

One of the most difficult questions has involved city managers or school superintendents who become the major issue in city council or school board elections. In 1992, the Fifth Circuit Court was faced with the dismissal of Dr. Nolan L. Kinsey, superintendent of the Salado Independent School District in Texas. During the school board election, Dr. Kinsey had openly supported candidates for the school board who were opposed by candidates running on the promise to fire Dr. Kinsey if elected. His opponents won the election, fired him, and he sued, arguing that he had been fired for his political affiliation (with the former board members who had been defeated at the polls). The court ruled against him, finding that he was not fired for his political affiliation but rather the other way around—his supporters had been fired by the voters for their affiliation with him and the victorious school board members were simply carrying out the mandate of the people (*Kinsey*).

Free Speech for Private Employees

Some states have very broad civil rights laws, as Vanessa Redgrave proved in Massachusetts (*Redgrave*). Vanessa Redgrave had a contract with the Boston Symphony to narrate a series of concerts. When the public found out, they called the symphony to protest her appearance. Apparently people objected to her stand on the Palestinian issue. The Boston Symphony canceled the contract, and Vanessa Redgrave sued. The case took 16 days in a federal district court. The jury decided that the Boston Symphony had broken her contract without good cause so she got the money she had been promised in the contract. Redgrave also argued that her rights had been violated under the Massachusetts Civil Rights Act because the symphony had fired her because of what she said on an important public issue. The symphony argued that it was only doing what the patrons asked it to do. The federal judges sent a question to the Massachusetts Supreme Court: Is bowing to the wishes of someone else a defense in a civil rights case under Massachusetts law? The answer from the Massachusetts Supreme Court was no. If that were true, people who interfered with someone's civil rights would say that they did it because they had been asked to.

This case stands for the general proposition that, in Massachusetts, a private employer cannot fire an employee because it does not agree with that employee's "comments on matters of public concern." Private employees have the same protection that public employees have because of the Massachusetts Civil Rights Act. Whether other state supreme courts will interpret their state civil rights acts the same way remains to be seen.

In 1983, the Connecticut legislature passed a special statute dealing with this issue. The statute reads:

> Any employers including the state and any instrumentality or political subdivision thereof, who subjects any employee to discipline or discharge on account of the exercise of such employee of rights guaranteed by the first amendment of the United States Constitution or section 3, 4, and 14 article first of the constitution of the state, provided such activity does not substantially or materially interfere with the employee's bona fide job performance or the working relationship between the employee and the employer, shall be liable to such employee for damages caused by such discipline or discharge, including the costs of any such action for damages. If the court determines that such action

was brought without substantial justification, the court may award costs and reasonable attorney's fees to the employer.

In other words, in Connecticut, the right of free speech applies to everyone, not just to public employees. At the same time, the Connecticut statute recognizes the same kind of "harmony among co-workers" defense that applies in public-employee cases. No other state has such a general statute.

California, Louisiana, and Ohio have statutes that keep employers from influencing the "political activities" of their employees. Pennsylvania has a statute that keeps employers from influencing the "political opinions" of their employees, while statutes in Indiana, New York, South Dakota, and Montana say employers may not influence employee "political opinions or actions." New Mexico and South Carolina have statutes that keep employers from discharging employees because of their "political opinions," while a Missouri statue says employers may not discriminate because of an employee's "political beliefs or opinions." Over half the states have statutes that keep employers from influencing how their employees vote (see Table 11.1).

If your state does not have a special statute, and your state civil rights act does not cover this situation, then it becomes a question of wrongful discharge.

You saw in Chapter 6 that the judges in many states have decided that people cannot be fired for "wrongful" reasons, such as refusing to do something illegal or reporting criminal activity to the authorities. Would it be wrongful for an employer to fire an employee because it did not like what the employee said about a "matter of public concern"? In many states, it probably would be. The New Jersey Supreme Court said it is wrongful to discharge employees for reasons that violate public policy and that we find public policy expressed in constitutions and statutes. The New Jersey Constitution says "every person may freely speak, write, and publish his sentiments on all subjects" (N.J. Const. Art. I, para. 6). If a private employer fired an employee in New Jersey because it did not like what that employee had said, the New Jersey Supreme Court would probably find that to be a case of wrongful discharge.

In 1988, the Third Circuit Court took the New Jersey Supreme Court at its word and ruled that it was wrongful discharge and a violation of New Jersey public policy for a private employer to fire an employee for the exercise of the right of free speech (*Zamboni*).

Administrators may not be as free to express their opinions as other private employees. In one case, a General Motors executive said he had been fired because he refused to lie to a government agency (*Percival*). The Eighth Circuit Court refused to do anything about it. The court said that, even if true, this was not a case of wrongful discharge because employers should be free to hire and fire people in "high and sensitive managerial positions."

Table 11.1   Statutes Protecting Free Speech or Voting Activity

Alabama	Boss may not influence vote.	17-23-10, 11
Alaska	Schoolteachers may speak out.	14.20.095, 100
Arizona	Boss may not influence vote.	16-1012
California	Boss may not influence political activity.	Labor Code 1102
Colorado	Boss may not influence vote. Boss may not prevent political participation.	1-13-719 8-2-108
Connecticut	Boss may not influence vote. Boss may not discharge because of exercise of free-speech right.	9-365 31-51q
Delaware	Boss may not intimidate vote.	15-5162, 5163
District of Columbia	Boss may not discriminate because of political affiliation.	1-2512
Florida	Boss may not fire because employee did or did not vote for any candidate or measure.	104.081
Indiana	Boss may not influence political opionions or actions.	3-14-3-21
Iowa	Boss may not influence vote.	49.110
Kentucky	Boss may not direct vote.	121.310
Louisiana	Boss may not influence political activity or discharge because of political opinions.	23:961, 962
Massachusetts	Boss may not influence vote.	Ch. 56, sec. 33
Minnesota	Boss may not influence vote.	211B.07

Table 11.1—*Continued*

Mississippi	Boss may not direct or coerce vote.	23-15-871
Missouri	Boss may not coerce vote or discriminate because of political beliefs or opinions.	130.028
Montana	Boss may not influence political opinions or actions.	13-35-226
Nebraska	Boss may not influence vote.	32-1050, 1050.01, 1223
Nevada	Boss may not prevent employee from engaging in politics.	613.040
New Jersey	Boss may not influence vote.	19:34-27
New Mexico	Boss may not coerce or discharge employees because of political opinions, beliefs, or vote.	1-20-13
New York	Boss may not influence political opinions or actions.	Election 17-150
Ohio	Boss may not influence political activity.	3599.05, 06
Oklahoma	No one may intimidate voters.	Title 26, sec. 16-113
Pennsylvania	Boss may not influence political opinions.	Title 25, sec. 3547
Rhode Island	Boss may not influence vote.	17-23-6
South Carolina	Boss may not intimidate or discharge because of political opinions.	16-17-560
South Dakota	Boss may not influence political opinions or actions.	12-26-13
Tennessee	Boss may not direct or coerce vote.	2-19-134

Table 11.1—*Continued*

Utah	Boss may not influence vote.	20-13-7
West Virginia	Boss may not affect vote.	3-9-20
Wisconsin	Boss may not influence vote.	103.18
Wyoming	Boss may not interfere with political rights.	22-26-116

Note: The law is always changing. Consult an attorney about your situation.

12

The Right to Due Process

Due Process Rights for Public Employees

The Fourteenth Amendment to the U.S. Constitution says that governments cannot deprive people of "life, liberty, or property without due process of law." That means that someone cannot have his or her home confiscated by government without a condemnation hearing or be thrown into prison without a trial. What does that have to do with public employees?

In 1972, the U.S. Supreme Court handed down decisions in the *Roth* and *Sindermann* cases. Roth, an assistant professor at Wisconsin University–Oshkosh, was hired with a one-year written contract. At the end of that year the university did not give him another contract. Roth sued, claiming he had been deprived of his property without due process of law. The Supreme Court held that if he had a property right in his job, then he was entitled to due process before being deprived of it. Persons could have a property right in their job either because a state civil service law gave them such a right or because they had a union or individual contract. In Roth's case, since his contract had run out and he was not protected by civil service, he did not have any "property" rights in his job. Roth lost.

There was no civil service statute or contract in Sindermann's case either, but Sindermann argued that there was an implied civil service system at his college, that people were given a kind of implied tenure, and that he had earned tenure under the implied rules. The Court said that a property right could arise from such an implied contract, and sent the case back for trial.

In other words, the U.S. Supreme Court held that if a public employee has tenure under a civil service system, or works under an employment contract, he or she has a kind of property. The U.S. Constitution does not require governments to give this kind of property to its employees. All the

158

employees could be at-will as far as the U.S. Constitution is concerned. But, once the government does give tenure or a contract to an employee, it cannot take it away without giving that employee the appropriate due process. The question then becomes, What kind of due process is appropriate?

The Supreme Court has answered that question in two cases. In the first, *Arnett*, in 1974, the employee was covered by the federal civil service system. Before his dismissal he was given the chance to respond in writing to the charges made against him. He was also given a trial-like hearing *after* his dismissal. Arnett argued that he should have been given a trial-like hearing *before* his dismissal. No more than three Supreme Court justices could agree.

Justice Rehnquist wrote an opinion joined by Chief Justice Burger and Justice Stewart. In his opinion, Justice Rehnquist argued that if the property right flows from a statute, then that same statute ought to be able to set up the procedure that is required to take the property away. Justice Rehnquist argued that the employee was entitled only to the process set out in the statute, in this case a chance to respond in writing before dismissal, followed by a trial-like hearing after dismissal.

Justice Powell, joined by Justice Blackmun, felt that only the Constitution, and the Supreme Court interpreting the Constitution, could say what procedure was due once a property right had been recognized. However, Powell felt that a trial-like hearing was not required by the Constitution before dismissal, provided the employee is given such a hearing soon after dismissal.

Justice Marshall, joined by Justices Brennan and Douglas, felt that the Constitution requires a trial-like hearing before dismissal.

These three different opinions in the *Arnett* case confused everyone until the Supreme Court handed down the *Loudermill* decision in 1985. This time Justice White wrote the majority opinion, which was signed by six other justices. Loudermill was a security guard with the Cleveland School District. When the school board discovered that he had failed to put on his job application that he had been convicted of a felony, they fired him. There was no hearing, and he was not even given a chance to tell his side of the story before being dismissed. The federal district judge ruled that Loudermill had all the due process that was coming to him because "the very statute that created the property right in continuing employment also specified the procedures for discharge, and because those procedures were followed, Loudermill was, by definition, afforded all the process due." In other words, the district judge read Justice Rehnquist's opinion and thought that that was the majority opinion in *Arnett*.

The justices of the circuit court disagreed. They said Loudermill was entitled to a full trial-like hearing before being dismissed. The circuit court thought Justice Marshall's opinion was the majority opinion in *Arnett*.

They were both wrong. It turns out that Justice Powell's opinion was the real majority opinion in *Arnett*. Justice White said that Loudermill was "entitled to oral or written notice of the charges against him, an explanation of the employer's evidence, and an opportunity to present his side of the story" *before* dismissal. He could be allowed to respond in person or in writing. At some point *after* the dismissal, public employees who have a property interest in their jobs have to be given a trial-like hearing.

People have a property interest in their government job if they are nonprobationary employees under a civil service law (which could be a local ordinance, regulation, or handbook) or have an employment contract that still has time to run (which could be a union or individual contract). If the employee is just an at-will employee, he or she does not have a property interest in the job and is not entitled to any due process (*Durepos; Kendrick; Adams County*).

The next question is, What kind of process is required? As you have just seen, employees are entitled to know why they are being dismissed, and they must be given at least a chance to respond to the charges before being dismissed. Employees are also entitled to a trial-like hearing soon after dismissal if they were not given a hearing before dismissal. The hearing should be similar to a trial. Employees are entitled to have an attorney present (*Francis*); to have notice of what they are accused of (*Pickles*); and to cross-examine the witnesses who testify against them (*Tron*).

Above all, the employee is entitled to a fair and impartial judge. In some situations, the school board or city council is not fit to be the judge. As the Pennsylvania Supreme Court said in reviewing a teacher-dismissal case, the "minimum requirements of due process demand that a litigant have, at some stage of a proceeding, a neutral fact finder" (*Belasco*). The court went on to say that most school boards act as both prosecutor and judge and therefore are by definition not neutral. However, in Pennsylvania, because the state secretary of education reviews the case and is considered an impartial judge, that provides dismissed teachers with due process.

Many situations depend on whether the employee can show that the board or council was biased before the hearing began. In one case, the federal district judge said that the board should not be allowed to be the judge in a dismissal hearing if:

1. They have made up their minds that the employee is guilty before the hearing.
2. They have made up their minds on important facts before the hearing.
3. They have some personal interest in the outcome of the hearing.
4. They have some personal animosity against the employee that would prevent an unbiased decision (*Salisbury*).

In those situations, the school board or city council should hire an impartial hearing officer to hear the case and make a determination of the facts.

While the U.S. Constitution provides the minimum procedure that must be followed, if the state or local government has set up even stricter procedures, these stricter procedures must be followed. In one case in the city of St. Albans, Vermont, the employee handbook was not followed (*Furno*). The jury awarded $31,000 in compensatory damages and $10,000 in punitive damages to compensate the employee for this violation of his right to due process.

In another case, the city had rules that probationary employees could be fired only for incompetence or disqualification (*Hayes*). The city was stuck with its own unique rules.

The U.S. Supreme Court has told us what the minimum procedure required by the U.S. Constitution is. Every state supreme court is free to decide that more is required by their state constitution's requirement that due process be given before property is taken. In 1987, the Supreme Court of Washington decided that the Washington Constitution did not require more than the U.S. Constitution (*Danielson*). The New Mexico Supreme Court decided in 1987 that the New Mexico Constitution required more. The court ruled that a civil servant is entitled to a trial-like hearing *before* being demoted (*Lovato*).

In some limited circumstances, a government employee is entitled to a due process hearing even though the employee does not have a property interest in the job. If the supervisor has said bad things about the employee while firing him or her, then the supervisor has probably made it difficult for that employee to find another job. The judges say that the supervisor has interfered with the employee's "liberty interest" because the employee is no longer at liberty to get another job (*Codd*).

In one U.S. Supreme Court case, a police chief was fired one day after a city councilman, in open session, charged him with misappropriation of public funds. The police chief requested a hearing on the charges to clear his name, and the city council refused. The U.S. Supreme Court ruled that by "blackening" his reputation at about the same time the city fired him, the city had deprived the police chief of liberty without due process of law (*Owen*). However, in 1991, the U.S. Supreme Court ruled that injury to reputation by itself is not a liberty interest protected by the Constitution. The case involved a federal employee who believed his supervisor's defamatory statements kept him from getting a better federal job (*Siegert*). Apparently, the defamation must be accompanied by more, such as being fired, before the "liberty interest" is involved.

If the charges are told to the employee in private, there is no deprivation of liberty and no need for due process (*Ortwein*).

What happens if the court decides the government employee has had his or her liberty interest interfered with? Usually the judge will order the government involved to give the employee a name-clearing hearing. The employee may also be entitled to damages if he or she really had trouble getting a job and lost wages as a result (*White; Selcraig*).

Due Process Rights for Private Employees

Generally, private employers do not have to give a hearing to employees accused of wrongdoing. However, in many dismissal cases the employee has the option of suing because some right we have explained in this book was violated. Often, whether they sue or not depends on whether they believe they have been treated fairly. In other words, while the law does not require it, employers should consider giving employees a hearing if they have been charged with misconduct. The employer may even decide, after learning all the facts, to keep the employee.

Getting a Government License

More and more jobs require a license. This puts great power into the hands of government. The purpose of the due process requirement is to make sure government exercises its power in a fair and impartial way. For many people, this due process requirement comes into play in two situations: when they apply for a license and when that license is revoked.

People who are denied a license are generally not entitled to a full trial-like hearing, but they are entitled to know why they did not get the license (*Valdes*). They are also entitled to appeal the denial and to explain, in writing, why they should have been given the license (*Curran*).

People are also entitled to be treated in a way that is not arbitrary or capricious. This means that the board in charge of giving out licenses must have rules that spell out when someone is entitled to get the license. They must also tell people why they did not qualify under the rules.

When an adult-bookstore owner in New Jersey was denied a license to sell lottery tickets, he appealed. The New Jersey Appeals Court ruled that this denial was "arbitrary and capricious." The court said the agency must have rules that set standards on when someone will be given or denied a license. The court also said that the store owner had a right to a written statement explaining why he did not get the license. As the judge put it, "Administrative officers should articulate the standards and principles that govern their discretionary acts in as much detail as possible" (*Corp. 613*).

Having a Government License Revoked

Once someone has a license from government, he or she has a piece of property that cannot be taken away without due process. Before the license is revoked, the person has a right to know why and should be given an opportunity to respond to the charges. At some reasonable time after the revocation, the person has a right to a trial-like hearing.

The agency should have regulations that are fair and reasonable. In one case, Newton Tattrie appealed the revocation of his license to promote wrestling matches. When a deputy commissioner from the athletic commission asked Tattrie for a doctor's fee of $150 and a referee's fee of $100, he refused to pay because $100 and $60 are standard in the industry. The athletic commission revoked Tattrie's license, and the Pennsylvania Appeals Court overturned the revocation. The judges said that the commission must set a fee schedule and put the schedule into a regulation, not make up things as it goes along (*Tattrie*).

In 1987, the Idaho Supreme Court overturned the revocation of an engineer's license because nothing in the regulations gave this engineer any warning that what he was doing could result in revocation of his license. The court said his right to due process had been violated (*HV*).

People who work in highly regulated industries have a duty under the law to find out what those regulations say. Ignorance of the law (and the regulations) is no excuse. In one case, a doctor was suspended from the Medicaid program for three years because he did not follow the proper record-keeping procedures. The doctor objected because the agency had never given him a copy of the regulations. The court did not care. It was his duty to get the regulations and follow them (*Del Borrello*).

Entities That Act as if They Were Governments

In some cases a private group has great economic power and provides a kind of license without which it is almost impossible to practice some professions. The best example is hospitals. Doctors who are not admitted to practice at the local hospital can forget about practicing medicine in the community. Courts in many states have ruled that entities such as hospitals have to provide a kind of due process to applicants just as if they were a government agency. This means that the hospital has to have reasonable rules concerning who is admitted to practice. In one recent New Jersey case, a doctor was refused the right to practice at the local hospital. The hospital had a rule that a doctor would be admitted to practice at the hospital only if he or she was affiliated with a doctor who was already admitted to practice at the hospital. The New Jersey Supreme Court said the hospital could refuse to allow a doctor to practice at the hospital for good reasons, but this was not a good reason (*Desai*).

The Problem of State Immunity

One problem for state employees who want to sue for violations of their constitutional rights is the problem of state immunity. In many states, a state cannot be sued in state court without its permission, which it seldom gives. The U.S. Supreme Court has interpreted the Eleventh Amendment of the U.S. Constitution in a way that prevents state employees from going to federal court in many circumstances. Employees should realize that there are many exceptions to these two doctrines that should be explored with an attorney. For example, employees of cities, counties, and school districts are not considered state employees under the Eleventh Amendment and can sue in federal court. Also, in 1991, the U.S. Supreme Court reaffirmed the principle that while the state itself cannot be sued, the state official can be sued "personally" in federal court without violating the Eleventh Amendment. The case involved the Pennsylvania auditor general who was sued personally for violating employee constitutional rights (*Hafer*).

In 1992, the North Carolina Supreme Court handed down a decision with potentially far-reaching implications. The court ruled that a state employee in North Carolina could sue the state directly for violations of the state constitution and that such lawsuits are not barred by the doctrine of sovereign immunity (*Corum*). Because most state constitutions provide protection for rights such as the right of free speech and the right to due process, this provides state employees with a powerful new weapon in their fight for fair treatment from state government employers.

13

The Right to Privacy

Creating Common-Law Privacy

Privacy became a part of the American legal system primarily because of the efforts of one man, Louis D. Brandeis. In 1890, Brandeis and another Boston attorney, Samuel Warren, wrote an article for a new journal, the *Harvard Law Review*, entitled "The Right to Privacy." During the decades that followed, common-law privacy came to protect four specific rights: (1) the right of people to commercially exploit their own name or likeness to advertise products; (2) the right to keep potentially embarrassing facts secret; (3) the right to keep facts that could be easily misconstrued from the general public (facts which could put the person in a "false light"); and (4) the right to be free from unwanted intrusions to physical privacy (not be searched). While this chapter is primarily concerned with the fourth category, employees can sue for the first three types of privacy invasions as well. Each type is illustrated by a recent case.

Ms. Staruski, an employee of the Continental Telephone Company, opened her newspaper one morning to find that her picture had been included in a telephone company advertisement without her consent. She sued for the wrongful use of her name and picture in an advertisement and won. The Vermont Supreme Court ruled that it did not matter that she was an employee of the company. By coming to work for the employer, she had not agreed to have her privacy invaded in this way (*Staruski*).

When Betty Dee Young had a partial hysterectomy, she tried to keep it a secret. Her supervisors told other employees about the hysterectomy when those employees expressed concern about her hospital stay. Betty had worked in a highly contaminated area of the Grand Gulf Nuclear Power Station and her co-workers were afraid the radiation had caused her trip to the hospital.

165

The Mississippi Supreme Court ruled that Betty Dee Young had a right to keep this private fact private, even from her co-workers. However, it also ruled that the supervisors had a conditional privilege to reveal this kind of information when necessary, and it was necessary in this case (*Young*).

The third type of privacy invasion, false light, was involved when Mr. Mendez was told to clean up the work area and he took home a handful of nails instead of throwing them away, as was the usual practice. His employer fired him and told everyone that he had been fired for theft of company property. While this was technically true (and, thus, technically not a case of defamation of character), putting it this way clearly gave people the wrong impression about Mendez and put him in a "false light." The Texas Appeals Court ruled that he could sue for this "false light" invasion of privacy (*Diamond Shamrock*).

Creating Constitutional Privacy

In 1916, President Wilson appointed Louis D. Brandeis to the U.S. Supreme Court. In 1928, Brandeis began to move the concept of a right to privacy into the interpretation of the U.S. Constitution. The case involved the Fourth Amendment, which says that people have a right to be "secure in their persons, houses, papers and effects against unreasonable searches and seizures" but does not specify what makes a search "unreasonable." That has been left to the courts. In 1928, the U.S. Supreme Court was faced with the conviction of Mr. Olmstead and more than 70 other people who had been engaged in a conspiracy of "amazing magnitude" to transport and sell intoxicating liquors in violation of the National Prohibition Act (*Olmstead*). Most of the FBI's evidence had been obtained by wiretaping several telephones. Because the wiretaps were made without physically trespassing on anyone's private property, a majority of the U.S. Supreme Court ruled that there had been no violation of the Fourth Amendment.

Justice Brandeis, in what became a famous dissenting opinion, argued that, while there had technically been no trespass on private property, Olmstead's rights had been violated. Brandeis argued that the question should be whether the person was engaged in a private activity and, if they were, that privacy should be protected from government intrusion. Almost four decades later, in 1967, a majority of the U.S. Supreme Court finally agreed with Justice Brandeis (who retired from the Court in 1939 and was replaced by Justice William O. Douglas). The case involved an FBI wiretap of a telephone booth that intercepted conversations about illegal gambling activities (*Katz*). The Court decided that the Fourth Amendment did protect privacy and threw out the evidence. More specifically, the Court ruled that the Fourth Amendment protected people's reasonable expectations of privacy. That meant that the people involved had to believe that they were engaged in private activity (or were in a private location) and that expectation had to be reasonable (one that society was willing to acknowledge as appropriate). The question then became, Where can people have a reasonable expectation of privacy?

While the basic principles of constitutional privacy have been developed in the context of police searching for evidence of criminal wrongdoing, the same principles apply when the government is an employer. The principles involved are also similar when a private employer wants to invade the privacy of an employee with one crucial exception. The courts have held that private employees can consent to having their privacy invaded and be threatened with dismissal if they refuse to consent. Public employees cannot be forced to consent to having their constitutional rights violated.

Searches of Lockers and Desks at Work

Whether an employer, public or private, has the right to search lockers and desks at work depends on whether the employee has a legitimate expectation of privacy in those lockers and desks. In one Texas case, a private employer provided the employee with a locker and told her she could use her own lock to keep things inside the locker private. In other words, the employer gave the employee an expectation of privacy in the locker. The employer then searched the locker. The jury awarded $100,000 in punitive damages for invasion of privacy, and the Texas Appeals Court upheld that jury verdict (*Trotti*).

Whether an employee has a legitimate expectation of privacy in a locker or desk at work is going to depend on the individual circumstances. An employer who intends to search lockers and desks has a duty to tell the employees (remove the employee's expectation of privacy). The same rule applies to government employers. In one case, security guards at the U.S. Mint searched all the employee lockers and found one that contained a bag of freshly minted quarters. The regulations stated that "no mint lockers in mint institutions shall be considered to be private lockers." In other words, the regulations removed any expectation of privacy, and the court said this was not an invasion of privacy (*Donato*). In a similar case, postal inspectors searched a post office employee's locker. Because the postal manual stated that the lockers were "subject to search by supervisors and postal inspectors," the court found no invasion of privacy (*Bunkers*).

In 1987, the U.S. Supreme Court handed down its first decision in a desk-search case. The Court said that an employer could remove the expectation of privacy in the desk with notice or regulations, just as these earlier courts had ruled. Because in this case the employer had not done this, the employee did have a reasonable expectation of privacy in his desk at work. The Court ruled that the employer needed "reasonable suspicion" to believe he would find something in this employee's desk before he could invade this employee's privacy by searching it (*O'Connor*). In 1991, the Ninth Circuit Court ruled that a navy engineer engaged in "classified" work did not have a reasonable expectation of privacy in either his desk or his office (*Schowengerdt*).

Searches of Purses, Briefcases, and Clothing

People have more of an expectation of privacy in their own purses, briefcases, and clothing. Generally employers, public and private, must have a good reason to suspect that something is contained there before a search would be legitimate.

In one case, a customs-service supervisor searched the jacket of an employee after a package containing $152,190 worth of emeralds disappeared. The jacket was hanging on a coat rack in the employee's office, and the package would have passed through this employee's hands. The Second Circuit Court ruled that the search was reasonable because the supervisor had good reason to suspect this individual employee (*Collins*).

It is not clear to what extent employers may take away their employees' expectation of privacy in the employees' own purses, briefcases, and clothing. It will probably depend on the nature of the work. The New Jersey Supreme Court has ruled that casinos may take away their employees' expectation of privacy because casino employees handle cash, and the industry is highly regulated (*Martin #2*).

Nonelectronic Surveillance

In most cases, employees have not successfully sued for privacy invasion simply because their employer hired someone to follow them around and observe their activities. For example, an injured employee said that any kind of work was too painful to perform and that he should be entitled to continued worker's compensation payments. The employer then hired a private investigator who followed the employee around and took pictures of the employee rototilling his garden and mowing his yard. The employee sued for invasion of privacy, but the Oregon Supreme Court ruled that these activities were open to public view, including the view of the employer (*McLain*). In a Maryland case, investigators observed an employee having an extramarital affair and revealed this to his union and his wife. The court said that because the investigators had simply followed the employee around, there was no invasion of privacy (*Pemberton*).

A few states, such as California and Nevada, have laws that regulate the use of "spotters" and "shoppers" (people brought into the workplace to spy on the employees). They generally require that the employee be given a copy of the report prepared by the spy and an opportunity to confront the spy before the employee is disciplined or dismissed.

Electronic Surveillance

Modern technology makes electronic surveillance an inexpensive way to observe employees. The extensive use of computers and telephones by employees also makes electronic monitoring easy and inexpensive. Studies suggest that a majority of employees who use computer terminals or telephones are routinely monitored by their employers.

Title III of the federal Omnibus Crime Control and Safe Streets Act of 1968 made it a federal crime to "intentionally intercept . . . any wire, oral or electronic communication" (18 U.S.C. sec. 2511 (1)(a)). This means that, as a general rule, wiretapping (listening to a phone conversation) and bugging (listening to any conversation) are federal crimes. Also, the victims of wiretapping and bugging may sue for damages. As far as employers are concerned, the law has three exceptions: (1) employees may consent to the monitoring; (2) an employer may listen on a telephone extension during the "ordinary course of business," and (3) companies that provide communication services may monitor those services to check the quality of transmission. When employers may listen to their employees phone conversations is illustrated by two cases. In one, the employer listened to the employee's phone conversation to determine whether or not the employee was giving away trade secrets to a competitor. The court found that this met the "ordinary course of business" requirement (*Briggs*). In another case, the employee sued her former employer for violating the law, charging that the employer listened to personal as well as business calls. The Eleventh Circuit Court ruled that while an employer could monitor calls at work and might inadvertently intercept personal calls, once the employer knew a call was personal he had a duty to stop listening. Because this employer continued to listen, this constituted a violation of the law (*Watkins*).

The federal law does not require that the customer on the other end of the phone line be informed that the conversation is being monitored. On several occasions bills have been introduced in Congress to require the use of an "audible beep" when phone conversations are being monitored; however, they have so far failed to become law. At least 37 states have wiretapping laws, but most are similar to the federal law. Statutes in California, Delaware, Florida, Illinois, Maryland, Massachusetts, Michigan, Montana, New Hampshire, Pennsylvania, and Washington require the consent of both parties before a phone conversation can be listened to or recorded, making routine phone monitoring by employers in those states all but impossible.

There is no "ordinary course of business" exception for bugging. Without the consent of at least one party to the conversation, intercepting a nonphone conversation by electronic means anywhere, even at work, is going to be a violation of federal law and subject to criminal penalties and possible lawsuits. While federal law and most state laws allow bugging with the consent of one party to the conversation, statutes in California, Delaware, Florida, Illinois, Maryland, Massachusetts, Montana, Michigan, New Hampshire, Oregon, Pennsylvania, and Washington require the consent of both parties before a conversation can be listened to or recorded. One supervisor who taped an exit interview without the employee's consent found himself in court for violating the Illinois Eavesdropping Act (*Cebula*). The court ruled that because it was not company policy to violate the law, the employee could not sue the company; however, he could sue the supervisor individually for violating the statute.

At least three states—Connecticut, Delaware, and Michigan—forbid the use of hidden cameras in areas of the workplace where people reasonably expect privacy (bathrooms and locker rooms, for example). In states without specific statutes on the subject, the use of hidden cameras in areas where most people have a reasonable expectation of privacy might be considered a common-law invasion of privacy similar to the searches discussed earlier.

As yet there are no statutes or court cases concerning the monitoring of computer display terminals by employers. Presumably, without specific legislation to the contrary, courts will view this as being equivalent to a boss looking over an employee's shoulder to observe work being done, something employers generally have the right to do. However, there are several lawsuits pending in California over employer monitoring of employee electronic mail.

Drug Testing

Drug testing in the United States has become common in many large corporations and government agencies. The standard process involves having the employee provide a urine sample, which is subjected to a simple and inexpensive chemical test (an enzyme-multiplied immunoassay test, or EMIT). If this test is positive, then the sample is subjected to a more expensive test (a gas chromatography/mass spectrometer, or GC/MS, test is commonly used). The more expensive test is also more accurate and less likely to show a false positive, that is, report the presence of drugs that are not really present. Even the more expensive tests are not perfect, however. Some nonprescription drugs and even some foods can set off chemical reactions in the body that may create by-products that appear to be the by-products of illegal drug use. Also, unlike blood or breath tests for alcohol consumption, drug tests cannot tell how "impaired" the person is or even when or how much of the drug the person ingested. People have tested positive for marijuana use simply because they had been around people who were smoking marijuana.

For public employees, the issue has been whether a drug test is a search (and thus subject to the the Fourth Amendment) and, if it is, when it is reasonable for a government to subject its employees to such a search. The U.S. Supreme Court has considered two drug-testing cases, both in 1989. The Court ruled that testing public employees for drugs is a search subject to the restrictions of the Fourth Amendment. It also ruled in both cases that the particular drug-testing program under review was "reasonable" and not a violation of the constitutional right of privacy.

In *Skinner v. Railway Labor Executives' Association*, the federal government published regulations requiring railroads to test workers for drugs and alcohol after an accident involving death, serious injury, or property damage (*Skinner*). The railroad workers sued to stop the tests, arguing that their constitutional right to privacy would be violated. In a seven-to-two decision, a majority of the U.S. Supreme Court found this drug-testing program to be reasonable and constitutional. While agreeing that these tests are "searches," the Court ruled that a search warrant would not be required. The Court also ruled that probable cause to believe a particular individual was suffering from drug use was also not required. Given the fact that in the circumstances of an accident it would be difficult if not impossible to determine who did what, the Court apparently felt it was reasonable to allow all the employees to be tested while the evidence of drug use was still present in their bodies.

In *National Treasury Employees Union v. Von Raab*, the Court split five to four in favor of testing (*Von Raab*). The program involved drug testing for customs-service employees who would be working in the drug interdiction program. The Court allowed the tests, finding that the invasion of privacy was small compared with a significant need on the part of the government to guarantee that drug law enforcers are not themselves the victims of drug abuse. Justices Scalia and Stevens, who had sided with the majority in *Skinner*, joined the dissenting Justices Brennan and Marshall in this case. The justices pointed out that this was the first time in 200 years that the U.S. Supreme Court had allowed a "search" without either "individual suspicion" (a reason to think the particular person has used drugs) or "special circumstances" (such as a railroad accident that would make the determination of individual suspicion all but impossible).

Both of these cases involved employees whose drug abuse could have devastating consequences to the public safety. Lower federal courts had ruled before these decisions that governments needed individual suspicion to test for drugs in most cases. They had also ruled that employees involved in public safety could be tested for drugs without individual suspicion. The U.S. Supreme Court appears to have agreed with this analysis. The question then becomes, Which government employees are involved in public safety? The Sixth Circuit Court has drawn the line between police and nuclear power plant employees who may be tested at any time for no reason, and teachers and firefighters who can only be tested if there is reason to believe the particular person has used drugs (*Lovvorn*).

It is important to remember that federal courts only interpret the U.S. Constitution. Every state constitution also protects people from unreasonable searches, and state courts are free to interpret their own constitutions to give people even more privacy rights. For example, in 1989, the Massachusetts Supreme Court ruled that employees involved in the horse-racing industry could not be tested for drugs by government regulators without individual suspicion (*Horseman*). The court said these workers were not involved in public safety. The Washington Supreme Court allowed nuclear power plant employees to be randomly tested for drugs because they were involved with the public safety (*Alverado*). While these two courts appear to have drawn the line in a way that is similar to rulings by federal courts, not all state courts agree.

Appeals courts in Florida, New York, and New Jersey have all ruled that police may not be tested for drugs unless there is reason to suspect the individual officer of drug abuse, rejecting the distinction developed by federal courts (*Bauman; Caruso; Newark*). In all three cases, the courts ruled that the state constitutions gave greater privacy protection than the federal constitution.

In the private sector, the analysis is different but it may ultimately lead to the same result. First, private employees can be asked to consent to the test under threat of job loss without triggering a lawsuit for invasion of privacy in most states. The question then becomes one of wrongful discharge. Is it against public policy to fire employees because they refuse to submit to random drug testing? Only one state supreme court, Alaska's, has squarely faced this question. The case involved two oil-field workers who were fired when they refused to submit to a drug test (*Luedtke*). The court analyzed the case as federal courts had analyzed drug-testing cases involving public employees. The court said that because these employees were involved in dangerous work where their impairment could endanger their fellow workers it was not against public policy to force them to take random drug tests. This analysis suggests that, at least in Alaska, private employers may not test non-safety-related employees for drugs without individual suspicion. It remains to be seen how other state supreme courts will rule in this area.

In one state, California, the state appeals courts have ruled that the privacy right contained in the state constitution applies to private employers in exactly the same way that it applies to public employers. In one case, the court said the private employer, a railroad, violated the privacy rights of an employee by discharging her when she refused to take a random drug test. The employee was a computer operator so there was no question of her being involved with "safety" (*Luck*).

To spell out when private-sector employees may be tested for drugs; a number of states have passed statutes on the subject. The statutes fall into three categories.

First, there are statutes like Utah's (Utah 34-38-1 to 15). The Utah statute is a license for employers to test for alcohol and drugs. The statute allows employers to test all their employees for drugs and alcohol on a routine or random basis "as a condition of hiring or continued employment," but it also requires employers and management to "submit to the testing themselves on a periodic basis." The statute requires that any positive reading be validated by using one of the more reliable (and more expensive) methods of testing before any action is taken against the employee. The statute makes it difficult, if not impossible, for an employee to sue an employer because adverse action was taken based on a false drug test. Florida, Louisiana, Maryland, and Nebraska have similar statutes (Fla. 440.101 to 102; La. 49:1001–1015; Md. Health Code 17–214.1; Neb. 48–1901 to 1910).

Second, there are statutes like Rhode Island's (R.I. 28-6.5-1). The Rhode Island statute prohibits urine and blood testing by employers unless the employer "has reasonable grounds to believe, based on specific objective facts, that the employee's use of controlled substances is impairing his ability to perform his job." If the employer does have "reasonable suspicion," it must follow the procedures required in the statute and must have a "bona fide rehabilitation program" for those who test positive. Violation of the statute is a crime, and employees may also sue for actual damages, punitive damages, and attorney's fees. Vermont and Iowa have similar statutes (Vt. tit. 21 sec. 511 to 519; Iowa 730.5).

Third, there are statutes like Minnesota's (Minn. 181.950 to 956). The Minnesota statute is a compromise between these two extreme positions. Employers may conduct random or routine drug tests of employees in "safety-sensitive positions." Employers may test other employees for drugs if they have "reasonable suspicion" to believe the employee is under the influence of drugs or the employee has been injured or has caused an accident. The statute has many provisions to guarantee the reliability, fairness, and privacy of the tests. If the statute is violated, the employee may sue "in a civil action for any damages allowable at law." The judge may also award attorney's fees. Montana, Maine, and Connecticut have similar statutes (Mont. 39–2–304; Me. 26–681 to 690; Conn. 31–51t to 51aa).

We have seen in earlier chapters that flunking a drug test does not necessarily preclude receiving unemployment compensation. Also, if the employee is a drug addict, he or she may be able to sue under the state handicapped-discrimination law. The Utah and Florida drug-testing statutes specifically say that a person shall not be considered "handicapped" solely because he or she tested positive on a drug test. That seems to suggest that if persons can prove they are bona fide alcoholics or drug addicts with other evidence, they are protected by state handicapped-discrimination statutes.

Is flunking a drug test going to be "good cause" for dismissal under civil service laws and union contracts? Almost every drug-testing case that has come before an arbitrator interpreting a union contract has been lost by the employer. The arbitrators do not consider flunking the drug test alone to be good cause for dismissal. That is because drug tests cannot tell us how "impaired" the employee is by the drug use. Also, arbitrators have generally held that if the employer wants to start drug testing, it has to negotiate with the union about it first.

Honesty Testing

The first lie-detector tests were developed in the 1920s to aid police in determining who was telling the truth. The standard polygraph test measures changes in perspiration, heart rate, and blood pressure as the subject is asked a series of questions. The examiner then interprets these changes to signify lying or truth telling. In 1923, a court first faced the question of whether the results of a polygraph examination could be introduced into evidence at a criminal trial (*Frye*). The court refused, finding that there was not enough scientific evidence to support the validity of these tests. That is still the rule in American criminal courts three-quarters of a century later. Throughout the twentieth century more and more employers used polygraph tests to screen job applicants and to investigate employees suspected of wrongdoing.

In 1988, Congress passed the Employee Polygraph Protection Act (EPPA) (29 U.S.C. sec. 2001). This law attempts to balance the interests of employers in protecting their business with the interests of employees in protecting their privacy. The law prevents private employers from using lie-detector tests unless they have reason to believe the particular employee has caused "economic loss" which, in most cases, means the employee is suspected of theft or industrial espionage. In a case involving economic loss, employees may attempt to prove their innocence by taking a lie-detector test. The employee may end the test at any time. Special rules allow wider use of lie-detector tests by private security firms and employers who make or distribute drugs, but even they cannot use the results of the test (or the refusal to take a test) as the sole basis for firing or not hiring an employee. Strict rules control the conduct of these tests in the workplace, and employees may sue if the law is violated.

There are many misconceptions about the EPPA. Some people believe that the law covers only polygraph tests. The law commands that most private employers not "request, suggest, or cause any employee or prospective employee to take or submit to any lie-detector test," and defines *lie detector* to include a "polygraph, deceptograph, voice stress analyzer, psychological stress evaluator, or any similar device (whether mechanical or electrical) that is used, or the results of which are used, for the purpose of rendering a diagnostic opinion regarding the honesty or dishonesty of an individual." It then allows the use of polygraphs, and only polygraphs, in a few limited cases such as security or drug-related employment or in cases of economic loss.

Even within these limited categories there are special limitations. For example, not all security personnel may be tested, only those who are specifically listed in the law, such as those who work at nuclear power stations or other "facilities" that have a "significant impact" on health or safety. Employers who make or dispense drugs may ask job applicants to take the test only if they will have direct access to the drugs. They may only test current employees "in connection with an ongoing investigation of criminal or other misconduct" involving the drugs. The test results or refusal to take the test may not be the sole basis for an adverse action against the employee.

The EPPA contains several testing prerequisites. There must be a pretest phase in which employees receive written notice of the time and place of the test and are advised that they may consult with an attorney before taking the test. Employees must sign a notice stating that they understand they may refuse to take the test, that they understand statements made during the test may be used against them, and that they know they may sue the employer and the examiner if the law is violated. Employees must be allowed to review all questions before the test and must be told that they have a right to end the test at any time. The test must last at least 90 minutes, and degrading questions may not be asked. Employees may not be asked about religion, racial matters, political or union beliefs or activities, or sexual behavior or life-style. After the test, employees must be told the results and must be given a copy of any opinions or conclusions based on the test. Employees must also be given a copy of the questions asked and the chart of the responses. Employers may not disclose the results of the test to anyone other than the employee; governmental agencies, if the results involve an admission of criminal conduct; and others pursuant to a court order.

The EPPA does not preempt more restrictive state or local laws. In New York and the District of Columbia, for example, private employers may not use polygraph tests results, regardless of whether the test fits within one of the exceptions in the EPPA. In Massachusetts, Michigan, Rhode Island, and Vermont, employers may not "subject employees to" or "administer" a test. In Alaska, Delaware, Connecticut, Maine, Minnesota, New Jersey, and West Virginia, employers may not "request" that a test be taken. Of the states just mentioned, only New Jersey, Vermont, and West Virginia make exceptions for specific job categories.

Employees may also be able to sue for common-law wrongful discharge. For example, a Maryland Appeals Court allowed employees to sue for common-law wrongful discharge even though Maryland had a statute regulating polygraph use by employers. The court upheld a jury verdict of $1 million in punitive damages for each of four employees (*Moniodis*). The Nebraska Supreme Court ruled the same way in a similar case (*Ambroz*).

The federal government is exempt from the EPPA and any state laws controlling lie-detector use. Also, the EPPA does not apply to state and local governmental workers. However, half the states have laws controlling the use of lie detectors with government employees, and most outlaw their use except with police officers. Just because a state does not have a specific statute does not mean that state and local employees must submit to a lie-detector test. In 1987, the Texas Supreme Court ruled that the state of Texas could not require its employees to take polygraph tests even though there was no Texas statute on the subject (*TSEU*). The court said it would be a violation of the constitutional right of privacy contained in the Texas constitution. While the court recognized that "unique circumstances" might justify requiring police officers to take polygraph tests, the court did not believe any circumstances justified their use with other government employees. The California Supreme Court came to the same conclusion in a similar case (*Long Beach*).

While many state statutes appear to allow the use of polygraphs with police officers, these employees are also protected by the Fifth Amendment, which protects people against self-incrimination. In a recent North Carolina case, the court ruled that a police officer working for a state university "could take the fifth" and refuse to answer the polygraph operators questions (*Truesdale*). Because a polygraph is not perfect and may condemn the innocent, even innocent people would be justified in "taking the fifth" when asked to take a polygraph test.

The statutes and cases discussed above have meant the end of widespread polygraph use in the American workplace. They have been replaced in many cases by paper and pencil tests that purport to measure "honesty." Whether these tests actually measure honesty in any meaningful sense is still an open question. Only Rhode Island has passed legislation regulating the use of written truth tests (R.I. 28–6.1–1).

Off-Duty Sexual Behavior

Does the right to privacy include the right "not to be fired" for reasons unrelated to actual workplace conduct? Most of the cases are concerned with employees fired for off-duty sexual conduct that the employer did not approve of. So far no state supreme court has ruled that it is against public policy to fire private-sector employees for this reason. The argument could be made that both the common-law and constitutional right to privacy provide the necessary "statement of public policy" in support of allowing sexual conduct to remain a matter of private concern, and it is not unimaginable that some state supreme courts could come to that conclusion in the coming years.

The public-sector cases are contradictory. For example, both a librarian and a state trooper sued after they were dismissed for committing adultery, and the courts ruled that this was not a violation of their constitutional rights (*Hollenbaugh; Suddarth*). On the other hand, the Sixth Circuit Court overturned the dismissal of a part-time police officer who was fired for living with a woman who was not his wife (*Briggs #2*). The court felt that this was a violation of his constitutional right to privacy. Another federal court ruled that a teacher could not be dismissed just because she was pregnant and unmarried (*Ponton*). The court felt that the teacher's right to bear children out of wedlock was greater than the school district's need to protect children from the sight of an unmarried, pregnant schoolteacher.

Personnel Files

There are two sides to the privacy coin. On the one hand, there are things employers want to know that employees want to keep private. On the other hand, there are things employees want to know that employers do not want to reveal. This is particularly true of the employee's own personnel records. Over a dozen states have statutes that grant employees the right to see their own personnel files (see Table 13.1). Illinois had such a law until the Illinois Supreme Court overturned it because it felt the law's provisions were too vague to be enforceable (*Spinelli*).

In states without specific statutes, employees may still be able to get access to their files. For example, the New Jersey Supreme Court ruled that a woman had been wrongfully discharged when she was fired for asking to see her

Table 13.1 Employee Access to Personnel Records

Alaska 23.10.430	Employees may see file.
California Labor Code 432	Employees may see file.
Connecticut 31-128	Employees may see file and insert rebuttal information.
Delaware 19-730 to 735	Employees may see file and insert rebuttal information.
Iowa 91B.1	Employees may see file.
Maine 26-631	Employees may see file.
Massachusetts Ch. 149, sec. 52C	Employees may see file and insert rebuttal information.
Michigan 423.501 to 512	Employees may see file and insert rebuttal information.
Minnesota 181.960	Employees may see file and insert rebuttal information.
Nevada 613.075	Employees may see some records.
New Hampshire 275.56	Employees may see file and insert rebuttal information.
Oregon 652.750	Employees may see some records.
Pennsylvania Title 43, sec. 1321 to 1324	Employees may see file.
Rhode Island 28-6.4-1 to 2	Employees may see file.
Washington 49.12.240	Employees may see file and insert rebuttal information.
Wisconsin 103.13	Employees may see file and insert rebuttal information.

personnel file (*Velantzas*). She argued that she wanted to see the file to find out if she was being treated the same as male employees. The court felt that New Jersey public policy supported the right of employees to examine their own personnel files for this purpose. The same argument could be made in most states without specific statutes on the subject.

In many states, "open records" acts also spell out when public employees may have access to their own personnel files. In some cases, the individual employee has access to the personnel files just like any other citizen.

When employers can reveal information contained in the personnel file is another privacy issue. As discussed at the beginning of the chapter, if the information is highly private or might tend to put the employee in a "false light," the employee may be able to sue if the information is revealed. In one case, a United Airlines flight attendant sought a waiver of the weight limit. She believed her reproductive system was causing her to gain extra weight, and she submitted medical records to the company doctor on this issue. That doctor discussed her case with several administrators. A jury found this to be an invasion of privacy and awarded $14,000 in damages (*Levias*). On the other hand, several courts have ruled that supervisors who need to know highly personal information contained in personnel files may have access to them. In one case, the court felt supervisors had a right to know that a chemical plant employee was suicidal and a possible safety threat (*Monsanto*).

Most states have statutes that dictate who has access to medical information. Many allow employers to ask employees for permission to inspect their medical files. The California Confidentiality Act, for example, requires employers to create procedures guaranteeing that medical information about employees is protected from unauthorized use. The act also bars the disclosure of medical data kept by employers without the written permission of the employee, and limits the kind of data that an employer can receive from an employee's physician without the employee's permission. The federal Americans with Disabilities Act of 1990 requires that medical information be kept separate and confidential except that managers may be informed if the employee's medical condition will require accommodation at work and safety personnel may be informed if the employee's disability might require emergency treatment. Also, government officials investigating compliance with the act may also have access to this information.

In 1977, the Privacy Protection Study Commission issued a set of recommended guidelines. These guidelines suggest that references and test scores be kept confidential; that employees be granted access to their own personnel files; that employers allow employees to correct inaccurate information and place notices of dispute in their personnel files; and that payroll, security, medical, and insurance records be kept separate from the rest of the personnel file and made available within the company only on a need-to-know basis. While these are only recommendations, they should be considered by employers who would like to stay out of court and on good terms with their employees.

The Future

We live in amazing technological times. Computers that were undreamed of 20 years ago are now available to the average person for home use. Electronic-information retrieval, storage, and transmission capabilities are beyond the wildest dreams of even George Orwell. The idea of human testing has taken on a life of its own apart from any consideration of whether the tests are actually valid or whether their usefulness outweighs their intrusion into privacy. The Minnesota Multi-Phasic Personality Inventory (MMPI) test is administered daily to thousands of job applicants across the country even though many experts question its usefulness or validity. This test asks people to respond true or false to such questions as: "I have strong political opinions"; "I have no difficulty starting or holding my urine"; "I have never indulged in any unusual sex practices"; "I believe in the second coming of Christ"; "Women should not be allowed to drink in cocktail bars"; and "I am strongly attracted to members of my own sex." In 1992, the California Supreme Court is expected to rule on the use of the MMPI test by California employers.

Early in the twenty-first century, employers will be able to compile a complete genetic profile of each employee. What use will they be allowed to make of that information? How will that impact laws designed to protect people from sex, race, national origin, or handicapped discrimination? When we have the capability of reading people's brain waves, will employers be allowed to do that as well? When, and under what circumstances? If employers are prevented from obtaining a great deal of information about prospective employees, will the law also protect them from lawsuits for negligent hiring when the employees they do hire injure consumers or fellow employees? How should the need to protect public safety be weighed against the need to protect employee privacy? These questions have yet to be answered.

PART

FIVE

RIGHTS UNDER WAGE, HOUR, AND LABOR LAWS

14

Wages and Hours

The Past

When millions were killed by the Black Plague, the demand for workers increased, driving wages up. In 1350, King Edward of England enacted the Statute of Laborers, which required all able-bodied men to work and kept workers from charging more than a "reasonable" wage. In 1875, the English Parliament repealed the statute. By that time workers were so abundant that there was no longer any need to control their wages. In fact, some politicians worried that workers were being paid so little that they could not survive.

There was also a concern about the long hours employees were expected to work and the use of children in mines and factories. A number of American states and the U.S. Congress tried to pass laws to prohibit child labor and to control the number of hours people could work in a week. In 1905, the U.S. Supreme Court declared a New York statute that limited the hours bakers could work to 60 hours a week and 10 hours a day to be unconstitutional. The justices said the law interfered with "the freedom of master and employee to contract with each other in relation to their employment" (*Lochner*). In 1918, the Supreme Court overturned a law by which Congress tried to prohibit the interstate transportation of products made with child labor (*Hammer*).

In 1932, Franklin Delano Roosevelt was elected president. From 1934 to 1936, the Supreme Court declared most of the New Deal legislation unconstitutional. In 1936, Roosevelt won a landslide victory and, in 1937, one member of the Court changed his mind. That year the Court upheld a state law that set a minimum wage for women, even though several years before the Court had declared a similar law to be unconstitutional (*West*

Coast Hotel). In 1941, the Court upheld the federal Fair Labor Standards Act of 1938 (*Darby*).

The Fair Labor Standards Act

Overtime Pay

The Fair Labor Standards Act was passed in 1938 to help achieve full employment. One weapon in the fight for full employment is to control the number of hours worked in a week. The target is 40. The Fair Labor Standards Act tries to enforce this goal with overtime pay. Workers are supposed to be paid 1½ times their usual hourly wage for every hour over 40 worked in a week. (The Fair Labor Standards Act is encoded at 29 U.S.C. section 201.)

The act *requires* overtime payment for more than 40 hours of work a week. A common misconception is that employers can provide "comp. time" instead of paying for overtime. That is not true. If employees covered by the act work more than 40 hours during a week, they are entitled to time and a half regardless of whether they are given compensatory time off in the future.

A difficult problem has been deciding when employees who are "on call" or "sleep on the job" must be paid for that time. Employees who are at home but on call must be paid if their movement is so restricted that they cannot really do the things they would normally be doing if they were not working. For example, in a 1991 case, on-call firefighters were required to be able to get to the fire station within 20 minutes of the call and could expect to be called four or five times a day. The Tenth Circuit Court said this kept them from going to a movie or out to dinner and therefore they were entitled to be paid for the on-call time (*Renfro*).

If employees are allowed to sleep on the job and work less than a 24-hour shift, they must be paid for that time. If they work a 24-hour shift, 8 hours can be deducted if the employees are allowed to sleep and the working conditions are such that they really can get a good night's sleep. If the employees' sleep is interrupted so much during the night that they cannot get a night's sleep, they must be paid for the 8-hour sleep period (*Hultgren*).

Minimum Wage

The federal minimum wage is currently $4.25 an hour. A few states have higher minimum-wage levels. For example, Alaska's minimum wage is $4.75 and state law requires the state minimum wage to be 50¢ more than the federal minimum wage. If the employee receives tips, 50 percent of the minimum wage may be displaced by tip income. However, the employee must actually make enough in tips so that total hourly income is at least at the minimum wage level.

Child Labor

The Fair Labor Standards Act also prohibits child labor. The minimum age is 14 for most nonmanufacturing, nonmining jobs that do not interfere with school or threaten the child's health. The minimum age for most purposes is 16, but 18 is the minimum age for jobs declared hazardous by the secretary of labor. The major exceptions are for farm work, newspaper delivery, and the making of wreaths. Most states also have child-labor laws that apply if they are more restrictive than the federal law.

Coverage

The federal Fair Labor Standards Act applies to almost every employee in the United States. It does not apply to independent contractors (see Chapter 5 for a discussion of the difference between employees and independent contractors). For a time there was some confusion over whether the federal law applied to state and local government employees but in 1987 the U.S. Supreme Court decided that it did (*Garcia*).

There are many exceptions. People who work on small farms, baby-sitters, fishermen, and amusement-park employees are not covered. There are additional exceptions from the 40-hour-a-week provision for cabdrivers, live-in domestic help, and car salesmen. There are also special provisions for seasonal workers, hospital employees, firefighters, and retail salespeople who are on commission.

The major exception is for executives and professional employees. Executives and professionals can be asked to work more than 40 hours a week without paying them overtime pay, but they must be true executives and professionals. While lawyers are considered professionals by the Labor Department, for example, paralegals are not. Executives exercise discretion and supervise other employees. Executives and professionals must also be treated like executives and professionals by their employer for this exemption to apply. If their wages are docked for hours missed during a week, they are not being treated like executives and must be paid overtime. In one 1991 case, the employer reduced the pay of so-called professional employees if they missed a fraction of a workday. The Second Circuit Court ruled that this kind of treatment meant the employees were not really professionals and were entitled to time and a half for overtime. A real professional is compensated for a full week if he or she works any time during that week. Any other policy means that they are not really professional employees (*Martin #3*).

Enforcement

Persons who think the Fair Labor Standards Act has been violated, or just want to know how the law applies to them, should call the Wage and Hour Division of the U.S. Labor Department. Usually, a complaint to the Labor Department will take care of the problem. Of course, sometimes the employee has to sue. He or she can sue in either state or federal court to enforce this federal law. If the employer has violated the time-and-a-half or minimum-wage provisions in bad faith, it can be ordered to pay double the wages owed and will also have to pay for the employee's attorney. In one case, the employee, Martin Cuevas, sued his employer for violations of the act. Cuevas was a busboy at Junction Eating Place in DeKalb, Illinois. After being fired, he filed a complaint under both the Illinois and the federal law. Cuevas testified that he worked from 7 A.M. to 5 P.M., seven days a week, with half an hour each day for lunch. While Cuevas did live in an apartment provided by the employer and ate meals provided by the employer, the Illinois Appeals Court did not allow any credit for this because the employer failed to keep the records required by the Labor Department. The appeals court also held that Cuevas was entitled to twice the wages owed to him because the employer did not try in good faith to comply with the act (it takes only a phone call to the Labor Department). The appeals court also ordered the employer to pay for Cuevas's attorney. Finally, the appeals court sent the case back to see if Cuevas should be allowed three years' back wages. While employees can usually recover only two years' back wages, the federal act allows the court to award damages covering the last three years if the judge finds that the employer willfully disregarded the act (*Cuevas*).

In 1988, the U.S. Supreme Court decided that an employer will not be considered to have willfully violated the act unless the employer "knew or showed reckless disregard for the matter of whether its conduct was prohibited by the statute." Simply not bothering to find out whether or not it is in compliance will not qualify as a "willful" violation (*Richland Shoe*).

Both employers and employees should call the U.S. Labor Department and the state labor commissioner if they have any questions about these statutes.

Wage Assignment or Garnishment

In many states, an employee can voluntarily assign part of his or her wages to someone else. Different states have different procedures that must be followed (call the state labor commissioner).

When a person gets a court order telling the employer to pay him or her part of the worker's wages directly, it is called garnishment. While assignment is voluntary, garnishment is not. It means the person has sued the worker and gotten a judgment against him or her. This judgment is then enforced by getting a court to order the employer to hold back part of the employee's wages and pay it to the person with the judgment. The Federal Consumer Credit Protection Act of 1968 (15 U.S.C. sec. 1671) sets a maximum on how much can be garnished from a worker's wages. A creditor cannot take more than 25 percent of the worker's disposable income (meaning the money left over after taxes and minimum living expenses have been subtracted). The federal law allows up to 60 percent of disposable income to be garnished if it is for child-support payments. Most states also have laws on this subject. If there is a conflict between the state and federal law, the one that allows the smallest amount to be garnished controls. Because the federal law does not set up any priority list concerning which debts get paid first, the state priority list applies. In many states, child-support payments have priority (*Com. Edison*).

For a century, any kind of wage garnishment was illegal in Texas. The Texas constitution was recently amended to allow for garnishment to pay for child support (Texas Const. Art. 16 sec. 28).

If you have any questions about wage assignment and garnishment, call the state labor commissioner.

Child Support Enforcement Act

Under the federal Child Support Enforcement Act, employers are required to withhold wages if ordered to do so for child-support purposes (42 U.S.C. sec. 666). Employers who fail to withhold the wages may themselves have to pay the amount that should have been withheld. The act makes it illegal for employers to discipline, fire, or refuse to hire people because their wages are subject to withholding for child support.

State Wage-Payment Provisions

Different states have different provisions regarding when wages must be paid. Some states require a paycheck every two weeks, which means, as one Ohio court said, 26 checks a year, not 24 (*Ohio Council 8*). Other states, such as Indiana, require biweekly paychecks only if the individual employee asks to be paid biweekly (*Pope*). Some states have a wage-assurance fund that pays employees up to two weeks' wages if the employer goes out of business and cannot meet the payroll (*Seeley*).

Many states also have statutes that control when wages must be paid if an employee is discharged. In New Hampshire, the employer has three days to pay. If he does not pay, he has to pay an additional 10 percent of the wages owed for every business day he delays up to the amount of wages owed (*Ives*). As you can see from Table 14.1, different states allow the employee to collect different penalties if forced to sue to collect back wages. In Arizona, the judge can award up to three times the amount of wages owed and order the employer to pay the employee's attorney's fees (*Patton*). In Colorado, the penalty is 50 percent of the wages owed and attorney fees. In one Colorado case, the employee collected $93,740 in back wages, $46,870 in penalties, plus attorney fees (*Mulei*).

On the other hand, many states have little or no penalty. The employee can sue for back wages, but without an award for attorney fees many employees cannot afford to sue. In these states, the employee should contact the state labor department for help in collecting wages.

Most states say that everything the employee is owed counts as wages for the purposes of these statutes. That includes bonuses and deferred compensation, as well as payments for accrued vacation and sick leave. These provisions apply to government as well as private employers (*Figgie; O'Hollaren; Golden Bear; Hammond; Matson*).

Maine has a statute that requires an employer to pay severance pay if 100 or more employees are laid off because of a plant closing. The employees get one week's pay for each year they worked for the employer. In 1987, the U.S. Supreme Court was asked whether this state statute had been preempted by federal law. The Court, in a five-to-four decision, ruled that the statute was not preempted by any federal law. While the Employee Retirement Income Security Act (ERISA) (see Chapter 19) controls employer benefit plans, wages and bonuses are "wages," not "benefit plans," and states can continue to control how and when they are paid as well as allow penalties for nonpayment (*Ft. Halifax*).

The Agricultural Worker Protection Act

The federal Agricultural Worker Protection Act is designed to protect migrant farm workers from abuse (29 U.S.C. sec. 1801). The act requires employers, farm-labor contractors, or agricultural associations that recruit migrant farm workers to disclose in writing to each worker: the place of employment; the wage rate; the kind of work; the period of employment; the transportation, housing, and other benefits available (and if there will be a charge for these benefits); whether there is a strike or slowdown at the farm in question; and if the employer has an agreement to receive a kickback from any goods or

Table 14.1 Wage Collection Statutes

Alabama* 37-8-270	Public-service corporations must pay wages every two weeks or semimonthly.
Alaska 23.05.140 to 280 23.10.040 to 047	Terminated†—must be paid within 3 working days. Penalty—up to 90 days' wages. Labor Dept. will help collect wages owed.
Arizona 23-350 to 361	Wages must be paid semimonthly. Fired—must be paid within 3 working days. Penalty—up to triple the wages owned. Labor Dept. will help collect owed wages if less than $2,500.
Arkansas 11-4-301 to 405	Corporations must pay wages semimonthly. Executives may be paid monthly. Fired—must be paid within 7 days. Penalty—go back on the payroll until paid. Must sue within 60 days.
California Labor Code 200 to 272	Wages must be paid semimonthly. Professionals and executives may be paid monthly. Fired—must be paid immediately. Quit—must be paid within 72 hours. Penalty—go back on the payroll for up to 30 days. Refusal to pay wages may be a crime.
Colorado 8-4-104, 105, 114	Wages must be paid monthly. Fired—must be paid immediately. Penalty—50% of wages owed and atty. fees.
Connecticut 31-71, 72, 73	Wages must be paid weekly (exceptions may be granted). Quit—must be paid by next payday. Fired—must be paid by next business day. Laid off—must be paid by next payday. Penalty—double the wages owed and atty. fees. Labor Dept. will help collect owed wages.
Delaware* 19-1101 to 1115	Wages must be paid monthly. Terminated—must be paid by next payday. Penalty—10% of wages owed per day up to amount owed. Labor Dept. will help collect owed wages.
District of Columbia 36-101 to 110	Wages must be paid semimonthly. Fired—must be paid by next working day. Penalty—pay atty. fees. Mayor will help collect owed wages. Refusal to pay wages may be a crime.

Note: The law is always changing. Consult an attorney about your situation.

*Pro-boss state.

†Terminated means the employee quit, was fired, or was laid off. Employers may pay sooner than required.

Table 14.1—*Continued*

Hawaii 388-1 to 42	Wages must be paid semimonthly.
	Employees may vote to be paid monthly.
	Quit—must be paid by next payday.
	Fired or laid off—must be paid by next working day.
	Penalty—double amount of wages owed and atty. fees.
	Labor Dept. will help collect owed wages.
	Refusal to pay wages may be a crime.
Idaho 45-601 to 617	Wages must be paid monthly.
	Terminated—must be paid by next payday or in 10 days, whichever is earlier.
	Penalty—go back on payroll for up to 30 days and atty. fees. In some cases triple damages.
	Labor Dept. will help collect owed wages if less than $2,000.
	Must demand wages in writing before suing.
Illinois Ch. 48, sec. 39m-1 to 39m-15	Wages must be paid semimonthly or every two weeks.
	Terminated—must be paid next payday. Must be paid for earned vacation.
	Labor Dept. will help collect owed wages.
	Refusal to pay wages may be a crime.
Indiana* 22-2-4-1 22-2-5-1 to 3 22-2-9-1 to 7	Wages in mining and manufacturing must be paid every two weeks.
	Other workers must be paid semimonthly or every two weeks if the worker requests it.
	Terminated—must be paid by next payday.
	Penalty—10% of wages owed per day up to double the amount owed and atty. fees.
	Labor Dept. will help collect owed wages.
	Farmers are exempt from most of this.
Iowa 91A.1 to 91A.13	Wages must be paid monthly.
	Terminated—must be paid next payday.
	Penalty—atty. fees.
	Labor Dept. will help collect owed wages.
Kansas 44-314 to 327	Wages must be paid monthly.
	Terminated—must be paid next payday.
	Penalty—1% of wages owed per day.
	Human Resources Dept. will help collect owed wages.
Kentucky 337.020 to .385	Wages must be paid semimonthly.
	Terminated—must be paid by next payday or within 14 days, whichever is earlier.
	Penalty—double the amount of wages owed and atty. fees.
Louisiana* 23:631 to 653	Wages for some employees must be paid semimonthly or every two weeks.
	Terminated—must be paid within 3 days.
	Penalty—go back on the payroll for up to 90 days and atty. fees.

Table 14.1—*Continued*

Maine 26-625B to 626B	Terminated—must be paid by next payday or two weeks after demand for wages, whichever is earlier. Penalty—double the wages owed and atty. fees. Labor Dept. will help collect owed wages. Special severance provisions for some workers.
Maryland Labor Code 3-501 to 509	Wages must be paid semimonthly or every two weeks, except for executives and professionals. Terminated—must be paid next payday. Penalty—up to triple the wages owed. Labor Dept. will help collect owed wages. Refusal to pay wages may be a crime.
Massachusetts Ch. 149, sec. 148	Wages must be paid weekly for most workers. Wages must be paid semimonthly or every two weeks for salaried employees. Quit—must be paid by next payday. Fired—must be paid the same day. Labor Dept. will help collect owed wages. Refusal to pay wages may be a crime.
Michigan 408.472 to .489	Wages must be paid semimonthly. Terminated—must be paid as soon as wages can be determined. Penalty—triple the wages owed and atty. fees. Workers must take their complaints to Labor Dept. Refusal to pay wages may be a crime.
Minnesota 181.08 to .17	Wages must be paid monthly. Quit—must be paid in 5 days. Fired—must be paid in 24 hours. Penalty—15 days' wages. Labor Dept. will help collect owed wages.
Mississippi* 71-1-35	Large manufacturers must pay wages semimonthly or every two weeks.
Missouri 290.080 to 120	Corporations and manufacturers must pay wages semimonthly. Executives and professionals may be paid monthly. Fired—must be paid in 7 days. Penalty—go back on the payroll for up to 60 days.
Montana 39-39-101 to 706	Wages must be paid every two weeks except for professionals, supervisors, technicians. Terminated—must be paid in 3 days. Fired for cause—must be paid immediately. Penalty—5% of wages owed per day for up to 20 days and atty. fees. Labor Dept. will help collect owed wages.
Nebraska 48-1230 to 1232	Terminated—must be paid in two weeks or by the next payday if sooner. Penalty—atty. fees.

Table 14.1—*Continued*

Nevada	Wages must be paid semimonthly.
613.030 to 170	Quit—must be paid in 7 days or by the next payday
607.170	if sooner.
608.020 to 195	Fired—must be paid immediately.
608.300 to 330	Penalty—go back on the payroll for up to 30 days
	and atty. fees.
	Labor Dept. will help collect owed wages.
	Employee has a lien on employer's property for owed
	wages.
	Refusal to pay wages may be a crime.
New Hampshire	Wages must be paid weekly (exceptions may be
275:43 to 56	granted).
	Quit—must be paid next payday.
	Fired—must be paid in 3 days.
	Penalty—10% of wages owed per day up to the
	amount owed and atty. fees.
	Labor Dept. will help collect owed wages.
New Jersey	Has a very elaborate wage collection process.
34:11	See an attorney or call the Labor Dept.
New Mexico	Wages must be paid semimonthly. Some workers may
50-4-2 to 12	be paid monthly.
	Quit—must be paid next payday.
	Fired—must be paid in 10 days.
	Labor Dept. will help collect owed wages.
New York*	Penalty—25% of wages owed and atty. fees.
Labor sec. 190 to 199	Labor Dept. will help collect owed wages.
North Carolina*	Wages must be paid monthly.
95-25.6 to 25.22	Terminated—must be paid next payday.
	Penalty—up to double the wages owed.
North Dakota	Quit—must be paid next payday.
34-14	Fired—must be paid next payday or in 15 days if
	sooner.
	Labor Dept. will help collect owed wages.
Ohio*	Wages must be paid semimonthly.
4113.15	
Oklahoma	Wages must be paid semimonthly.
Title 40, sec. 165.1 to	Public employees may be paid monthly.
165.4	Terminated—must be paid next payday.
	Penalty—2% of wages owed up to the amount owed
	and atty. fees.
Oregon	Quit—must be paid in 48 hours.
652.110 to 445	Fired—must be paid immediately.
	Penalty—go back on the payroll for up to 30 days
	and atty. fees.
	Labor Dept. will help collect owed wages.

Table 14.1—*Continued*

Pennsylvania* Title 43, sec. 251; Title 43, sec. 260.1 to 292	Wages must be paid semimonthly. Terminated—must be paid by next payday. Penalty—25% of wages owed up to $500 and atty. fees. Labor Dept. will help collect owed wages. Refusal to pay wages may be a crime.
Rhode Island* 28-14	Terminated—must be paid next payday. Labor Dept. will help collect owed wages.
South Carolina 41-11	Terminated—must be paid next payday. Penalty—go back on the payroll until wages paid. Labor Dept. will help collect owed wages. Must sue within 60 days.
South Dakota 60-11	Quit—must be paid next payday. Fired—must be paid within 5 days. Penalty—double the wages owed and atty. fees. Labor Dept. will help collect owed wages. Refusal to pay wages may be a crime.
Tennessee 50-2-103	Wages must be paid semimonthly. Labor Dept. will help collect owed wages.
Texas Art. 5155 to 5159; Civil Prac. & Rem. Code 38.001	Wages must be semimonthly or monthly depending on the type of work. Quit—must be paid by next payday. Fired—must be paid within 6 days after demand for wages is made by employee. Labor Dept. will help collect owed wages. Refusal to pay wages may be a crime.
Utah 34-27-1 34-28	Wages must be paid semimonthly. Wages may be paid monthly for salaried employees. Quit—must be paid in 72 hours. Fired—must be paid in 24 hours. Penalty—go back on the payroll for up to 60 days and atty. fees. Labor Dept. will help collect owed wages. Must sue within 60 days.
Vermont Title 21, sec. 342 to 347	Wages must be paid semimonthly or every two weeks. Quit—must be paid next payday. Fired—must be paid in 72 hours. Penalty—double the wages owed and atty. fees. Labor Dept. will help collect owed wages. Refusal to pay wages may be a crime.
Virginia 40.1-29	Wages must be paid semimonthly or every two weeks. Salaried employees may be paid monthly. Terminated—must be paid next payday. Labor Dept. will help collect owed wages. Refusal to pay wages may be a crime.

Table 14.1—*Continued*

Washington 49.48.010 to .090	Terminated—must be paid next payday. Penalty—atty. fees. Labor Dept. will help collect owed wages. Refusal to pay wages may be a crime.
West Virginia 21-5	Quit—must be paid next payday. Fired—must be paid in 72 hours. Penalty—go back on the payroll for up to 30 days and atty. fees. Labor Dept. will help collect owed wages.
Wisconsin 109.03 to .11	Wages must be paid monthly. Quit—must be paid in 15 days. Fired—must be paid in 3 days. Penalty—the penalty goes up depending on the length of time wages are not paid. Labor Dept. will help collect owed wages. Refusal to pay wages may be a crime.
Wyoming 27-4	Wages must be paid semimonthly by some employers. Quit—must be paid in 72 hours. Fired—Must be paid in 24 hours. Penalty—18% interest and atty. fees. Labor Dept. will help collect owed wages. Refusal to pay wages may be a crime.

services that will be sold to the workers. It is generally believed that these written statements would qualify as written employment contracts under state law in most states.

The act also requires employers to provide each migrant worker with a written pay statement that explains how the wages were determined; the number of piecework units earned, if wages are based on piecework; the number of hours worked; the total pay earned; any amount withheld and the reason it was withheld; and the net pay. Employers must keep a copy of these records for at least three years. Also, employers may not force workers to buy goods or services exclusively from them.

The Worker Adjustment and Retraining Notification Act

The federal Worker Adjustment and Retraining Notification Act (WARN) requires employers to provide notice if they are about to close a plant or lay off a lot of employees (20 U.S.C. sec. 2101). The federal law applies to employers with 100 full-time employees or enough full-and part-time employees so that 4,000 hours of work are performed in a week (exclusive of overtime). A few states have plant-closing laws that apply if the employer has 50 or more employees in the state (Hawaii 394B-9; Tenn. 50-1-602; Wis. 109.07).

The act requires advance notice of at least 60 days to employees, unions, and state and local government if a plant or a major section of a plant is to be closed or a "mass layoff" is to take place. A plant closing is defined as "the permanent or temporary shutdown of a single site of employment, or one or more facilities or operating units within a single site" where the shutdown will cause work loss for 50 or more full-time employees. Notice of a temporary shutdown is required if it will result in 50 or more employees being terminated, laid off for more than six months, or having their hours reduced by more than 50 percent for any six-month period. Workers who are currently on temporary layoff and have a "reasonable expectation of recall" are counted in these calculations. The act also requires notice if a "mass layoff" will occur; a mass layoff is defined as a reduction in force that, during any 30-day period, will cause an employment loss for 33 percent of the employer's work force (if that percentage amounts to at least 50 workers) or where the number of affected workers is 500 or more, regardless of the percentage.

The act does not apply if the closing or layoff is the result of a labor dispute (strike or lockout) or natural disaster, or if the project was temporary and workers were told that at the beginning. It also does not apply if the company is seeking financing and has a "realistic" chance of obtaining financing and avoiding the layoff or closing. This "faltering company" exception does not apply to a company that is trying to negotiate a sale of the company (*Local 397*). The notice period is reduced to the "longest period practicable" if the layoff or closure is the result of unforeseeable business circumstances. In a 1990 case, the employer was told by a customer (that accounted for 40 percent of the business) that it was taking its business elsewhere. The court ruled that the employer should have provided the WARN notices at that point instead of hoping the customer would change his mind (*Kayser-Roth*).

Employers who fail to provide the required notice may be sued by their employees for back pay and benefits for each of the 60 days they did not receive the notice, and fined up to $500 a day. An employer can avoid this by transferring the employees or by paying them severance pay (not already required by a contract or agreement) that amounts to 60 days' back pay and benefits.

The Thirteenth Amendment

The Thirteenth Amendment to the U.S. Constitution outlaws slavery and "involuntary servitude except as a punishment for a crime." Congress also made it a crime to knowingly and willfully hold another person to involuntary servitude (18 U.S.C. sec. 1584). However, it is not always easy to tell when someone is being held to involuntary servitude. A 1988 Supreme Court case involved two mentally retarded men who were found working for no pay on a Michigan dairy farm. The farmer, his wife, and son were convicted of violating the federal law. The men had been told that if they left the farm they would be institutionalized. The conviction was overturned because the law only applies to physical or legal coercion, not psychological coercion (*Kozminski*).

In 1992, the U.S. Supreme Court will review what has become the most famous Thirteenth Amendment case of the twentieth century. The case involves mental patients at Indiana mental institutions who were forced for decades to work with little or no pay at everything from scrubbing the floors to washing the dishes. They were told that if they did not do the work they would be put in solitary confinement or given electric shock treatments. An Indiana judge ordered the state to pay the patients $28 million in damages, but in June 1991 the Indiana Supreme Court overturned that decision. The court felt that this kind of forced work was akin to jury duty and other "civic duties" that a state has a right to ask its citizens to perform (*Bayh*). The U.S. Supreme Court has agreed to review that decision.

15

Labor Unions

The Past

The history of labor unions is a history of struggle. From the Civil War to the Great Depression, unions had to contend not only with employers but also with the legal system. Judges put labor leaders in jail and used the power of injunction to stop strikes and picket lines.

Two centuries ago English judges found labor unions to be "criminal conspiracies" and put union leaders in jail. In 1836, the High Court of New York also found union leaders guilty of criminal conspiracy (*Fisher*). In 1842, the Supreme Court of Massachusetts began the movement to allow the existence of labor unions when it found that just forming a union was not "criminal conspiracy" (*Hunt*).

An injunction is a court order telling someone to stop doing something. This order was invented by the English judges to use against people who were in the process of injuring private property. During the Industrial Revolution, American judges reasoned that a business is private property; strikes and picket lines hurt business; therefore strikes and picket lines hurt private property.

In 1896, the Massachusetts Supreme Court upheld an injunction against peaceful union picketing. Justice Oliver Wendell Holmes wrote a famous dissenting opinion in which he said it was wrong to prohibit "organized persuasion" if it was free from the "threat of violence." He felt that the majority of the justices of the Massachusetts Supreme Court made the unwarranted assumption that all union picketing leads to violence (*Vagelahn*). Most American judges made that assumption. One federal judge in 1905 said, "There is and can be no such thing as peaceful picketing, any more than there can be chaste vulgarity, or peaceful mobbing, or lawful lynching. When men want to converse or persuade, they do not organize a picket line" (*Gee*).

197

In 1932, Congress passed the Norris-LaGuardia Act, which took away from federal judges the power to use injunctions to stop strikes and picket lines. Some leaders hoped that would be the end of it. Others felt that more would be required to end the conflict, not only between union and employer but also between union and union.

The National Labor Relations Act

Congress passed the National Labor Relations Act—also called the Wagner Act—in 1935. The act had two purposes: to end labor conflict (including the conflict among rival unions) and to set up a system under which fair collective bargaining could take place. To accomplish this, Congress created a new entity, the National Labor Relations Board (NLRB), to enforce and interpret the new law. The board also acts as a court and hears disputes that relate to the law.

The Wagner Act made it illegal to fire or not hire workers simply because of their union membership. If workers feel that has happened, they must take the case to the NLRB within six months. The NLRB can order the employer to hire back the employees and pay them the wages they would have been paid if they had been hired, or not fired, in the first place.

The purpose of the Wagner Act was to end conflict not only between union and management but also between union and union. The staff at the NLRB oversees elections in which employees decide if they want to be represented by a union, and which union they want to represent them. Once a union wins that election, it becomes the workers' exclusive voice. The employer cannot bargain with another union.

The NLRB also determines what the appropriate "bargaining unit" will be. A bargaining unit is a group of workers who will be dealt with as a group for the purposes of collective bargaining. Bargaining units might be set up to differentiate between skilled and unskilled workers, blue-collar and white-collar workers, or workers in different parts of the country.

Section Seven of the act states that employees "shall have the right to self-organize, to form, join or assist labor organizations, to bargain collectively through representatives of their own choosing" and to do anything else necessary for their "mutual aid or protection." How are these rights enforced? By allowing the NLRB to punish employers who interfere with these rights.

The act also created a new concept in the law, the concept of an unfair labor practice. Section Eight explains what an unfair labor practice is. First, it is an unfair labor practice for an employer to interfere with the right to organize spelled out in Section Seven. It is unfair for employers to form company unions or to help one union win an election contest over another. It is unfair to discriminate against union members in any way, or to discriminate against employees who file charges with, or testify before, the NLRB.

It is also an unfair labor practice for an employer to refuse to bargain. This means that the employer cannot refuse to: (1) meet with the union, (2) sign a contract with the union that embodies the terms that have been agreed to, or (3) turn over information to the union. The employer also cannot change wages and working conditions during the negotiations unless the negotiations reach an impasse.

While the statute set out the broad outlines of this new concept of unfair labor practices, it has been up to the National Labor Relations Board and the U.S. Supreme Court to fill in the details.

Can an employer keep union members from talking about the union at lunch or on coffee breaks? No, but an employer can keep nonemployees (such as outside union organizers) off its property. The employer has to treat union organizers fairly. If the employer allows others to solicit on the premises, it has to let the union organizers do the same thing. That is why most factories have a big sign that forbids all nonemployees from coming onto the property (*Republic Aviation; Babcock & Wilcox*).

Does the employer have to let the union have a meeting in the company cafeteria? No, but it cannot discriminate against the union. If the employer rents the cafeteria to other groups, it has to rent it to the union as well (*Stowe Spinning*).

Unlawful Coercion by Employers

Can the employer talk to the employees about unions and their disadvantages? Yes, as long as the employer is not trying to coerce the employees into not joining the union (*Va. Electric*). It is often difficult to tell where talk ends and coercion begins. In a 1991 Seventh Circuit case, management told employees the corporate bylaws contained a provision that required the company to shut down if the employees voted for union representation. The court ruled that telling the employees this amounted to coercion and an unfair labor practice. While management may make reasonable "predictions" about the future, they may not make "threats"; the court ruled that this was a threat, not a prediction. The mere fact that such a statement was contained in the corporate bylaws did not mean that such a shutdown would actually take place (*Wiljef*).

Hiring Back Strikers

If the employees go on strike, can the employer hire workers to keep the business going? Yes. When the strike is over and the strikers ask for their jobs back, can the employer refuse to rehire them? It depends on why the workers went on strike and what the permanent replacement workers did while the strike was in progress. If the workers went on strike to protest unfair labor practices by the employer, the employer has to take them back and fire the replacement workers (*Mastro Plastics*). If the workers went on strike for economic reasons (wages and working conditions), then the employer can refuse to hire them back immediately, and the employer does not have to lay off less senior replacement workers to reinstate more senior strikers (*TWA #2*). When new job openings occur, the employer cannot discriminate against the former strikers (*Mackay Radio*). However, the employer can refuse to hire back workers who engaged in criminal activity during the strike even if the illegal activity consisted of trespassing on the employer's property (*Fansteel*).

In 1991, the Eighth Circuit Court ruled that while permanent replacements may be hired for economic strikers, it is an unfair labor practice to fire the striking employees until the permanent replacements have actually been hired (*American Linen*). Also in 1991, the Second Circuit Court upheld a ruling by the NLRB that an employer can refuse to reinstate strikers only if the replacement workers actually held the jobs in question or were in training for the jobs in question during the strike. If the particular job was left open during the strike, the striking worker gets the job back after the strike (*Waterbury*). State laws that attempt to limit or control the hiring of permanent replacements for striking workers are preempted by federal law (*Justies*).

Taking Concerted Action for Mutual Aid and Protection

Workers have a right under the National Labor Relations Act to take "concerted action" for their "mutual aid and protection," and it does not matter whether the workers belong to a union or whether there is a union at the place of employment. In one case, the workers walked off the job because they believed it was too cold to work. The NLRB ordered the employer to hire them back (they had been fired because of the walkout), and the U.S. Supreme Court enforced the order (*Washington Aluminum*).

Many cases involve employees who complain to management and are fired for their trouble. In one case, the company hired a new supervisor who, during his first week on the job, requested the sexual favors of six different female employees. When the women refused to start work one morning until the plant manager agreed to listen to their complaints, he fired them (the new supervisor left town). The NLRB ruled that these women had engaged in "concerted action" and ordered them reinstated with back pay; the Sixth Circuit upheld the order (*Downslope*). This right does not protect employees who are simply insubordinate, but it is not always easy to draw the line between insubordination and protected concerted action. In a 1991 case, two employees posted a sarcastic letter thanking management for the company picnics and employee appreciation dinners (there were none). They were fired and the NLRB ordered them reinstated. The Fourth Circuit Court refused to enforce the order, finding this to be more insubordination than concerted action (*New River*).

An employee who acts alone is generally not considered to be engaged in "concerted action." The employee must either be acting with other employees or be supported by other employees in taking the action (*Ewing*).

The Taft-Hartley Act

By 1947, Congress felt that the labor statutes needed to be revised. The Wagner Act had allowed the closed shop. The Taft-Hartley Act outlawed the closed shop. It appeared to allow the union shop, but after the Supreme Court interpreted the act, what it really allowed is the agency shop. A *closed shop* is an agreement between the employer and the union that the employer will hire only union members. In a closed shop, persons cannot get a job unless the union first accepts them as members. This kind of agreement is now forbidden by federal law. The act appeared to allow the *union shop*, which is an agreement that within a certain period of time new employees must join the union. They do not have to belong to the union to get the job in the first place, but they must join if they want to keep the job. The act says that the employer cannot make them join the union until they have worked for 30 days.

An *agency shop* is an agreement that within a certain period of time new employees must start paying union dues. They do not have to actually join the union, but they must pay the dues. While Taft-Hartley appears to allow a union shop, the Supreme Court has decided that people have a right not to belong to organizations they do not want to belong to. Congress cannot pass a law that requires people to join a union, but Congress can require people to pay union dues, and that is what Taft-Hartley really does. In other words, while the language of the statute appears to allow union shops, it really allows only agency shops. States are allowed to pass right-to-work laws that outlaw even the agency shop (*General Motors*). See Table 15.1 for a list of states with right-to-work laws.

In one case, employees resigned from the union during a strike and went back to work. The union tried to fine them, but the U.S. Supreme Court said the union could not fine people who were no longer members of the union. While these workers were still required to pay dues under the agency-shop agreement, they could not be fined by an organization to which they no longer belonged (*Pattern Makers*).

Table 15.1   States with Right-to-Work Laws

Alabama	Kansas	South Carolina
Arizona	Louisiana	South Dakota
Arkansas	Mississippi	Tennessee
Florida	Nebraska	Texas
Georgia	Nevada	Utah
Idaho	North Carolina	Virginia
Iowa	North Dakota	Wyoming

People who are forced to pay union dues because of an agency-shop agreement do not have to pay to support political causes they do not agree with. Unions must refund that portion of union dues that goes to support political causes. The U.S. Supreme Court has ruled that unions must provide a reasonably prompt opportunity for nonmembers to challenge the amount of dues the union collects, and the decision on the amount of dues to be refunded must be made by an impartial decision maker (*Chicago Teachers*).

The other major change brought about by the Taft-Hartley Act was the addition of unfair labor practices that unions could commit. Unions cannot coerce employees or employers, refuse to bargain, charge excessive dues, or insist on featherbedding (requiring employers to pay people who do not work). It is not always easy to tell what constitutes featherbedding. In one case, the Supreme Court allowed a union to demand that newspaper type be set twice a day even though the second set was not used. In another case, the Court allowed a union to demand that a theater hire a local orchestra to play at intermission, even though the traveling road shows brought their own orchestras to play during the performances. In other words, the U.S. Supreme Court has interpreted featherbedding narrowly to mean having workers standing idly by and not doing any kind of work. That is something a union cannot ask an employer to do. Unions can ask employers to pay workers who do useless work. Of course, the employer is free to refuse to agree to that kind of clause in the union contract (and face a strike or picket line that might destroy the company). Many employers think Congress should amend the law to include useless work in the definition of featherbedding. So far Congress has not responded (*American Newspaper; Gamble*).

The Taft-Hartley Act also allows the president of the United States to stop a strike if he or she determines that health and safety are threatened. The president can order the workers back to work for up to 80 days (a cooling-off period), during which time the two sides must work to try to settle the dispute. The act also requires either side to give the other side 60 days' notice before asking to negotiate a new contract. They must also notify the Federal Mediation and Conciliation Service that they intend to negotiate a new contract. Some legal scholars believe that requiring union members to go back to work violates the Thirteenth Amendment's prohibition against "involuntary servitude," but the U.S. Supreme Court has never ruled on this question.

The Landrum-Griffin Act

In 1935, the Wagner Act was passed to protect unions from employers. In 1947, the Taft-Hartley Act was passed to protect employers from unions. In 1959, the Landrum-Griffin Act was passed to protect workers from unions. The part of the act we are concerned with is called the Labor-Management Reporting and Disclosure Act (LMRDA). It set out a Bill of Rights for union members.

Equal Rights within the Union

The first right listed is the right to be treated equally. All members of the union have the same right to nominate candidates, vote in elections, and attend meetings. All union members also have the right to vote on dues increases.

The Right of Free Speech and Assembly

The LMRDA guarantees the right of free speech and assembly to all union members. This includes the right to speak at union meetings. If one group of union members shouts down another group of union members, they have violated this right (*Scovile*).

This also includes the right to criticize union leaders or union policy. In 1989, the U.S. Supreme Court ruled that a local union official could sue the international union when he was removed from his union office for speaking out against a dues increase (*Lynn #2*). In 1991, the Fourth Circuit Court ruled that a longshoreman kicked out of the union for using offensive language toward a union official could sue the union for violating his right of free speech (*Kowaleviocz*).

This right of free speech also includes the right of free assembly, which means that union members can get together in groups to discuss union business without fear of retaliation from the union leadership (*Kuebler*).

The Right to Sue the Union

The LMRDA allows union members to sue the union. At the same time, it allows unions to require members to bring problems to the union before they file a lawsuit. The act says a member "may be required to exhaust reasonable hearing procedures" (not to exceed a four-month lapse of time) within the union. The U.S. Supreme Court has ruled that, because the statute says "may be required" instead of "shall be required," it is up to the district judge to decide if he or she will delay the trial to give the union a chance to solve the problem internally. The judge does not have to do this. Also, the judge may award attorney's fees to union members who have to sue their own union (*Marine*).

The Right to Fair Discipline Hearings

It is common for union constitutions to contain provisions that allow members to be disciplined for doing things not considered in the best interest of the union. Discipline might include a fine or expulsion from the union. The LMRDA guarantees union members the right to a fair hearing before being disciplined. The union member must be "(*a*) served with written specific charges; (*b*) given a reasonable time to prepare; and (*c*) afforded a full and fair hearing." Courts have said that a full and fair hearing includes the right to cross-examine witnesses, to have a lawyer if the union has a lawyer, and to have an unbiased judge and jury (*Kiepura; Cornelio; Semancik*).

The Right to Fair and Open Elections

The LMRDA guarantees fair and open elections. Local union officers must be elected at least every three years, national officials at least every five years. A secret ballot is required in local elections. Higher officials may be elected at a convention. Unions are allowed to set "reasonable" qualifications for candidates. In one case, a union required candidates for major office to have served in a lower office. The Supreme Court declared this rule invalid because it disqualified 93 percent of the union members (*Wirtz*). In another case, the Supreme Court declared invalid a rule that required candidates to have attended at least half the union meetings during the three years preceding the election. This rule disqualified 96 percent of the members (*Steelworker's #2*).

Unions have to treat all candidates equally and distribute their campaign literature to the members at the candidate's expense. A union cannot use union funds to support a particular candidate. The union must provide members with a reasonable opportunity to nominate candidates and notify members at least 15 days before an election. Union members who are unhappy with a union election cannot sue directly. They have to get the U.S. secretary of labor to sue for them to set aside the union election.

The Right to Review Financial Information

Unions are required to file annual financial reports with the U.S. secretary of labor. Union members have a right to examine these reports. Union officials have a fiduciary duty to use great care in handling union funds.

The Right of Fair Representation

Once a union is certified as representing a bargaining unit, it represents all employees in the unit, even those who refuse to join the union. The certified union is the only entity that can negotiate a group contract for these employees. The union has a duty to represent all the employees fairly, even those who do not belong to the union but are covered by the union contract. In one case, a union tried to negotiate different benefits for black and white employees. The Supreme Court held that this violated the union's duty to represent all the workers fairly (*Steele*). The union must also treat all employees fairly in grievance and arbitration procedures and may not act in bad faith or arbitrarily to exclude any employee (*Anchor Motor*).

The union has a duty to "make an honest effort to serve the interests of all its members without hostility to any" (*Ford Motor Co.*). If the union breaches this duty, the injured employee can sue. If the union has done a bad job of representing the employee at the arbitration hearing, the employee is usually stuck with the arbitrator's decision unless the union was "dishonest," acted in "bad faith," or was "discriminatory." On the other hand, the union should have a good reason for not taking the case to arbitration and has a duty to follow up on leads provided by the employee (*Anchor Motor*).

An employee who feels that the union has breached the duty of fair representation must sue both the employer and the union together. The employee has to prove two things: that the employer violated the union contract, and that the union did not live up to its duty to represent the employee fairly in the grievance and arbitration proceedings. If an employee does prove both these things, the judge can order both the employer and the union to pay damages (*Vaca*).

Arbitration

Over the last century, more and more disputes in the area of labor relations have come to be settled by arbitration. Arbitration is used for two purposes: contract formation and contract interpretation.

Contract Formation

Because a strike can be costly to both sides, labor and management have an incentive to find better ways to settle disputes over what the union contract should contain. One approach is *mediation*. With mediation, a neutral third party is chosen by both sides to help them come to an agreement. A mediator does not have the power to impose an agreement, only to help the parties achieve the result they want, a fair contract. In some situations, the federal government will provide a mediator.

Another approach is *fact-finding*. A fact finder looks at the company books or the market for the product and presents both sides with a set of facts. These facts might relate to the profitability of the company or the effects of competition on the company.

In some situations, mediation and fact-finding do not help, and both sides agree to abide by what an *arbitrator* decides. Several industries, including the coal and apparel industries, have used arbitrators over the last half century to reach agreements and avoid strikes.

Contract Interpretation

While arbitration is not a common way of making union contracts, it is a very common way of interpreting union contracts. Many union contracts require both sides to submit a dispute about the interpretation of the contract to an arbitrator. Most disputes over the contract involve whether or not the employer had a right under the contract to fire a particular employee. Many union contracts require the employer to have good cause before firing an employee protected by the union contract. The contract may define good cause in great detail or leave it up to the arbitrator to decide what constitutes good cause. Some contracts recognize two types of good cause. Heavy-duty good cause consists of those things for which the employee can be fired without a warning and a chance to improve. Dishonesty, insubordination, being drunk on the job, or fighting at work are often considered heavy-duty sins for which the employee can be fired immediately. Lesser infractions and plain old incompetence require a warning and a chance for the employee to improve. In most situations, an employee who wants to have his or her case heard by an arbitrator must first file a grievance with the employer. This gives the employer a chance to change its mind. If the employer does not, the case is presented to an arbitrator. Both sides present evidence and the arbitrator makes a decision. While the arbitrator can award back pay and order the employer to reinstate the employee, arbitrators usually will not award punitive damages or attorney fees. Arbitration is supposed to be a quicker and easier way of settling disputes than going through a court battle.

Labor arbitrators have developed a set of principles that they live by. The arbitrator is supposed to determine whether the employee actually did what he or she was accused of doing and, if so, what the appropriate penalty should be. The arbitrator is more likely to go along with the punishment decided on by the employer if the employer conducted a fair investigation. More and more arbitrators are ordering employers to take back employees who are alcoholics or drug addicts if the employee promises to get treatment in a rehabilitation program. Arbitrators will usually not allow employees to be disciplined or dismissed because of conduct that takes place off the job unless there is a clear relationship between the off-the-job conduct and the interests of the employer.

The U.S. Supreme Court has ruled that an employee protected by a union contract has a right to be represented by a union representative at the earliest stage in the process in which discipline might result (*Weingarten*). If the employee gets no satisfaction from the grievance procedure, then the union can take the case to an arbitrator. Usually the union represents the employee at the arbitration hearing, and the employee is not allowed to bring his or her own attorney to the hearing. The hearing is informal. Witnesses testify and are cross-examined just the way they are at a trial. The arbitrator is not bound by the normal rules of evidence and can hear any testimony he or she feels might be helpful. Generally, if the employee does not testify on his or her own behalf, the arbitrator is going to consider that a black mark against the employee (criminal defendants have a constitutional right not to testify at their own trial but the same does not apply in a labor arbitration hearing).

The award of the arbitrator can be enforced in court. In 1960, in a series of decisions involving the Steelworkers Union, the U.S. Supreme Court laid down the fundamental principle that the award of the arbitrator is to be enforced in almost all situations. The Court said it was the intent of Congress that disputes over the interpretation of union contracts be handled by arbitration whenever possible and that the arbitrator's decision should not be overturned except in extraordinary circumstances (*Steelworkers Trilogy*).

Generally, courts will overturn an arbitrator's decision only if the decision does not follow the contract, if it violates public policy, or if there were gross defects in procedure. Of course, courts can disagree about what violates public policy. In one case, the Fifth Circuit Court overturned the arbitrator's decision. The arbitrator had found that the employee had not used marijuana at work as alleged. The circuit court believed that he had and that to allow him to work around heavy machines under the influence of marijuana was a violation of public policy. The U.S. Supreme Court overturned the circuit court's decision and reinstated the arbitrator's decision. The Supreme Court said that the whole purpose of arbitration is to have a quick and final decision. Courts cannot second-guess the arbitrator in most situations (*Misco*).

Federal Preemption

Federal labor law preempts state law. This means that if workers have a complaint that falls within the jurisdiction of federal labor law, they have to file a complaint with the NLRB or the U.S. secretary of labor, not in state court. In many situations the workers must file the complaint within six months. If the employer mistreats or discharges them because they are union members, it is a matter for the NLRB. If they have a complaint about the way the union has treated them, they should call the U.S. Labor Department.

While federal law has generally preempted the field, there are some employers that the federal law does not reach. While there is no size limit written into the federal statute, the NLRB has decided it will not deal with small employers. It is often unclear how small is too small. Generally, any employer or employee in the private sector should assume federal labor law applies to them until an attorney tells them otherwise.

Federal labor law does not cover state and local government employees.

There are many state statutes that were passed decades ago and are still on the books, even though federal law has preempted this area. It will be up to your attorney to decide if they still apply. For example, many states have criminal laws that prohibit blacklisting. If the workers are being blacklisted because of their union membership, that is a matter for the NLRB, not the local police. Many states have laws that purport to control strikes, picketing, and boycotts by unions. Many of these state statutes either violate the U.S. Constitution or have been preempted by federal labor law. Many states also have laws against rioting that were designed to be used against strikers. Some of these criminal laws have been declared unconstitutional by the U.S. Supreme Court (*Medrano*). In 1988, Texas and Nebraska statutes against "mass picketing" were also declared unconstitutional. These laws tried to limit the number of people that could be on a picket line at any one time (*Howard Gault; UFCWI*).

One important issue to many unions has been whether they can have a contract clause that requires the employer to place union information in employee mailboxes at the workplace. This has been of particular interest to teacher unions. In 1988, the U.S. Supreme Court ruled that such an agreement would be a violation of federal postal laws. Union letters must have a stamp and go through the post office just like other letters (*Regents*).

Suing the Boss

What if employees are covered by a union contract and want to sue their employer for wrongful discharge or a tort such as defamation of character?

The U.S. Supreme Court has ruled that it depends on whether the dispute is "inextricably intertwined" with the union contract (*Lueck*). For example, in a 1988 case, the employee was suing under Illinois law for wrongful discharge. The question was whether the discharge violated Illinois public policy. There was no need to interpret the union contract to make that determination. Because of this, the U.S. Supreme Court said that the employee could sue in state court and did not have to submit the dispute to arbitration under the union contract (*Lingle*). It is important to remember that one purpose of federal labor law is to guarantee that union members and employees covered by union contracts are not placed at a disadvantage. If the Court had ruled that they could not sue as other employees could, it would have discouraged workers from joining unions and working under union contracts. It is also important to remember that the contract in this case simply said that disputes concerning the interpretation of the union contract would be submitted to arbitration. That does not mean a union and an employer could not agree to have every dispute between employees and the employer settled by arbitration, including civil rights and wrongful discharge claims. The 1991 ruling by the U.S. Supreme Court in *Gilmer* (discussed in Chapter 10) said that individual employees can contract away their right to take even civil rights claims to court, and union employees should also have that right through their union contract.

Unions and the Right of Free Speech

In the early 1900s, the American Federation of Labor published a list of companies that refused to bargain with the AFL, hoping consumers would stop buying products made by the companies on the list. Bucks Stove and Range Co. was on the list because it refused to bargain with the stove worker's union. A federal judge issued an injunction against publishing the list. The head of the AFL, Samuel Gompers, argued that he had a right of free speech that included the right to publish a list like this, but the U.S. Supreme Court disagreed. While it struck down this particular injunction on a technicality, it declared that these kinds of lists could be enjoined by judges concerned with protecting private property (*Gompers*).

Unions argued that they had a right of free speech under the First Amendment that protected their right to picket and boycott. In 1940, the Supreme Court finally agreed, holding that peaceful picketing against employers with whom the union has a direct labor dispute is protected by the First Amendment and cannot be prevented by statutes. The case involved an Alabama statute that made peaceful picketing by unions a criminal offense (*Thornhill*).

The next year, the Court applied the same logic to strike down an injunction by a state court that tried to prevent a union picket line (*Swing*).

In 1959, federal labor law was amended to outlaw picket lines against people who are not directly involved in a labor dispute. This means unions cannot put a full union picket line around a company in an attempt to get the picketed company to stop doing business with the employer the union has a dispute with. In 1964, the Supreme Court made a distinction between a full picket line and an informational picket line. The case involved union picket lines around supermarkets. The union asked consumers not to buy apples from Washington state. The union did not ask employees to refuse to work, and it did not ask customers to boycott the store. It only asked consumers to boycott Washington apples. The Supreme Court said the union had a right to do that. The Court felt that this kind of informational activity was not the kind of coercive picket line that may not be used against parties not directly involved in a labor dispute (*Tree Fruits*).

It is generally believed that a union can use other methods of speech, short of a full picket line, to inform consumers about a labor dispute and ask them to boycott in support of the union. The federal labor laws specifically allow "publicity, other than picketing, for the purpose of truthfully informing the public, including consumers," about a labor dispute. The U.S. Supreme Court had to interpret this provision in 1988. The case involved a dispute between construction unions and the owner of a shopping mall in Florida. The construction unions passed out handbills at the entrances to the shopping mall urging consumers not to shop there because a department store was being added to the mall and the construction company was paying, in the union's opinion, substandard wages and benefits. The U.S. Supreme Court upheld the right of the union to pass out handbills. The Court made much of the fact that the union did not form a picket line, and did not ask anyone to stop work or refuse to make deliveries to the mall. The Court allowed this kind of informational activity and made it clear that any other interpretation of the statute would raise "serious constitutional problems" (*DeBartolo*).

State supreme courts are also protecting the free-speech rights of union members. One 1987 case involved union members in Connecticut who were arrested for picketing in front of the home of the president of the company against which they were striking. Connecticut had a statute that made it a crime to picket in a residential neighborhood. The Connecticut Supreme Court struck down the statute as an unconstitutional infringement on the right of free speech. The attorney trying to save the statute argued that it did not infringe the right of free speech because the statute was used only against union members (presumably this attorney assumed union members do not have the same rights as everyone else). The Connecticut Supreme Court ruled that union members do have constitutional rights and struck down the statute

(*French*). However, in 1991, a New Jersey court used an injunction to stop union picketing in front of a company president's house when the court felt the picketing had become coercive and intimidating (*K-T Marine*).

There are still many unanswered questions concerning the extent to which the First Amendment's right of free speech protects union members. However, some things are fairly well settled. People have a right under the First Amendment to form groups, including labor unions (while states and the federal government may be able to prevent public employees from going on strike, they cannot prevent them from joining a union). People have a right to picket employers with whom they have a direct conflict. Judges can limit the use of full picket lines against businesses that are not directly involved in a labor dispute because these kinds of picket lines involve more than just speech (the law still believes that full picket lines are coercive). Finally, people have the right to form informational picket lines or pass out leaflets to inform their fellow consumers about a business and its practices.

16

Immigration

Not very many years ago the subject of immigration law would have been of interest only to those hoping to immigrate to the United States and their relatives. After 1986, it became of interest to every American. That was the year Congress made it a federal crime to hire aliens who are not authorized to work in the United States and required most employers to ask job applicants to prove that they are either United States citizens or eligible to work in the United States.

The Past

Between the American Revolution and the Civil War, Congress showed little interest in immigration. With increased immigration after the Civil War, Congress began both to formalize the procedure for "naturalization" and to put limits on who could immigrate to the United States. From 1875 to 1921, Congress added more and more restrictions in an effort to keep out undesirables such as prostitutes, convicts, and lunatics. As a reaction to the possibility of greatly increased immigration from China, the Chinese were the first ethnic group to be singled out as undesirable. In 1917, the law was amended to keep out most Asians. To keep out people with strange ideas, both polygamists and anarchists were put on the list of those who were not allowed to immigrate to the United States.

Early in the twentieth century, the influx increased, with more than a million new immigrants arriving in some years. Congress ultimately decided it could not control this flood with "literacy tests" and restrictions on "subversives," so in 1921 the first quota law was passed limiting the number of immigrants from eastern and southern Europe.

In 1952, Congress rewrote the immigration laws, setting out in detail the reasons why people could be kept out of the United States and setting quotas to limit immigration. In 1965, Congress put an end to special quotas for particular countries but set a general limit of no more than 20,000 immigrants from any one country except countries in the Western Hemisphere, which would have a total hemisphere quota of 120,000 per year. Total immigration from the rest of the world was limited to 170,000 per year. In 1986, Congress put into place the first criminal sanctions against employers who hire illegal aliens and set in motion the greatest amnesty program for illegal aliens in American history. In 1990, the law was again subjected to major changes, including a significant increase in the number of immigrants that would be allowed in (675,000). This revision also changed the titles of some provisions. For decades people were allowed to immigrate under the "third" or "sixth" preference if they met certain "employment" criteria. Critics asked why these employment preferences couldn't be grouped together, and that is exactly what Congress did in 1990. The "third" and "sixth" preferences were replaced by the first, second, and third "employment-based preferences."

Immigration Procedures

Immigration is controlled by the Immigration and Naturalization Service (INS), which is a branch of the U.S. Department of Justice. In most situations, the INS works with the State Department to issue visas to appropriate people. However, it is always the INS that has the last word. Someone may come to the border with a visa issued by the State Department and still be denied admission by the INS.

Throughout this book, the discussion is about rights. When it comes to immigration, there are no rights; no one has a right to enter the United States. Congress could keep everyone out or let in only people of one particular ethnic group. There is nothing in the Constitution that says immigration laws have to be "fair" or "just." Once someone makes it into the United States, he or she does have a right to a fair hearing before the person can be thrown out again, but that does not include the right to a jury trial, a court-appointed attorney, or a court-appointed translator (*Ardestani*; *El Rescate*).

The decision of the INS or an administrative-law judge may be appealable to a review board or a federal court, but the people involved may have as little as 30 days to appeal. That is why anyone who has received a negative decision in this area should contact an attorney immediately or risk losing the right to appeal.

Nonimmigrants

Immigration law divides people who want to enter the United States into two groups: immigrants and nonimmigrants. Immigrants are people who want to reside in the United States permanently and eventually become citizens. Nonimmigrants only want to visit for a while to see the tourist sights, conduct business, or get an education.

Different nonimmigrant visas have different letters, depending on the type of visit the person will be making. Visitors for business or pleasure get a B visa; people in transit through the country receive a C visa; crewmembers on planes or ships temporarily in the country get a D visa; special business people who will conduct foreign trade or make investments receive an E visa; students get an F or an M visa; temporary workers get an H visa; foreign journalists get an I visa; visitors and students under special exchange programs get a J visa; engaged persons coming into the country to get married get a K visa; people coming because they work for an international company and have been transferred to the United States get an L visa; and the representatives of foreign countries or international organizations get an A or a G visa.

The 1990 revisions created several new nonimmigrant categories. So-called special immigrants receive an N visa. This catchall category includes lawful permanent residents returning from a trip abroad; former citizens wishing to reacquire citizenship; former and current employees of the United States government or the old Panama Canal Company, if they meet certain criteria; and some people associated with international organizations. Aliens with extraordinary ability and achievement in the sciences, arts, education, business, or athletics get an O visa; athletes and entertainers who are part of a performing group get a P visa; aliens who come in through some international cultural exchanges get a Q visa; and ministers, priests, and others who are employed in religious work get an R visa.

Eighty percent of nonimmigrant visitors come as tourists. How difficult it is for them to get into the country depends on which country they are coming from. Business visitors receive different kinds of visas, depending on how long they intend to stay and whether or not they will receive a salary from an American company while in the United States. There are also provisions for temporary workers. An entertainer or athlete would receive an H-1 visa to come and perform in the United States. A worker coming to provide a skill that is in short supply receives an H-2 visa, while an alien coming as a trainee receives an H-3 visa. People who are being transferred from one branch of a company to another are given an L-1 visa. People coming to the United States temporarily to carry on a trade with a foreign country (import-export) or to invest in an American business come on E-1 and E-2 visas.

Most temporary workers are nurses, agricultural workers, or people of "distinguished merit and ability." For each of these three categories, special procedures apply. Generally, the United States is considered to have a shortage of nurses, so nurses may be hired as temporary workers with a minimum of procedure. Employers who wish to employ agricultural workers and people of "distinguished merit and ability" do not need to apply for the usual labor certificate discussed below, but they must contact the U.S. secretary of labor for a special certification. For agricultural workers (H-2A visa), the employer must receive certification from the secretary of labor that there are not sufficient agricultural workers and that the import of such workers will not adversely affect wages or working conditions. The secretary is required by law to act quickly on these applications (presumably because the crops are ready to be picked). An employer wanting to hire someone of "distinguished merit and ability" must demonstrate to the secretary of labor that he will be paying prevailing wages and that there is no strike or lockout. The employer must also notify the appropriate labor union representative or, if there is none, post a notice in a conspicuous location that a request has been filed with the secretary of labor.

Immigrants

An immigrant is someone who wants to come to the United States as a permanent resident in the hopes of becoming a citizen at some point in the future. Two main categories of people are allowed to immigrate: the immediate relatives of current citizens (and permanent residents), and those with special skills that are needed by the American economy. Until the 1990 changes, people were allowed to come in under six major "preferences." Since the changes, things have been renamed and reorganized. There are now five types of relatives given special treatment. The first are the unmarried minor children, parents, or spouses of citizens. These relatives receive the highest priority and are not subject to quota limitations.

After this special preference, there are four family-preference categories with limits on how many people may come in under each category. In the first category are adult unmarried children of United States citizens. In the second are the spouses and unmarried children of permanent residents. In the third are the married sons and daughters of citizens, their spouses, and children. In the fourth are the brothers and sisters of adult citizens, their spouses, and minor children.

There are now three employment-preference categories (these replaced the old "third" and "sixth" preference categories). In the first employment-preference category are what the law calls "priority workers." These are people of "extraordinary ability," such as college professors, researchers, business executives, and managers. In the second employment-preference category are professionals, people with advanced degrees, and people with "exceptional ability" in the sciences, arts, and business. In the third employment-preference category are skilled and unskilled workers, with very few places reserved for the unskilled category. Generally, alien workers must be more "able, willing and qualified" than workers already in the country, unless they are coming as teachers or as people with exceptional ability in the sciences and arts, in which case they only have to be equally qualified. Also, as a general rule, people entering the country to work (either temporarily or permanently) must not adversely affect the wages and working conditions of similarly employed workers already in the United States.

The Labor Certificate

A labor certificate is not required for nurses, farm workers, or people with "extraordinary ability" but is required for almost everyone else coming into the United States to work. The labor certificate procedure is designed to make sure alien workers will not be taking jobs away from workers who are already legally in the country. The process usually begins when an American employer applies to the state job-placement service for certification that there are no citizens or current permanent residents "able, willing and qualified" to take a particular job. The state job service will supervise advertising the job opening to ensure that this is indeed the case. Their opinion will ultimately be turned over to the U.S. Labor Department, which will certify to the INS that the foreign worker will not displace a worker already legally in the United States and that the compensation that will be paid will be commensurate with prevailing wages in the area. A few jobs do not require the labor certificate procedure because the jobs are listed on Schedule A. Schedule A is a list of highly skilled jobs for which there is a recognized labor shortage. Most of these jobs are in the medical field. The INS will review the Labor Department opinion with an eye to the fact that the burden is always on employers to prove that they tried and failed to recruit a U.S. worker.

Special Provisions of the 1990 Act

The 1990 Act brought into the law several new provisions. First, 10,000 immigrant visas are reserved each year for people coming to the United States to invest at least $1 million in a new business that will provide at least 10 new jobs. If the investment will be in a rural or high-unemployment area, it can be as little as $500,000. For investments in high-employment areas, a higher investment may be required. This has been dubbed the "Fat Cat Preference."

Also new in 1990 was a provision to attempt to bring in people from countries that were discriminated against in the past. It is not clear exactly how it will be determined who qualifies for this status; however, during the first three years of the law, 40 percent of these special visas will go to Irish nationals. For this reason, this has been dubbed the "Irish Preference." There are currently 40,000 of these special-diversity visas issued each year, and that is scheduled to increase to 55,000 by 1993.

The 1990 changes also made visas more easily available for people from Hong Kong, Lebanon, and selected other countries, with 10,000 special Hong Kong visas being issued each year until 1994.

Hiring Workers

The 1986 revisions attempted for the first time to control the hiring of illegal aliens by making it a crime for employers to hire illegal aliens knowing that they were either in the country illegally or not authorized to work. It also required employers with more than three employees to fill out a form I-9 for every new employee. This form requires new employees to present proof of both their identity and their employability in the United States. The following documents will serve both purposes simultaneously: a U.S. passport, a certificate of U.S. citizenship or naturalization, an unexpired foreign passport with employment authorization from the INS, a permanent-resident card (commonly called a green card although they are currently white in color), an INS temporary-resident card, or an INS employment-authorization card if it has a picture of the worker. Most citizens do not have any of these documents. For them, proof of citizenship will usually be established by first proving identity with either a valid state driver's license or state ID card and, second, by producing a Social Security card or birth certificate to prove citizenship. The United States has so far rejected the idea of providing every citizen with a picture identification card that proves citizenship.

Employers charged with knowingly hiring illegal aliens can use a properly filled out I-9 form as a defense. Employers can give new employees three business days to present the proper documents unless they are being hired for less than three days, in which case they must present proper documentation on the first day of work. Employers must retain these I-9 forms for one year after the date an employee is terminated or for three years if the employee works for the employer for less than two years. People who knowingly recruit or refer illegal aliens for employment are also subject to criminal penalties.

Employers cannot require employees to post a bond or otherwise indemnify them for the expenses they may incur if the worker turns out not to be authorized to work in the United States. Employers who hire illegal aliens face fines of up to $10,000 and six months in jail. In 1991, the Eighth Circuit Court ruled that these criminal penalties may be applied to the chief executive officers of corporations that hire illegal aliens (*Steiben*). Also in 1991, the Ninth Circuit Court ruled that employers cannot be expected to spot forged Social Security cards given that there are currently 16 different types of legal Social Security cards in circulation (*Collins Foods*).

This 1986 revision also preempted state law in this area. In other words, state laws against hiring illegal aliens are no longer enforceable.

Discrimination

The 1986 immigration law also made it illegal for employers (with four or more employees) to discriminate against alien workers. Specifically:

> It is an unfair immigration-related employment practice for a person or other entity to discriminate against any individual (other than an unauthorized alien) with respect to the hiring, or recruitment or referral for a fee, of the individual for employment or the discharging of the individual from employment—
> (A) because of such individual's national origin, or
> (B) in the case of a citizen or intending citizen, because of such individual's citizenship status. (8 U.S.C. sec. 1324)

The intent of this section was to prevent discrimination against workers who look or sound like they might be illegal aliens. There is some concern that this has not had the desired effect and that American citizens or permanent residents are being discriminated against because they look or sound foreign. This provision also seems to authorize discrimination against aliens who do not "intend" to become United States citizens. It is not clear from the law exactly how employers are to decide if alien workers "intend" to become citizens (*Todd Corp.*). In 1990, the General Accounting Office issued a report that concluded that "widespread discrimination" had resulted from the 1986 act. Nineteen percent of employers surveyed said they had begun discriminating on the basis of appearance, accent, or citizenship status.

Amnesty

One of the most controversial aspects of United States immigration law is the amnesty provision. This allows the INS to grant permanent resident status to illegal aliens who have resided in the United States for so long that it no longer makes sense to send them back. The general amnesty provision is called the "registry." Under current law, if someone entered the United States before January 1, 1972, resided continuously in the United States since that time, and is of good character, then the attorney general at his discretion may grant that person permanent resident status. This date is changed every few years as time passes.

By the 1980s, there were so many illegal aliens in the United States that a special one-time amnesty provision was placed in the 1986 Immigration Act. This provision guaranteed amnesty to illegal aliens who could prove that they had been in the United States illegally since January 1, 1982, or had worked in "perishable agriculture" for at least 90 days prior to May 1, 1986. Many of the reasons that would usually prevent such people from receiving amnesty, such as poverty, were waived in this special amnesty provision. Over three million people applied for permanent residency under this program.

Refugees

Granting political asylum or refugee status is one of the most controversial areas of United States immigration law. In November 1991, a wave of small boats began leaving Haiti, causing the U.S. Coast Guard to divert ships from the drug interdiction program to intercept these potential illegal aliens. A special detention camp was built at the U.S. naval base at Guantanamo Bay, Cuba, to hold them until the INS and the federal courts could decide what to do with them.

The asylum and refugee programs were designed to help people who face death or imprisonment because of their race, religion, nationality, membership in social groups, or political beliefs. It is not supposed to be used by people who simply want to improve their standard of living. However, it is often hard to tell whether people from many Third World countries are motivated by fear of political persecution or a desire for a better life.

The law says the person must have a "well-founded" fear of persecution. The U.S. Supreme Court has ruled that this means it must be "more likely than not" that the person will be persecuted (*Stevic*). The persecution may be from a source other than the government. For example, in one case a former member of the Provisional Irish Republican Army (PIRA) claimed he would be executed by the PIRA if he returned to Ireland. He was granted asylum (*McMullen*). The fact that someone will have difficulty finding a job in their home country is not enough. For example, in one case a member of the Zoroastrian religion from Pakistan argued he would not be able to get a government job in Pakistan because of religious discrimination. The court said that this was not enough to justify the granting of asylum (*Minwalla*). In 1992, the U.S. Supreme Court ruled that the possibility of being drafted by either side in a civil war also did not justify the granting of asylum (*Elias-Zacarias*).

Aliens may be entitled to reside and work in the United States temporarily under Temporary Protected Status. This status is given to aliens fleeing from armed conflict or natural disasters such as floods, droughts, and epidemics. Such aliens may remain in the United States until the attorney general determines that it is safe to go home or until they violate the terms of their visa.

Deportation

Deportation means throwing noncitizens out of the country because they are undesirable. Generally, people are deported either because they entered the country illegally, have committed a crime, pose a threat to national security, or have violated some provision of their visa. However, aliens can be deported for many other reasons. If they fall into one of the categories listed as reasons to exclude aliens in the first place, they can be deported for the same reason. They can also be deported because they failed to maintain their employment, their marriage was a "sham," or they are simply "undesirable."

People who face deportation are not entitled to a jury trial, but they do get a fairly extensive hearing if they want one. Furthermore, the government has to prove its case. People are entitled to have an attorney with them at a deportation hearing, but they are not entitled to have an attorney at government expense if they cannot afford one for themselves (*Ardestani*).

It is a defense in a deportation case if the alien has resided continuously in the United States for at least seven years and is of good moral character, and if deportation would result in extreme hardship. Of course, it is often difficult to prove that extreme hardship will result. People who are deported and return to the United States may be imprisoned and fined. The burden is always on aliens to prove they entered the country legally.

Becoming a Citizen

The most difficult step in the immigration process is obtaining permanent-resident status. Once someone obtains that, remains in the United States on a continual basis, pays taxes, holds down a job, and stays out of jail, he or she can expect to become a citizen at some point in the future. Most people are eligible to apply for citizenship five years after becoming permanent residents. They can become a citizen faster if their spouse or parents are citizens, they are ministers or priests, or they served in the United States military. To become a citizen, a person must pass a test that demonstrates a basic knowledge of how the American government works and of American history. The person also needs to be able to speak English, be of good moral character, and take a loyalty oath.

Of course, people born in the United States are already citizens, as are people born in Puerto Rico, the American Virgin Islands, and Guam. People born outside of the United States who have at least one parent who is an American citizen are eligible to establish citizenship if they meet certain criteria. The rules on this have changed several times during the course of the twentieth century, so only the INS or an attorney can tell if someone meets the right criteria, given the date of their birth.

Generally, people cannot have their citizenship taken away unless they "voluntarily renounced" their U.S. citizenship or made "willful misrepresentations" in the process of becoming naturalized citizens and those misrepresentations were "material" enough that they might have influenced the INS when it was making its original decision to grant permanent-resident status (*Afroyim*; *Terrazas*; *Fedorenki*; *Kungys*).

There Is Always Another Way

No one has a right to enter the United States or to become a United States citizen. At the same time, this is one area of the law where there is always another way. If the usual procedures do not work, the attorney general or the president may be persuaded to allow the person to enter or remain in the country. In some cases, congressmen can be persuaded to put through a "private bill" letting someone into the country or making the person a permanent resident. When it comes to immigration law, one thing is clear: never say never.

PART
SIX

RIGHTS AFTER INJURY

17

Accidental Injury and Worker's Compensation

The Past

A century ago, English and American judges ruled that employers owed several duties to workers (they still do). The major duties were (and still are):

1. The duty to provide and maintain a safe workplace
2. The duty to provide safe tools and machines
3. The duty to provide a competent group of co-workers
4. The duty to promulgate and enforce safety rules
5. The duty to warn of known dangers

If an employer breached one of these duties and a worker was injured as a result, the worker could sue. Of course, to recover, the worker had to prove the employer was negligent (breached one of these duties). In major-injury cases, workers managed to prove that about 20 percent of the time. This meant two things. First, 80 percent of seriously injured workers received nothing. Second, the 20 percent who did win received a lot of money, so much money that people were afraid the Industrial Revolution would come to a halt.

In 1837, the case of *Priestly v. Fowler* came before the English House of Lords (in England the House of Lords is the Supreme Court) (*Priestly*). Lord Abinger wrote an opinion that denied the worker a recovery for two reasons. The first reason was that a fellow servant had been partly responsible for the injury. Lord Abinger said the injured worker should sue the person really responsible for the injuries, the fellow servant, not the employer. Lord Abinger also said that when a worker goes to work in a dangerous industry, the worker assumes the risk of injury. If workers do not want to assume that risk, they should get some other kind of job.

In 1842, the Massachusetts Supreme Court adopted these ideas (*Farwell*). Eventually every state supreme court agreed, and Lord Abinger's opinion evolved into the three defenses that came to be called the unholy trinity. The first, *contributory negligence*, said that if the worker was the least bit at fault, he or she could not recover anything in damages. The *fellow servant doctrine* said that if a fellow servant was the least bit responsible, the injured worker could not recover from the employer. The *assumption of the risk doctrine* said that anyone taking a job in a dangerous industry knew at the time that it was dangerous and thus assumed the risk of injury.

The English legal system had been built on the idea of fault. English law believed that making the person at fault pay for the damages prevented injuries, as well as providing damage awards to injured people. Of course, if no one was at fault, there was no compensation. With the invention of the unholy trinity, it was even less likely that an injured worker was going to recover anything from an employer, even if the employer was at fault (negligent). Stories appeared of mine owners who saved mules rather than men in flooding mines because mules cost money to replace. In 1897, the English responded by passing a Worker's Compensation Act that required the employer to compensate the injured worker (or his widow) regardless of fault. No longer was the concept of negligence to be used, or the three defenses. English economists believed the consumers of a product should pay the full cost of the product, including the cost of lost arms and lost lives. The English also felt that employers would have an incentive to save the workers rather than the mules because the workers would now cost more than the mules. American states followed the English model, requiring compensation for "injury by accident arising out of and in the course of employment."

The Worker's Compensation System

The easiest way to describe the worker's compensation system is to say that it replaced a system based on fault with a no-fault system. The employee gives up the right to sue and perhaps win a big award in exchange for quick but low compensation, and the employer passes along the cost to the consumers.

Employees Covered

Most employees are covered by worker's compensation. The major exceptions in most states are domestic servants and farm workers. Also, partners and business owners are usually not covered (or have the option in most states not to be covered). Some states have a separate system for state and local government employees, while the federal government has its own federal employee's compensation act (5 U.S.C. sec. 810). It is important to remember that worker's compensation is paid only to employees, not to independent contractors (see Chapter 5 for a discussion of the difference between employees and independent contracators).

Injury by Accident

The first requirement for qualification under worker's-compensation laws is that there be an "injury by accident." Early in the twentieth century most courts required an "impact" before they would find that an accident had occurred. If the worker had a heart attack or a hernia or slipped a disk, there was no impact and no recovery.

Over time, courts moved away from this impact requirement. Still, to be an accident, some judges felt the injury should be sudden. Also, many judges felt the injury should be unexpected. In one case, the District of Columbia court held that a bus driver who strained his back when he turned around quickly to tell passengers that they could not smoke on the bus had had an "accident." The judges said it was an accident because something "unexpectedly" went wrong with the human frame (*Wash. Metro.*).

Before some courts will find "something gone wrong with the human frame" to be an accident, the worker must be doing something other than routine work. Over the years, more and more courts have dropped this "other than routine work" requirement. Recently Indiana did just that when a worker suffered a herniated disk while picking up planks. Under the old interpretation, this injury would not have been covered by worker's compensation because this worker routinely picked up planks. Under the new interpretation, the appeals court found this to be an "accident" covered by worker's compensation (*Savich*). Today most back problems and hernias are found to be "accidents."

What if problems develop slowly over many months or years and are caused by doing the routine tasks of the job? Under the old interpretation, this would not be an accident either because it was not "sudden" enough or because it was caused by "routine work." More and more state supreme courts are allowing recovery for these types of injuries. The Illinois Supreme Court recently held that a laundry-room employee who suffered from "carpal tunnel syndrome" (compressed nerves caused by repetitive trauma to the hands) was suffering from an "accident." The court held that there should not be any requirement of "sudden mishap." The key should be whether the injury was work-related or not (*Belwood Nursing*). In the early 1990s, the Montana and

Nebraska supreme courts agreed that carpal tunnel syndrome was an injury, while courts in Idaho and Virginia ruled that it was not an injury but was still covered by worker's compensation as an occupational disease (*Kraft; Schlup; Kinney; Wood*).

Three areas that cause a great many problems are heart attacks, occupational diseases, and mental illness.

Heart Attacks

Heart attacks are something employers bring up as an example of how unfair the law is. If you look at the cases, it seems that persons are covered by worker's compensation if they have the heart attack at work and are not covered if they have the heart attack at home, even though heart attacks are caused by years of improper diet and lack of exercise.

The New York High Court developed the "greater than ordinary wear and tear of life" test for heart attacks. If the worker is doing something similar to what he or she would be doing if the worker had stayed home and has a heart attack, the New York court will not allow worker's compensation to pay benefits. In 1979, the New Jersey legislature added this requirement to the New Jersey Worker's Compensation Act. In New Jersey, a heart attack is not covered unless it was caused by work stress greater than what most people experience during the "wear and tear of daily living." In 1988, the New Jersey Supreme Court ruled that a heart attack caused by moving heavy doors in the heat of summer met this test (*Hellwig*).

Some states, such as North and South Carolina, require the heart attack to be the result of "sudden, unusual exertion" at work (*Dillingham; Cline*). North Dakota requires the worker to have the heart attack as the result of "unusual" work stress, and the North Dakota Supreme Court found working for a long time in 120-degree heat was not "unusual" enough to qualify (*Grace*).

Occupational Diseases

Occupational diseases were a problem for a long time. How can a disease be an accident? Most states have now amended their statutes to include occupational diseases if they meet certain requirements. Also, over time, more and more courts have come to regard illness as an "accident."

Mental Illness

Because most state legislatures did not deal with mental illness when they wrote their statues, the courts have had to come up with some way of dealing with claims that work stress caused mental illness.

Some courts require the mental problems to be the result of "abnormal" working conditions. A Pennsylvania court held that a worker who got anxiety depression after being transferred to the night shift was just reacting to "normal working conditions" and could not receive worker's compensation (*Andracki*). The Arizona Legislature amended the statute to deal with this problem (something every state legislature could do). In Arizona, a worker must prove that the mental illness was caused by "unexpected, unusual, or extraordinary stress" related to the job (*Lapare*). The Oregon law says that mental disorder is not covered unless the conditions that produced it were other than those "generally inherent in every working situation" (*Zimmerly*). In California, mental illness caused by normal working conditions is covered by worker's compensation.

Arising Out Of

The second requirement is that the injury "arise out of" the employment. This means that the job must in some way "cause" the injury. At the beginning of the twentieth century, many judges felt that the injury did not arise out of the job unless it was the kind of injury that was "peculiar" to that particular job. This is best illustrated by two early cases. In 1935, a workman suffered from frozen feet because his job required him to be outside all night in the Boston cold. The Massachusetts Supreme Court said that everyone had to accept the risk of bad weather, and the court did not let him receive worker's-compensation benefits (*Robinson's Case*). In 1938, a Texas judge saw things differently:

> In the case before us the very work which the deceased was doing for his employer exposed him to a greater hazard from heat stroke than the general public was exposed to for the simple reason that the general public were not pushing wheel-barrow loads of sand in the hot sun on that day (*Webster*).

Over time most judges came to agree with the Texas judge. Most modern judges ask if a particular job increased the probability of a particular injury. The Iowa Supreme Court adopted this new test in 1990 in a case involving a worker who sufferred from heatstroke (*Hanson*).

In a recent New Jersey case, a worker was lighting a cigarette during the lunch break when her hair caught on fire. The New Jersey Supreme Court found this to be a risk she took every time she lighted a cigarette and being at work did not increase the probability of this injury, so she did not receive compensation (*Coleman*).

Sherman Black and Allen Aylsworth were co-owners of a small furniture factory in Georgia and both were covered by worker's compensation. When

Aylsworth murdered Black, Black's widow sued for her worker's-compensation death benefits. The insurance company argued that Aylsworth killed Black for personal reasons (he may have been in love with Black's wife) that did not arise out of the job. Aylsworth testified that he killed Black for business reasons (he was tired of Black's coming to work late). The judges believed him. Aylsworth got a life sentence and Mrs. Black got the compensation (*Black*).

In the Course Of

The third requirement is that the injury occur "in the course of" employment. This refers to the location of the worker and the activity the worker was engaged in when the injury occurred. Generally, the worker has to be working to receive worker's compensation.

One difficult type of case is when the employee is injured while engaging in horseplay. Some courts simply hold that when employees engage in horseplay, they are not working and are not covered by worker's compensation. In one case, the Colorado Appeals Court refused to allow the worker to receive compensation. She had injured herself showing a fellow employee a new dance step (*Kater*).

Other courts take a more generous view. The North Carolina Appeals Court said horseplay was simply a "reality of human conduct" and should be covered (*McGraw*).

Injuries that occur commuting to work are another problem. The general rule is that workers are not covered by worker's compensation when they are commuting to work, but there are several exceptions to that rule. A Pennsylvania Appeals Court listed four major exceptions to the rule. The employee is covered by worker's compensation commuting to and from work: (1) if the employment contract includes transportation to and from work, (2) if there is no fixed place of work, (3) if the worker is on a special mission for the employer, or (4) if the worker is doing something that is furthering the employer's business (*Kear*).

Generally, once the employee reaches the employer's parking lot, the commute is over and the employee is considered to be at work and "in the course of" employment.

Many cases involve workers who are engaged in recreational activities. Generally, employees who are hurt playing on the "company team" get compensation. The team provides advertising and benefits the employer.

The 1979 changes in the New Jersey statute prevent recovery in most recreation cases. In a recent case, the employee was injured playing paddle ball during the lunch break. The New Jersey Supreme Court said he did not meet the new test. The statute requires the recreational activity to be a "regular incident of employment" and "a benefit to the employer beyond just improving the health and morale of the employees" (*Sarzillo*).

In a Connecticut case, Caryn Luddie drove to New London to meet with a client. After transacting their business, she was driving him to Hartford so he could catch a train. Along the way they went to the Plainfield dog track to watch the races, and then they headed for her house so she could take a shower. They were involved in a car wreck at 3:00 A.M. The Connecticut Appeals Court said the trip to the dog track and to her house were not benefiting her employer and therefore were not "in the course of" her employment. She did not receive compensation (*Luddie*).

The Modern Approach

Many modern judges are no longer trapped by the phrase "injury by accident arising out of and in the course of" employment. These judges believe the law should be interpreted liberally to achieve the purposes for which it was passed. The two main purposes were to provide compensation for injured workers and to transfer the cost of compensation to the consumers of a particular product instead of to the society in general. Today "injury by accident" means any kind of injury, mental or physical, caused by impact, work stress, or disease. "Arise out of and in the course of employment" means that the job increased the probability of getting this particular injury or illness. If the worker was more likely to suffer this injury at work than at home, he or she is going to receive worker's compensation.

Death

Worker's-compensation laws provide benefits to the dependents of workers who die on the job. Death benefits are usually limited to the maximum amount the worker would have been entitled to if he or she had lived and been totally and permanently disabled.

Most statutes require someone to be both a relative and actually dependent on the worker for support before he or she can receive benefits. Many statutes cut off widow's benefits if the widow (or widower) remarries—this encourages a lot of people to "live in sin." The Illinois act tries to avoid this by giving the widow(er) a lump sum equal to two years' benefits if he or she remarries (*Stewart*). The New Jersey act says children between the ages of 18 and 40 cannot be dependent on the worker, even if in reality they actually were (*Piscopo*).

The fact that more and more people in our society choose to live together rather than get married causes problems. Under most statutes, live-in boyfriends or girlfriends cannot collect benefits, even if they were dependent on the worker for their support at the time of the death, because they are not "relatives."

In one case, Rita Stone had lived with the worker for six years before his death, but during that time she was married to someone else. She filed for death benefits as a "concubine." Specifically, she asked the Rhode Island Supreme Court if a "concubine" who had been financially dependent on the worker for six years before his death is a "member of the family" for the purposes of the worker's-compensation statute. The court held that she was not a member of the family because she was not related by "blood or marriage" (*Stone*).

A few states have amended their statutes to deal with this problem. The Oregon statute allows a person who has "cohabitated" with the worker for at least one year before the worker's death, and who had a child with the worker, to collect death benefits. In a recent Oregon case, the couple cohabited for three years and had a child. However, one month before his death, the worker had moved out. The Oregon Supreme Court ruled that his girlfriend could not get death benefits because they were not cohabiting at the time of his death (*Cottrell*).

Disqualification

Most statutes have a list of things that will disqualify a worker from receiving compensation. Many states disqualify workers who are injured because of their own "willful misconduct." About half the states disqualify workers who "willfully disobey safety rules." Many states will not allow a worker to collect if he or she was intoxicated at the time of the injury. However, some courts say the intoxication must be the sole cause of the injury. If the injury would have happened regardless of the intoxication, the worker can still receive compensation and the burden is on the employer to prove that the accident was caused solely by the intoxication (*Bama Tran.; Poole*).

Many states will not allow dependents to collect death benefits if the worker committed suicide. There are two main exceptions to that rule: (1) if the worker was driven crazy by the job before the suicide, or (2) if the worker received an injury on the job that caused insanity which, in turn, caused the suicide. In one case, a security guard shot a robbery suspect and was so upset that he then shot and killed himself. The security guard's widow received benefits (*Globe Sec.*).

Weekly Benefits

In most cases, the worker receives a weekly payment equal to a percentage of his or her average weekly wage (up to a maximum set by law). This is another reason why everyone should keep track of wages. This can include overtime pay if the worker regularly received overtime pay (*Bradley*). If the worker has two jobs, then the wages are added together to get the worker's average weekly wage (*Boles*). The value of any fringe benefits may also be included (*Ragland*).

These statutes have complex rules concerning how much the worker's benefits are to be reduced if the worker is receiving a pension (*Baltimore*). The Social Security rules require that the combined worker's-compensation payments and Social Security disability payments add up to not more than 80 percent of what the worker was actually earning before he or she became disabled (*Larimer County*).

Second-Injury Fund

Most states have a second-injury fund. This fund pays if a worker who has already been injured is injured again, and the second injury is worse because of the prior injury. The idea is to encourage employers to hire disabled workers. Of course, in the real world, many employers will not hire workers if they know that they have received worker's-compensation payments in the past. This fact causes most employees to lie about previous compensation if asked. Withholding this information is usually not going to keep the worker from getting compensation unless keeping the prior injury a secret "caused" the new injury (*McDaniel; Ledbetter*).

Medical Expenses

Besides paying money to the worker to compensate for lost wage-earning capacity, worker's compensation is also supposed to pay medical expenses. Different states have different rules on such issues as who chooses the doctor and what expenses are included. In some states, such as Virginia, the worker has to go to the employer's doctor and, if he or she does not go, the employer does not have to pay the doctor bills. Of course, there are going to be times when employees should still go to a doctor of their own choosing. In one recent Virginia case, the only reason the worker collected anything from worker's compensation was because the worker had a doctor at the hearing who contradicted the employer's doctor (*Richmond Memorial*).

In some states, such as Kansas, if the worker is unhappy with the employer's doctor, he or she can ask the worker's compensation agency to pick a doctor (*IBP*). In many states, the employee is free to choose any doctor. In Oregon, the employee is even allowed to get a second opinion (*Welch*).

The employer, or the insurance company, also has to pay for other medical-type expenses that result from the injury. Recently the Pennsylvania Appeals

Court ordered the employer to pay for hand controls on the worker's car and for remodeling his home to accommodate a wheelchair. The court said that these expenses constituted "orthopedic appliances" and were therefore covered by worker's compensation (*Rieger*). Medical expenses can include the cost of home care (*Bello*).

Temporary or Permanent; Partial or Total

Worker's-compensation insurance is really several different kinds of insurance in one. First, it is life insurance. If the worker dies from a work-related injury or illness, his or her dependents are taken care of. Second, it is medical insurance. It pays the hospital and doctor bills for a work-related injury or illness. Third, it provides short-term disability payments for temporarily disabled workers. Fourth and finally, it provides compensation for the loss the worker has suffered. The worker may have lost a hand or an eye or been disfigured. Also, the worker may have suffered a loss in wage-earning capacity. In most states, worker's compensation does not provide long-term income-replacement payments to disabled workers. Social Security does, and we will discuss that in Chapter 19. What worker's compensation does provide is an amount of money intended to compensate the disabled worker for the physical loss and the loss in wage-earning capacity caused by the accident. This loss is figured in terms of number of weeks times the worker's average weekly wage. In most states, a totally and permanently disabled worker receives between 300 and 500 times his or her average weekly wage.

Most statutes have four basic kinds of coverage for workers who survive the accident. The worker can receive payment from any one of the four sources, and from all four over time, but he or she can receive only one type of payment at a time. The four categories are Partial Temporary, Total Temporary, Partial Permanent, and Total Permanent. Throughout this system, the payments are based on a percentage (between 50 and 70 percent) of the worker's average weekly wage (up to a maximum).

Temporary Partial coverage pays the worker who is injured, but can still work, for a temporary physical loss. Someone who can work only a limited number of hours a week, or who cannot use a hand or leg temporarily, would qualify for this.

Total Temporary disability means the worker is injured and cannot work at all for a while. In some states, a totally disabled worker goes on Total Temporary disability first to see if he or she is going to recover.

Partial Permanent disability means the worker can still work at some jobs but either has suffered a permanent loss (such as a lost arm or leg) or has suffered a permanent reduction in wage-earning capacity (can no longer do high-paying work).

Total Permanent disability means the worker is so disabled that he or she cannot do any kind of work.

Many worker's-compensation statutes also contain a Scheduled Injury section. This part of the law spells out what a lost hand or eye is worth. A lost thumb might be worth 60 weeks of wages. A lost eye might be worth 300 weeks of wages. Remember, the payment is to compensate for the *physical loss*, and whether or not the worker is still able to work is irrelevant (*Bethlehem Mines*).

In some states, if the worker has a "scheduled loss," he or she gets whatever the schedule says and that is the end of it. In other states, the schedule is only a minimum. If the worker is entitled to more through one of the four types of coverage, then he or she gets that instead. In a few states, the worker can recover from both the schedule and the other four types of coverage.

Recently the Tennessee and Arkansas supreme courts said that a worker must stop getting Total Temporary payments when either of two events occur: when the worker is able to go back to work, or when the worker attains the maximum level of recovery. At that point, the worker gets either some kind of permanent-disability payment or a payment from the schedule (*Roberson; Guffey*).

The question of whether someone is stuck with the scheduled amount often depends on the full extent of the injury. If the impact was to the leg, but the injury extends beyond the leg, then the worker has more than a scheduled injury. Recently the Kansas Supreme Court made this point in a case that involved injury to the left elbow (*Bryant*). The award of permanent partial disability instead of the scheduled amount for an arm was correct because the pain went up into the shoulder. The court said that the key is the location of the disability, not the impact. Generally, it is to the worker's advantage to have more than a scheduled injury and to find pain in the shoulder or hip if the arm or leg is injured. A total and permanent disability can "arise out of" a scheduled injury (*Mendez #2; Alva*).

In some cases, the award is for lost earning capacity even if the physical symptoms have disappeared. In a recent Rhode Island case, the worker was a cook who suffered a back injury. The doctor testified that the worker could no longer be a cook because doing the things required of a cook would cause the injury to recur. Even though the worker no longer had any physical symptoms, he was entitled to Partial Permanent compensation because he had suffered a loss in wage-earning capacity (*Herley*).

The largest award is for Total and Permanent disability. There is a big difference between the legal definition of *disability* and the medical definition of *incapacity*. A worker can be partially incapacitated and still be totally and permanently disabled. To illustrate, in a recent Utah case, the worker had been a coal miner for 39 years before a heavy cable fell on him. The doctors testified that before the accident the coal miner had a 14 percent impairment to the whole body as a result of previous injuries; after the accident he had a 31 percent impairment to the whole body. As the Utah Supreme Court pointed out, the degree of impairment is a medical finding; the degree of disability is a legal finding. The court said one must look at the individual's work history, educational level, age, and past injuries as well as the injury resulting from this particular accident. In this case, the miner managed to continue to work for several years after the injury, but he had to go to the hospital often for traction and he never recovered. The court found him to be totally and permanently disabled (*Norton*).

If an injured worker, because of age, education, and work history, is not able to get a job, then he or she is totally and permanently disabled (*Swan*). This is true even though a younger, better educated worker might be able to get a job and would not be disabled. In a recent Arkansas case, a man who worked with his hands suffered torn biceps tendons. He was 50 years old and had a high school education. The court awarded total and permanent disability (*Atchley*).

One of the things that is hard to understand is that a worker can receive compensation for Total and Permanent disability more than once. A worker can be totally and permanently disabled, get another job, have another injury, and be totally and permanently disabled again. Or, a worker can receive partial benefits for one injury and then total benefits for another injury. In a South Carolina case, the worker received 248 weeks of compensation for his first back injury. He received 500 weeks (the maximum for Total and Permanent) for his second back injury. In a sense, he was now one and a half times totally disabled (*Wyndham*).

Claims Procedure

Worker's compensation is controlled by a state agency. While different states have different names for this agency, many call it the Industrial Accident Commission. In many states, this commission has three members: one represents employers, one represents workers, and one is neutral.

Notice

The statutes require two kinds of notice when a worker feels he or she has had a work-related injury: notice to the employer and notice to the commission. Usually the worker must notify the employer quickly. In some situations, the worker knows about the injury but does not realize the injury is work-related. Generally, the worker's obligation to give everyone notice does not begin until he or she knows, or a reasonable person would have known, that the injury was work-related.

Recently the Tennessee Supreme Court had to tell Linda Sue Puckett that she could not receive worker's compensation (*Puckett*). The doctor told her in January 1984 that her arthritis-like symptoms were caused by her job. At that point, under Tennessee law, she had 30 days to notify her employer of a work-related injury. She did not and lost any chance of getting worker's compensation.

The worker also has to notify the commission before the deadline. In a recent Virginia case, Patricia Garcia was injured on February 25, 1982, and notified the commission on March 19, 1984. Because Virginia workers have two years to notify the commission, Patricia Garcia could not receive worker's compensation (*Mantech*).

There is something to consider before filing a claim for worker's compensation. We will discuss in Chapter 18 when a worker can sue the employer for a physical injury. In many states, if the worker files for worker's compensation, he or she cannot sue the employer later for the same injury. Workers who think that they might want to sue their employer for an injury should consult an attorney right away.

Settlements and Releases

The goal is for the injured worker and the worker's-compensation insurance company or state insurance fund to come to an agreed settlement. This happens in 90 percent of the cases. This is a dangerous time for the worker. Workers should not settle with an insurance company until they have discussed their case with an attorney. In some states, the Industrial Accident Commission has to approve the settlement. In other states, the worker can go to the commission and have the settlement overturned if it turns out to have been unfair.

In one case, the employer told the worker that if he would sign a little piece of paper, he would be put back on the payroll. The worker signed and was fired. The little piece of paper was a settlement agreement ending his worker's-compensation claim. The Pennsylvania court overturned this agreement because the employer had induced the worker to sign the agreement by misrepresentation and because the worker was still disabled. The worker had to prove both things to get out of the agreement (*Exxon #2*).

Reduction, Increase, Discontinuation, Reinstatement

In most lawsuits, there is a final end to the case. This is not true of worker's compensation in many states. If something changes, either the employer or the worker can go back to the commission to ask for more or less compensation or to ask to stop or restart compensation payments. What either side has to prove to accomplish this differs from state to state.

In Pennsylvania, if the employer wants to reduce the compensation, it has to prove not only that the worker is physically capable of doing work but also that there actually are jobs available for this particular worker (*Kachinski*).

In most states, the employer cannot just stop paying compensation when it hears that the worker has gotten a job. The employer has to go to the commission and get permission. In a recent case, the Rhode Island Supreme Court made the employer pay the worker 20 percent extra because the employer had stopped making compensation payments without permission (*Lavey*).

Generally, to get increased compensation, a worker has to prove that his or her physical condition has gotten worse and that the worsened condition resulted from the original injury.

There is a big difference between "recurrence" of an old injury and "aggravation" of an old injury. In a recent Rhode Island case, the court found that the worker had a recurrence of an old injury. He got compensation again, but at the old compensation rate. If it had been an aggravation (meaning his present job increased his old injury), then he would have been entitled to a higher rate based on his new, higher wages (*Mignowe*).

On Appeal

Different states have different appeal procedures. Once the hearing officer has made a decision, either side can appeal to the full commission. After that, in most states, the appeal goes to a district judge, then an appeals court, and finally to the state supreme court.

In most states, if either side wants to appeal the decision of the commission, they have to act quickly (usually within 30 days). Most courts use the "substantial evidence test." If the decision of the commission is supported by substantial evidence, then the court will uphold it. Of course, the courts are free to tell the commission how to interpret the statute. They are also free to decide what kind of procedure is acceptable. In other words, if you (employer or worker) feel there was not substantial evidence to support the decision against you, or your constitutional or procedural rights were violated, or the statute was not interpreted correctly, you should appeal your case to a court. In a few states, neither side is stuck with the facts as found by the commission, and each can get a whole new trial in front of a judge and jury. In other states, that is not possible. Once the commission decides the facts, those are the facts and no judge can change them.

Generally, the worker is going to need the help of an attorney. In Wyoming, the county attorney will help. In Minnesota, the attorneys at the state department of labor will help workers with worker's-compensation claims.

Federal Laws

Over the course of the last century, Congress has passed a number of special statutes for special groups of workers. Three groups of workers benefit from these laws: sailors, railroad workers, and longshoremen.

Sailors

There are three things for which a sailor can sue the employer when the sailor is injured. The first is *maintenance and cure*. In medieval law, a master had to care for an injured apprentice regardless of how the apprentice became injured. American judges did away with that duty for everyone except shipowners. The judges felt that many sailors are far from home when injured, therefore the employer has a special responsibility to care for an injured sailor.

Second, the employer has a duty to provide a *seaworthy vessel*. Because of the obvious risks that result from being on an unseaworthy vessel, judges require shipowners to provide a safe ship. This is an absolute duty. If the ship is unseaworthy and an injury results, the employer pays regardless of "fault" in the usual sense.

Finally, Congress passed a statute many years ago called the Jones Act (46 U.S.C. sec. 688) that allows an injured sailor to sue the employer for *negligence* and takes the unholy trinity of defenses away from the employer.

Anyone who works on a boat in a navigable waterway is a sailor, even if the boat is on a river or a lake. A sailor not only gets money to pay for his doctor bills and basic living expenses while injured (maintenance and cure), but he or she is also allowed to sue if the boat was unsafe in any way, or if the employer was negligent. In a sense, sailors have the best of all worlds. In a recent Illinois case, the jury awarded $1,250,000 to the injured sailor, far more than any worker would receive from worker's compensation (*Ruffiner*).

Longshoremen and Harbor Workers

Longshoremen and harbor workers are covered by a special federal worker's-compensation statute, called the Longshoremen and Harbor Workers Compensation Act (LHWCA), which is administered by the U.S. Department of Labor. It pays higher benefits than most state worker's-compensation statutes. Many workers who would be entitled to these payments do not get them because they do not realize that they are harbor workers under the law. The federal government has jurisdiction over any navigable waterway. That means people who work along most rivers and lakes in the United States are harbor workers and are covered by the act. In 1980, the U.S. Supreme Court held that a worker is entitled to receive the best of both worlds: if the state act is better in any way, the injured worker can recover under the state as well as the federal act (*Sun Ship*).

Railroad Workers

There are two federal laws for railroad workers. The first is the Federal Safety Appliance Act of 1893 (45 U.S.C. sec. 1). This law says that if a railroad employee is injured by a piece of railroad equipment, the railroad company pays the costs. The worker does not have to prove that the employer was negligent. In a recent case, the automatic coupling system failed to work and the switchman got hurt when he tried to couple the cars manually. The railroad had to pay. The court did not want to know if anyone, either the worker or the company, was at fault (*Leveck*). In another case, the worker hurt his back trying to release the hand brake. The jury awarded $470,000 in damages (*Geiser*).

The other federal law is the Federal Employers Liability Act (FELA) (45 U.S.C. sec. 51). This act allows an injured railroad worker to sue if the employer is negligent, just as all workers could do under the common law a century ago. In 1939, Congress amended the law and removed the unholy trinity of defenses from the railroads. Cases that are tried under this act give us an idea of what the world would be like if the judges had not invented the unholy trinity of defenses in the first place and the states had not responded with worker's-compensation insurance. First of all, the injured worker has to prove the employer was negligent. That means the employer breached one of the duties employers owe to employees.

For example, in a recent Georgia case, the injured railroad worker was hit by a piece of metal protruding from the side of a boxcar. The worker sued the railroad company for breach of the duty to provide a safe place to work and breach of the duty to warn workers about hazardous conditions. The jury awarded $561,282 in damages (*Seaboard*). In a recent Texas case, the worker hurt his shoulder when he was forced to jump off a runaway train. The jury awarded $400,000 for future physical impairment; $900,000 for lost future earning capacity; $343,000 for pain, suffering, and medical expenses; and $150,000 for punitive damages (finding the railroad company to be grossly negligent) (*Southern Pacific*).

Of course, the injured railroad workers do not always recover. They have to prove that the company was negligant or that the equipment caused the injury. In one case, the worker suffered a heart attack at the railroad yard in a situation where he would probably have collected under worker's compensation. The jury found that the railroad company was not negligent, and the worker got nothing (*Greenfield*).

Third-Party Defendants

In many cases, the worker is hurt on the job and worker's compensation pays. At the same time, there is a third party that the worker could sue and recover from. In these situations, it is in everyone's interest for the worker to sue that third party. In most states, the employer or his insurance company has a *right of subrogation*. That means that, if the worker recovers from the third party, he or she has to pay back the worker's-compensation benefits. This is an ideal system for the injured worker. He or she has a sure, if small, recovery from worker's compensation helping to pay basic living expenses. The worker also has a chance at a really big recovery in a court of law. The employer has an incentive to cooperate because, if the worker wins, the employer is off the hook for worker's compensation.

Manufacturers

Whom are we suing when we sue third-party defendants? Anybody other than the employer who had something to do with the injury. Often we are suing the maker of some piece of equipment that was defective and caused the injury. In one case, the worker lost a thumb and three fingers on his left hand while operating a radial saw that the jury decided was defective. The jury awarded $792,000 (*Bussell*). In another case, the worker lost an arm and received $35,000 from worker's compensation. He sued the machine's Italian manufacturer and received $800,000 from an American jury (*Mason*). In a 1991 case, the jury decided that an arm lost in a defective combine was worth $3.1 million (*Wheeler #2*).

In many of these cases, the manufacturer will sue the employer for contributing to the worker's injury. In 1991, the Illinois Supreme Court ruled that in such a case the employer's liability is limited to the amount it would have had to pay under the worker's compensation statute (*Kotecki*).

Medical Malpractice

Some injured workers die in the hospital because of medical malpractice. If the widow(er) sues and proves malpractice, then the worker's-compensation company is off the hook. If there is no malpractice, and the worker dies in the hospital, then worker's compensation pays just as if the worker had died instantly at the job (*Powell*).

The Landlord

In some cases, the employee sues the owner of the property that the employer leases. Even if the property owner is a parent company or subsidiary of the employer, it is a different entity and can be sued (*Kiehl*).

On the Streets

The streets of America are very dangerous. Many workers are hurt or killed in car accidents in circumstances in which worker's compensation must pay off. If the worker can sue and recover from the driver of the other car, everyone stands to gain.

Co-Workers

Generally, if a co-worker causes the worker's injury, the co-worker cannot be sued. He or she is protected by the worker's-compensation statute just as the employer is. However, there are times when the co-worker can be sued. The Arkansas Supreme Court recently said an injured worker can sue the co-worker if the co-worker's actions were willful or intentional (*Fore*). The Connecticut statute allows a worker to sue a co-worker if the case involves the use of a motor vehicle (*Kiriaka*).

A recent Indiana case illustrates how a co-worker might be sued even in a case involving simple negligence. Karen Seiler's supervisor was showing her how to use a pistol when it went off and injured her. The Indiana Appeals Court said that whether or not Karen could sue this co-worker, who happened to be the president of the company, depended on why he was showing her the gun. If he was showing her the gun so she could use it to defend herself at work (she was a bartender), then the co-worker could not be sued. On the other hand, if he was showing her the gun for personal reasons (to show it off), then she could sue him for her injuries (*Seiler*).

If the co-worker is the company doctor and has committed malpractice, some states will allow the worker to sue, even though the doctor is a co-worker (*Stover*).

Dual Capacity

On occasion, the employer acts in a dual capacity, as both employer and product provider. What if the worker is hurt, not because of on-the-job negligence but because the product is defective? In most states, the injured worker can sue the employer, not as employer but as product maker. In one case, a Uniroyal truck driver was injured when one of the Uniroyal tires on his truck blew out. The Ohio Appeals Court said he could sue Uniroyal as the maker of a defective product, just as any other consumer could (*Mercer*).

Suing the Insurance Company

Many times the worker feels more injured by the insurance company than by the original accident. In some states, the worker is prevented, either by statute or by court decision, from suing the worker's-compensation insurance company. That is not true of all states, and more courts are allowing these lawsuits.

Bad Faith

There is a general legal principle that says: Implied in every insurance policy is the promise from the insurance company that it will act with good faith toward both the person paying the premiums and the beneficiaries of the policy. While some state courts hold that this does not apply to worker's-compensation insurance, other states will allow such lawsuits. In 1987, the South Dakota Supreme Court allowed a worker to sue an insurance company for intentional, fraudulent, and bad-faith termination of worker's-compensation benefits (*Cert. Question*). In two 1991 Texas cases, the appeals court upheld awards of $1.5 million in punitive damages against insurance companies which the juries felt had breached the duty of good faith and fair dealing (*Borden; Puckett #2*).

A number of states have deceptive trade-practice acts and special insurance statutes that allow insurance companies to be sued for up to triple the actual amount owed if they acted deceptively or in bad faith. In a Minnesota case, the insurance company kept trying to terminate benefits. Finally, the worker's-compensation agency awarded a penalty to the worker under a special provision of the worker's-compensation statute. In addition, the Minnesota Supreme Court allowed the worker to sue the insurance company for triple damages (*Kaluza*).

Intentional Injury

In other cases, the worker has been allowed to sue the insurance company for things such as fraud or intentional infliction of emotional distress. In one case, Ms. Young was assaulted at work and suffered emotional trauma. The insurance company refused to pay the psychiatrist's bills. When she called the insurance company, the insurance agent told her that she was crazy and if it were up to him she "would not get a penny." Ms. Young then tried to kill herself. The Maryland Supreme Court said that she could sue the insurance company for intentional infliction of emotional distress (*Hartford*). In 1990, the Alabama Supreme Court upheld an award of $750,000 by a jury that decided the insurance company had intentionally inflicted emotional distress. The company had delayed paying the worker's doctor bills in an effort to force the worker to settle his claim for a very small amount (*Con. Cas.*).

Negligent Safety Inspections

Many worker's-compensation insurance companies perform safety inspections. If they do this negligently, should the injured workers be allowed to sue? Recently, the Massachusetts Supreme Court held that the worker could not sue the insurance company for negligently performing safety inspections. The court expressed the fear that if they were held liable, the insurance companies would stop conducting safety inspections (*Swift*).

The Supreme Court of Vermont recently held that Vermont workers could sue for negligent safety inspections by insurance companies. The Vermont Supreme Court felt "no inspection is better than a negligent inspection" (*Derosia*).

Should Employees Opt out of the System?

In New Jersey, South Carolina, Texas, Arizona, Kentucky, Rhode Island, Massachusetts, and Illinois (and possibly other states), workers can opt out of the system and take their chances with the common law. Should workers do this? That is a difficult question to answer. If workers could prove negligence, they would receive more than they would under worker's compensation. Take a recent case. Lorenzo Sanchez lost his right hand in a potato harvester and sued his employer. As a farm worker, he was not covered by worker's compensation. The Idaho Supreme Court upheld an award of $1,350,000 (*Sanchez*).

What about the unholy trinity of defenses? In many states, the concept of contributory negligence has been replaced by comparative negligence. Under contributory negligence, if a person is the least bit at fault, he or she receives nothing. Under comparative negligence, a person who is partly at fault can still recover some money from the other person. This would allow workers to receive some money even if they are partly responsible for the accident.

Several state supreme courts have done away with the idea that workers "assume the risk of injury" just by taking the job. The Texas Supreme Court did away with this concept in 1975, finding that once a system of comparative negligence is adopted, the concept of assumption of the risk no longer makes sense (*Farley*). The Nevada Supreme Court did the same thing in 1987 (*Central Telephone*).

What about the fellow-servant doctrine, which says that if a co-worker is involved, the injured worker cannot sue the employer? This doctrine grew out of and was tied directly to the assumption-of-the-risk doctrine. Logically, if one goes, so does the other. The odds are that a modern court would eliminate both given half a chance.

Several states have statutes or constitutional provisions that eliminate or limit these defenses. The Arizona Constitution eliminates the fellow-servant doctrine and says the question of assumption of the risk is strictly up to the jury (Ariz. Const. Art. 18, sec. 4,5).

Of course, injured workers have to prove the employer was negligent. Also, if workers opt out, they should make sure that their medical insurance will pay for a work-related injury. Many exclude this.

Workers who wish to opt out of worker's compensation must follow the state's rules. Texas and Massachusetts allow the worker to opt out only when first hired. Rhode Island and Illinois give the worker a chance to opt out once a year.

18

Intentional Injury and Suing the Boss

The law distinguishes between *intentional injury* and *negligence*. Someone is negligent if he or she has not been careful enough and an accident has resulted. If employees have been physically or emotionally injured at work because of negligence, worker's compensation is supposed to take care of them. They cannot sue.

If an employer or supervisor negligently causes injury other than physical or emotional injury, the employee can sue. If an employer or supervisor intentionally causes injury of any kind, even physical or emotional, the employee can sue (in most states).

There are four main reasons that employees sue employers: the employer lied to the employee, the employer lied about the employee, the employer intentionally caused emotional injury, the employer intentionally caused physical injury.

Lying to the Employee

If an employer tells an employee something that turns out to be untrue, the employee can sue. If the employer knew that what was said was untrue (or was reckless regarding the truth), it is called *fraud*. If the employer did not know it was a lie but was negligent in not trying to find out before speaking, it is called *misrepresentation*.

In a 1989 Illinois case, the employer told a salesman that he would never give away any of the salesman's accounts without his consent. At the time, the employer had already given some of the accounts away. This was a case of fraud (*Callahan*). In a 1990 Alabama case, the employer told the employee there would be stock options and bonuses that he never intended to provide. The Alabama Supreme Court affirmed an award of $800,000 in damages (*Ramsay Health*).

What if the lie was a result of negligence? Maria D'Ulisse-Cupo was a teacher at Notre Dame High School. Her supervisor told her several times in the spring that she would be rehired in the fall. She could have looked for another job if she had known she would not be rehired. She did not look for another job and she was not rehired after all. The Connecticut Supreme Court said she could sue for misrepresentation (*D'Ulisse-Cupo*).

At the beginning of the twentieth century, it was a common practice for employers to place ads in newspapers to recruit employees to work in another state. When the employees arrived, they often found that they had been hired to be strikebreakers or that the working conditions were nothing like the advertisements. This was particularly true of employers in the western states. Several states passed statutes to deal with this problem. These statutes are still on the books in at least nine states: Alaska (23.10.015 to 030), California (Labor Code 970 to 977), Colorado (8-2-104 to 107), Minnesota (181.64 and 181.65), Montana (39-2-303), Nevada (613.010 to 030), Oklahoma (tit. 40 sec. 167, 170), Tennessee (50-1-102), and Wisconsin (103.43). These statutes are virtually identical. They generally say that if an employer induces an employee to move (either into the state or from one place to another within the state) by "means of false representations" concerning the "character of the work," the "compensation," the "conditions of employment," or the existence of a "strike or lockout," then the employee can sue the employer for "all damages" and attorney fees. The California statute allows the court to award double the amount of actual damages. Most of these statutes also make this activity a crime for which the employer and the supervisor can be fined and put in jail for at least a year. Employers in these states should be particularly careful about what they say to prospective employees, particularly if the employees are going to have to move to accept the job.

Sometimes the worker can sue the employer, not because the employer lied, but because the employer did not tell the employee something. In a New Jersey case, a group of employees sued Du Point, alleging that the company doctors had known that these employees were suffering from diseases caused by asbestos exposure and had deliberately kept it from them (*Millison*). In a Michigan case, a research chemist alleged that Dow had hidden the potential dangers involved in working with "agent orange" (*Beauchamp*). Both cases involved *fraudulent concealment*. In some situations, the law says people have a duty to tell what they know to prevent harm. The allegations in these two cases are classic examples of this. An employer or supervisor has a duty to tell employees that they are being exposed to dangerous chemicals or are already suffering from such exposure.

The lower courts in both these cases granted summary judgment for the companies. The supreme courts of New Jersey and Michigan sent the cases back for trial. They said that, if the employees could prove their allegations, they should be allowed to recover for their damages. Both companies argued that worker's compensation should take care of this and that the employees should not be allowed to sue. Both supreme courts held that worker's compensation was intended to deal with negligence; if a worker could prove intentional conduct, he or she could sue in court to recover damages. Intentionally concealing a dangerous aspect of the working environment is something for which employees can sue their employers.

Lying about the Employee

If the employer lies about the employee, the law calls it *defamation*. If the lie is oral, it is called *slander*. If it is written, it is called *libel*. To prove defamation, the employee has to prove that the employer said something untrue about the employee; that the employer "published" it, meaning that the employer told it to someone other than the employee; and that the employee's reputation was damaged as a result. It is usually easy to prove that the employer said something that damaged the employee's reputation and that what was said was untrue. These cases usually come down to whether the employer abused the privilege and whether or not the defamatory statement was published.

The courts have always allowed some people to be privileged in our legal system. The idea is that a general good can be accomplished only if we allow people in certain situations to be free from the worry of being sued. There are two types of privileges: absolute and conditional.

An *absolute privilege* means someone cannot be sued. For example, judges have an absolute privilege relating to the decisions they make as judges. The law wants judges to do what they think is right without worrying about lawsuits.

A *conditional privilege* means the person has a privilege, but he or she can lose the privilege if it is abused. The law says that employers and supervisors have a privilege to speak about employees to people who need to know about the employees, such as other employers and supervisors. If the employer or supervisor happens to lie about the employee, that is usually acceptable. In other words, employers and supervisors have a privilege to defame their employees. However, this is a conditional privilege.

Employers and supervisors can lose the privilege if they know that what they are saying about the employee is false at the time they say it; if they are reckless about whether or not it is true; or if they talk to someone whom they are not privileged to talk to, such as their customers (*Shannon*).

In one case, a prospective employer called a school superintendent about a teacher. The superintendent said that the teacher had been a bad teacher. In fact, the teacher had an excellent record. The superintendent had never observed the teacher in class and had never received any negative comments about the teacher from parents or fellow teachers. The jury found that this superintendent lost his privilege because he either knew that what he was saying was untrue or showed a reckless disregard for the truth (*True*).

In another case, an Exxon auditor tracked the employee down at a crowded restaurant to accuse him of stealing money from the company. The court held that, while the auditor had a privilege to talk to some people about this problem, he was not privileged to tell it to the people who happened to be in that restaurant. At one moment the auditor had both published the defamation (told it to people other than the worker) and violated his privilege (by telling it to people not covered by the privilege) (*Exxon*).

A 1986 decision by the Minnesota Supreme Court has made it even easier for employees to win defamation suits against supervisors and employers (*Equitable*). Carole Lewis and three other former employees sued the Equitable Life Assurance Society for breach of the employee handbook and defamation. These employees were dental-claim approvers in the St. Paul office. In the fall of 1980, the company's Pittsburgh office asked for help to deal with a heavy work load. Lewis and her colleagues were sent to Pittsburgh for two weeks to help out. They had never traveled on company business before. The St. Paul office manager was responsible for explaining company travel-expense policy to them before the trip. Because he was out of the office at the time, this task fell to his secretary, who had never given these kinds of instructions before. The secretary did not tell them that detailed expense reports would have to be filled out when they returned. The employees were each given a $1,400 travel advance, which they spent in full. When the four employees returned to St. Paul, they each received a personal letter from management commending them on their job performance in Pittsburgh. They were also told to fill out detailed daily expense reports. They did this, but management was not happy. Apparently upper management thought each employee should give back about $200 from the travel advance. Over the course of several months, the employees were asked to revise the expense reports several times, and each time they were given a different set of guidelines to follow. The employees were ultimately fired for what their supervisor called "gross insubordination." Company officials admitted at the trial that these were good employees and that they should have been given written guidelines before the trip.

When these employees tried to find new jobs, their prospective employers asked why they left Equitable. They said they had been terminated for "gross insubordination." When these prospective employers called Equitable to find out more, they were told only the dates these employees had been employed and their final job title. Needless to say, these employees did not find work. When they sued for defamation, the employer argued that the defamation had not been published. The jury found that the employer had published the defamatory statements by telling the employees who in turn were forced to tell other people. This is called "compelled self-publication." The Minnesota Supreme Court ruled that an employee could sue even if the employer made the defamatory statement to no one other than the employee if the employee is later put in a position in which he or she must repeat the defamatory statement.

Now to the criminal charges. A century ago, defamation was a crime in every state. That is no longer true, but criminal-defamation statutes are still on the books in half the states. That means that a supervisor risks criminal prosecution as well as a lawsuit by the former employee (see Table 18.1).

On top of that, almost half the states have statutes that make it a crime to *blacklist* a former employee (see Table 18.1). Many of these laws were passed early in the twentieth century in response to union blacklists. These were lists of suspected union members. However, most of these statutes apply to more than just written lists of suspected union members. The Arizona statute defines blacklist to mean "any understanding or agreement whereby the names of any person or persons . . . or other means of identification shall be spoken, written, printed or implied for the purpose of being communicated or transmitted between two or more employers of labor, their bosses, foremen, superintendents, managers, officers or other agents, whereby the laborer is prevented or prohibited from engaging in a useful occupation" (Ariz. 23-1361). The North Carolina statute says blacklisting is preventing or attempting to prevent a "discharged employee" by "word or writing of any kind" from "obtaining employment" (N.C. 14-355).

Given the problems inherent in the concepts of "conditional privilege" and "compelled self-publication," the expensive nature of defamation lawsuits, and the vague wording of criminal-defamation and blacklisting statutes, the best advice any attorney can give to any employer or supervisor is to keep quiet.

The advice to any employee who has been discharged is: try to find out why you were fired. If the supervisor will not tell you in writing, then get the information orally. Write down what is said as soon as possible, when it was said, and who said it. You may want to use that information later in a lawsuit or in an unemployment-compensation hearing.

Table 18.1 Criminal Defamation and Blacklisting Statutes

Alabama	Defamation is a crime.	13A-11-160 to 164
	Blacklisting is a crime.	13A-11-123
Arizona	Blacklisting is prohibited.	Const. Art. 18, sec.
	Blacklisting is defined.	9
		23-1361, 1362
Arkansas	Defamation is a crime.	5-15-101
	Blacklisting is a crime.	11-3-202
California	Defamation is a crime.	Penal Code 258 to
	Blacklisting is a crime.	260
		Labor Code 1050
Colorado	Defamation is a crime.	18-13-105
	Blacklisting is a crime.	8-2-110 to 115
Connecticut	Blacklisting is a crime.	31-51
Florida	Defamation is a crime.	836.01 to .11
Georgia	Defamation is a crime.	16-11-40
Idaho	Defamation is a crime.	18-4801 to 4809
Indiana	Blacklisting is a crime.	22-5-3-1,2
Iowa	Blacklisting is a crime.	730.1 to .3
Kansas	Defamation is a crime.	21-4004
	Blacklisting is a crime.	44-117 to 119
Louisiana	Defamation is a crime.	14:47 to 50.1
Maine	Blacklisting is a crime.	17-401
Michigan	Defamation is a crime.	750.370, .371
Minnesota	Defamation is a crime.	609.765
	Blacklisting is a crime.	179.60
Mississippi	Blacklisting of telegraph operators is forbidden.	77-9-725 to 729
Montana	Defamation is a crime.	45-8-212
	Blacklisting—punative damages allowed.	39-2-801 to 804
Nevada	Defamation is a crime.	200.510 to 560
	Blacklisting is a crime.	613.210
New Hampshire	Defamation is a crime.	644:11

Table 18.1—*Continued*

New Mexico	Defamation is a crime.	30-11-1
	Blacklisting is a crime.	30-13-3
North Carolina	Defamation is a crime.	14-47
	Blacklisting is a crime.	14-355, 356
North Dakota	Defamation is a crime.	12.1-15-01
Oklahoma	Defamation is a crime.	Title 21, sec. 771 to 781
	Blacklisting is a crime.	Title 40, sec. 172, 173
Oregon	Blacklisting is prohibited.	659.230
South Carolina	Defamation is a crime.	16-7-150
Tennessee	Defamation is a crime.	39-2-401 to 404
Texas	Blacklisting is a crime.	Art. 5196, 5197
Utah	Defamation is a crime.	76-9-404
	Blacklisting is prohibited.	34-24-1,2
		Const. Art. 12, sec. 19
		Const. Art. 16, sec. 4
Virginia	Blacklisting is a crime.	40.1-27
Washington	Defamation is a crime.	9.58
	Blacklisting is a crime.	49.44.010
Wisconsin	Defamation is a crime.	942.01
	Blacklisting is a crime.	134.02

Note: The law is always changing. Consult an attorney about your situation.

Seven states have service-letter statutes that require employers to provide former employees with some kind of statement concerning their employment. Each statute is different (see Table 18.2). For example, in Minnesota employees have only five working days to request such a letter in writing. In 1990, the Eighth Circuit Court ruled that a request from an attorney is not enough; employees must make the request themselves (*Zeman*).

Intentional Infliction of Emotional Distress

Many employees would like to sue their employers and supervisors for driving them crazy. However, the courts will not allow this unless the employer or

Table 18.2   State Service-Letter Statutes

Indiana 22-6-3-1	Employee must make written request. Employer must provide reasons for departure. Does not apply to employers who do not require written applications or written recommendations.
Kansas 44-808	Employee must make written request. Employer must provide statement of length of work, wages, job classification.
Maine 26-630	Employee must make written request. Employer must provide reasons for discharge.
Minnesota 181.933	Employee must make written request in 5 working days after discharge. Employer must provide reasons for discharge.
Missouri 290.140	Employer must respond in 45 days. Employer must provide reasons for discharge, nature of job, and length of employment.
Montana 39-2-801	Upon request from employee, employer must provide reasons for discharge.
Nevada 613-210	Employee may demand and employer must provide reasons for departure.

supervisor behaved in an outrageous way. Just being harassed at work or fired from a job is usually not enough.

The supreme courts of California, Massachusetts, and Wisconsin have ruled that employees in those states may not sue their employers for intentional infliction of emotional distress and therefore, are stuck with worker's compensation (*Fair Oaks*; *Foley #2*; *Jenson*). Most state supreme courts have not agreed with these courts.

Leta Fay Ford began work for Revlon as a secretary in 1973. After several years, she had worked her way up to buyer. Revlon then hired Karl Braun to be her supervisor. On April 3, 1980, Braun invited her to dinner, at the end of which he announced that he "planned to spend the night with her." When she refused, he told her that she would "regret" it. On May 3, 1980, at the company picnic Braun walked up to her in front of witnesses and said, "I want to fuck you, Leta." Later that day, as she was leaving the ladies' room accompanied by a friend, he grabbed her and put her in a choke hold. He ran his hands over her body and told her he wanted to fuck her.

She complained to higher executives at Revlon, who discussed her case for six months without doing anything. Meanwhile the harassment continued and she developed high blood pressure, a nervous tic in one eye, and other symptoms of emotional stress. On May 28, 1981, Revlon gave Braun an official letter of censure. In October 1981, Ford tried to kill herself. On October 5, 1981, Revlon fired Braun. In April 1982, Ford sued Revlon and

Braun for assault, battery, and intentional infliction of emotional distress. The jury found Braun guilty of assault and battery but not intentional infliction of emotional distress. The jury found Revlon guilty of intentional infliction of emotional distress and awarded $10,000 in compensatory damages and $100,000 in punitive damages against the company. Revlon felt that it should not be liable for intentional infliction of emotional distress if Braun was not liable for intentional infliction of emotional distress. The Arizona Supreme Court disagreed. In this case, Revlon, acting through its higher executives, was guilty of inflicting emotional distress because it failed to take action to stop the sexual harassment. The Arizona Supreme Court had no trouble finding the behavior of Revlon's executives to be "outrageous," the first requirement of the tort of intentional infliction of emotional distress. Second, the court said Revlon either intended to cause the emotional distress or "recklessly disregarded the near certainty that such distress" would result. Finally, severe emotional distress did result. What about worker's compensation as an exclusive remedy in this case? The Arizona Supreme Court held that because the acts of Braun and the Revlon executives were intentional, not "accidents," worker's compensation did not prevent this lawsuit (*Ford*).

In 1988, the South Dakota Supreme Court agreed with Arizona. The case involved a supervisor who knew the employee was under a doctor's care for depression. When the supervisor saw this employee take a drink after work, he told the employee he had to join a company alcoholic-treatment plan or lose his job. When the employee asked for a few days to think about it, he was fired. The jury awarded $30,000 in compensatory damages and $100,000 in punitive damages (*Wanger*). In 1989, the Ohio Supreme Court ruled that employees who suffer from sexual harassment may sue for intentional infliction of emotional distress (*Helmick*). In 1990, the Vermont Supreme Court allowed an employee who was subjected to three hours of the "third degree" when he was suspected of theft and then fired to receive $19,000 in compensatory damages and $25,000 in punitive damages to compensate for the emotional damage he suffered at the hands of his employer (*Crump*). In 1991, supreme courts in Georgia, Maryland, and Washington agreed that employees may sue their employers for intentional infliction of emotional distress (*Federated Stores*; *Wilmot*; *Yarbrag*). All of these courts came to the conclusion that worker's compensation did not preempt these lawsuits.

Intentional Infliction of Physical Injury

Employees can sue their employers for intentionally inflicting physical injury on them. These cases are difficult because it is often hard to draw the line between "accidents" on the one hand and "intentional" conduct on the other.

As the Arizona Supreme Court said in the *Ford* case, it is intentional conduct if the employer consciously intends to cause harm, or "recklessly disregards the near certainty that such" harm is going to result. It is easy to call the conduct intentional when the target is known to everyone. For example, if an employer walks up to a particular worker with a stick of lighted dynamite and throws it at him, no court would have trouble finding that to be intentional conduct. The employer intended to harm a particular worker, and harm was certainly going to result.

What if the employer leaves a stick of lighted dynamite where workers frequently come and it kills one of them? Is that intentional behavior? It was no accident that the dynamite went off. It was highly certain that someone would be hurt, but the employer was not trying to kill a particular worker. During the past few years several state supreme courts have become so disgusted with the actions of some companies that they have allowed the workers or widow(er)s to sue in situations like this.

In 1986, a research chemist at Dow charged that Dow failed to tell him he was being exposed to "agent orange." He sued for (1) intentional misrepresentation; (2) fraudulent concealment of potential danger; (3) intentional infliction of physical injury; and (4) intentional infliction of emotional distress. The Michigan Supreme Court allowed him to sue for all four things, saying that "if the injury is substantially certain to occur as a consequence of actions the employer intended, the employer is deemed to have intended the injuries as well" even if he did not have a particular worker in mind when he did what he did (*Beauchamp*).

Over the years since that decision by the Michigan Supreme Court, several state supreme courts have adopted the "substantially certain to cause injury" rule, including the supreme courts of Texas and North Carolina (*Rodriquez*; *Woodson*). Courts in Ohio and West Virginia have handed down the most decisions in this area, in part because their legislatures put special provisions into the state worker's-compensation statutes dealing with this issue after the state supreme courts authorized these kind of lawsuits.

The West Virginia statute says employees may sue if the employer subjects them to a high degree of risk and there is a strong probability that harm will result. In a 1990 case, the employee was told to carry a large bucket of hot grease down a slippery slope. The employee fell and was badly burned by the grease. The West Virginia Supreme Court said this probably would not have met the "substantial certainty" test, but it did meet the new test provided in the statute and the employee was allowed to sue (*Mayles*).

In a 1991 case, the Ohio Supreme Court found an intent to injure when an employer removed the safety guard from a conveyor and ordered employees to clean the conveyor while it was still moving. The court said these facts suggested that the employer (1) knew about the dangerous process or condition, (2) knew that injury would result to a substantial certainty, and (3) continued to require employees to work under these conditions. This met the new statutory test (*Fyffe*).

Special Legal Provisions

More and more states have passed special statutes or have amended their worker's-compensation statute to deal with employers who violate safety regulations. In 1978, Connecticut amended its statute to require higher worker's-compensation benefits in cases where a safety regulation has been violated. The statute calls for an increase in benefits from 66 percent to 75 percent of average weekly wages (*Mingachos*). Several states have provisions like this, including Arkansas, Missouri, New Mexico, North Carolina, Ohio, South Carolina, Utah, and Wisconsin. In California, the compensation amount is increased by 50 percent. In Massachusetts, it is increased by 100 percent.

The Texas Constitution has a provision that allows the widow(er) to sue the employer for punitive damages. Section 26 of Article XVI of the Texas Constitution says:

> Every person, corporation, or company, that may commit a homicide, through willful act, or omission, or gross neglect, shall be responsible, in exemplary damages, to the surviving husband, widow, heirs of his or her body, or such of them as there may be, without regard to any criminal proceeding that may or may not be had in relation to the homicide.

In a recent Texas case, the jury awarded $450,000 in exemplary (punitive) damages. The trial judge decided for the employer anyway, ruling that the jury could not award exemplary damages because they had not awarded actual damages. This is a nice catch-22. The constitution does not allow them to award actual damages in a case controlled by worker's compensation. It allows them to award only exemplary damages. The Texas Supreme Court said it would be useless for the jury to make an award for actual damages in one of these cases and reinstated the jury's verdict (*Gifford-Hill*).

In some cases, the employer tries to have it both ways, arguing that the worker's injury is not covered by worker's compensation but that the worker cannot sue in court because of the worker's-compensation statute. Helen McCarthy worked for 10 years in an office where she was regularly exposed to "cigarette and other kinds of tobacco smoke." She sued her employer, arguing that he failed to live up to his duty to provide her with a safe place to work. Usually, when someone sues for breach of this duty, we call it a negligence lawsuit and say it is barred by worker's compensation. In this case, the state department of labor denied her worker's-compensation claim because they said her injury was not the result of a work-related injury or occupational disease. The Washington Appeals Court ruled that they cannot have it both ways. If this is not a case covered by worker's compensation, then McCarthy can sue in court under the common law (*McCarthy*).

Cigarettes

This Washington case illustrates a problem with the present system. In thousands of cases, the consumers of other products are made to bear the cost of injuries that are really caused by cigarettes. The 1979 changes in the New Jersey worker's-compensation statute require that worker's-compensation benefits be reduced by the amount of loss "attributed to cigarette smoking" (*Field*). The Pennsylvania Supreme Court decided in 1987 to do the same thing without a special provision in the worker's-compensation statute (*Martin*). What the New Jersey legislature and the Pennsylvania Supreme Court have not done is to require the makers of cigarettes to pay for the damages their products cause.

A decade ago, a New Jersey Appeals Court handed down a landmark decision in the fight for smoke-free air. A nonsmoking employee sued to get an injunction to stop the smoking at her place of employment. She had a severe allergy to cigarette smoke and seven of the thirteen employees in her department smoked heavily. When the employer refused to make them stop, the employee sued for violation of the duty to provide a safe place to work. The court held that she could not sue and collect money for a violation of this duty (that was preempted by the worker's-compensation statute) but she could sue and ask for an injunction to stop an ongoing threat to her safety and health (*Shrimp*).

Other Intentional Injuries

Fraud, defamation, intentional infliction of emotional distress, and intentional infliction of physical injury are the most common things for which employees sue employers. This does not mean they are the only things for which employees can sue employers. Anytime the employer or supervisor acts intentionally or recklessly and injures an employee, there is potential liability.

In one case, a jury awarded $80,000 in damages because an employer brought unfounded theft charges against the employee (*Eggleston*). The law calls that malicious prosecution.

In another case, the jury awarded $1.5 million for malicious prosecution, $1 million for defamation, and $500,000 for false imprisonment (being kept from leaving a room) (*Foley #2*).

Any worker who thinks he or she has been intentionally injured at work should talk to an attorney immediately, before filing a claim for worker's compensation and before talking to the employer's attorney or insurance agent. Employers should investigate situations that might involve intentional injury and act quickly to end the outrageous conduct.

Criminal Charges against the Employer

In recent years, district attorneys have become so disgusted with the behavior of some employers that they have prosecuted them under the state penal code. Three cases made headlines in the 1980s. In Michigan, a manager was charged with involuntary manslaughter when an employee died from carbon monoxide poisoning after being left in a company van (*Hegedus*). In Illinois, a company and five of its executives were charged with aggravated battery when 42 employees suffered various stages of poisoning. The company, Chicago Magnet Wire Corporation, allowed these employees to work around "poisonous and stupefying substances" without any effort to provide them with ventilation or safety equipment (*Chicago Magnet*). In New York, executives of a company that manufactured thermometers were charged with assault for exposing their employees to mercury vapor and hiding that fact from safety inspectors (*Pymm*). In all three cases, lower courts ruled that these indictments could not be brought because they were preempted by the federal Occupational Safety and Health Act. The argument was that because Congress had passed a law that attempted (and obviously failed) to regulate workplace safety, the states could not apply their penal codes to these kinds of workplace injuries. The supreme courts of Michigan, Illinois, and New York in 1989 and 1990 ruled that these cases were not preempted by federal law. The New York justices felt that

> it would make absolutely no sense to hold that employers who engage in willful criminal conduct, which coincidentally constitutes a violation of an OSHA standard . . . should be insulated from criminal prosecution. . . . Instead, we believe that the Act's penalties operate as a floor and that a State can supplement these penalties with sanctions authorized by their own criminal laws.

19

Social Security

The Past

The Social Security Act of 1935 created several new programs. The part most of us associate with the term *Social Security* is currently called the Federal Old Age, Survivors, Disability, and Hospital Insurance Program (OASDHI) (42 U.S.C.). It is funded by the Federal Insurance Contribution Act (FICA) (26 U.S.C. sec. 3101). That is why your Social Security deduction is called FICA on your paycheck stub. The national unemployment insurance system was also created by the 1935 Act (see Chapter 5). The 1935 Act also created the welfare system that has evolved into the system we have today. The original act set up federal grants to states to help fund local welfare programs. Part of this welfare system became a strictly federal program called the Supplemental Security Income (SSI) program (42 U.S.C. sec. 1381). This program helps old, disabled, and blind people who are too poor to help themselves. The rest of our welfare system is still a state-run system, with money coming from the federal government for things such as food stamps and Aid to Families with Dependent Children.

During the presidential campaign of 1936, Social Security was a major issue. Alf Landon campaigned against it. Many pay envelopes just before election day contained a flyer that read: "You're sentenced to a weekly pay reduction for all your working life. You'll have to serve the sentence unless you help reverse it on November 3." On November 3, 1936, Franklin D. Roosevelt won by a landslide. In 1937, Justice Cardozo wrote the Supreme Court decision finding the Social Security Act of 1935 to be constitutional (*Helvering*). (This tactic of putting campaign literature in pay envelopes caused half the states to make it a crime for employers to influence how their employees vote. See Chapter 11.)

259

The Social Security System

The present Social Security system consists of five basic parts: a retirement system, a life-insurance system, a disability system, a medical-insurance system, and the welfare system called SSI. Employers and employees each pay 7.65 percent of wages into Social Security. Self-employed people pay the whole amount themselves, 15.3 percent.

While most people pay Social Security taxes on all of their wages, there is a point beyond which Social Security taxes do not apply. As of 1992, the first $55,500 of wages are subject to tax. The first $130,000 of wages are subject to the Medicare Hospital Insurance portion of the tax (1.45 percent of the 7.65 percent). These amounts increase every year as average wages increase. Social Security taxes are only collected on wages, not on other types of income such as dividends, interest, rents, and pension payments.

Some people must pay income taxes on part of their Social Security retirement benefits. Up to half of Social Security retirement benefits are taxable if adjusted gross income, plus half of Social Security benefits, plus nontaxable interest income is over $25,000 ($32,000 for a couple filing jointly; zero for a married couple filing separately). In a simple example, a single person with $25,000 of other income and $5,000 of Social Security retirement benefits would pay income tax on $2,500 of the Social Security retirement benefits. If you think this might apply to you, get the Social Security pamphlet, *Part of Your Benefits May Be Taxable*. Many people have suggested making all of the Social Security retirement benefits taxable as a way to balance the federal budget.

The 1983 changes to the Social Security system added millions of people, including all newly hired federal civil service employees and the employees of nonprofit corporations, to the system. Also, state and local governments will no longer be able to get out of the system. If they are in now, or ever join, they cannot get out as they used to be able to do. The retirement age will start to rise above 65 in the year 2005. The retirement age will increase two months a year until it reaches 66 in 2010. It will do the same thing from 2022 to 2027 so that a person will have to be 67 to retire by 2027. The new law also changed the percent of retirement benefits people will get if they take early retirement (see Table 19.1).

Eligibility

The Social Security system is based on quarters of a year. Before 1978, a worker had to earn $50 or more in a quarter to earn a quarter's worth of credit in the Social Security system. After 1978, a worker earns a quarter's worth of credit for every so-many dollars earned during a year. He or she can

Table 19.1 Percent of Retirement Benefits Received if the Worker Takes Early Retirement

Age	Currently You Get	In 2010 You Will Get	In 2027 You Will Get
62	80.0%	75.0%	70.0%
63	86.7	80.0	75.0
64	93.3	86.7	80.0
65	100.0	93.3	86.7
66	103.0	100.0	93.3
67	106.0	108.0	100.0

only earn a maximum of four quarters of credit in any one year. In 1978, a worker earned a quarter's worth of credit for every $250 earned up to four quarters' worth of credit if he or she earned $1,000 or more during the year. In 1992, a worker earned a quarter of credit for every $570 earned during the year up to four quarters' worth of credit for a yearly wage income of $2,280. This amount goes up each year as average wages go up.

Retirement Eligibility. A worker is "fully insured" and eligible to retire when he or she is old enough and has 40 quarters of credit in the system (10 years).

Disability Eligibility. Workers who become disabled before age 24 need six quarters of credit during the last three years to be eligible for disability benefits. Between ages 24 and 31, they need credit for half the time between their 21st birthday and the time of the disability (a 25-year-old would need eight quarters). Between ages 31 and 42, a person needs 20 quarters over the last 10 years. Workers over 42 must meet two tests. First, they must have 20 quarters of credit during the last 10 years. Second, those over 42 must meet a "Total of Quarters" test (see Table 19.2). For example, a person disabled at age 54 must have 20 quarters over the 10 years just prior to disability, and a total of at least 32 quarters over his or her lifetime. Special rules apply to blind people.

Of course, in addition to the required number of quarters of credit, the worker must be *disabled*. Disability is different under Social Security than it is under worker's compensation. First of all, Social Security does not care if the disability is work-related. Second, there is no such thing as "partial" disability under Social Security. If persons are still physically able to get a job, Social Security does not care that they can no longer get the high-paying job that they had before becoming disabled.

The Social Security Administration (SSA) defines disability as:

inability to engage in any substantial gainful activity by reason of a medically determinable physical impairment, which can be expected to result in death or has lasted, or can be expected to last for a continuous period of not less than 12 months.

In other words, Social Security covers long-term disability. The SSA does take age, education, and work experience into account, but the primary concern is physical impairment. To decide on eligibility, the SSA goes down a list of questions.

1. Are the persons currently engaged in "substantial gainful activity" (do they have a job)? If they have a job, they do not get disability payments. If they do not have a job the question is:

2. Do the persons have a severe impairment? If they do not have a severe impairment, they do not get disability payments. If they do have a severe impairment the question is:

3. Is the impairment in the Listings? If the impairment is in the Listings, they get disability benefits. If the impairment is not in the Listings, the question is:

4. Does the impairment prevent the persons from getting work? If the impairment does not prevent the persons from getting work, they do not get disability payments. If the impairment does prevent the persons from getting work, they get disability payments. The U.S. Supreme Court has approved this method of processing claims (*Bowan*).

The *Listings* are simply a list of impairments that are so severe that the person is automatically qualified for disability benefits and the SSA does not

Table 19.2 Total Quarters Test
for Disability Benefits

Age	Lifetime Quarters Needed
42	20
44	22
46	24
48	26
50	28
52	30
54	32
56	34
58	36
60	38
62	40

need to go further. This list contains things such as loss of both feet, loss of both hands, cerebral palsy, and Parkinson's disease. If the impairment meets the requirements of the Listings, then the process is over and the person gets disability benefits. If the impairment does not meet these requirements, then the SSA looks at the physical impairment, along with the age, education, and work experience of the worker, and makes a determination whether he or she is too disabled to get a job.

In making the determination whether or not the person can get a job, the SSA uses the *grids*. The grids are simply charts that list age, education, and work experience along with level of impairment to help the SSA decide if the person is disabled or not.

Some people qualify for Social Security disability benefits not on their own but because their parent is covered by Social Security. A "disabled adult child" is a child of an insured worker, who is over 18, and who is disabled because of a condition that developed before the child reached 22. The "disabled adult child" is not entitled to benefits until the parent dies, retires, or becomes disabled.

Death

Surviving dependents of a deceased worker are eligible to receive benefits if the worker was eligible for (or receiving) retirement or disability benefits at the time of death. They are also eligible if the worker was "fully insured" (40 quarters) at the time of death. They are also eligible if the worker was "currently insured" (had 6 quarters of credit during the last 13 quarters) at the time of death. In addition, even if the worker was not receiving or was not qualified for either retirement or disability benefits, dependents may still qualify under a special rule. If the worker was 28 or younger and had a total of 6 quarters of credit, dependents are still eligible. If the worker was over 28, see Table 19.3.

If the worker is disabled and has enough quarters to qualify for death benefits but not disability benefits, and then dies, his or her dependents get death benefits. For example, suppose a worker is disabled at age 36 with 14 quarters. Because he needed 20 quarters over the last 10 years to qualify for disability benefits, he did not qualify. But if he dies, his surviving dependents would qualify for death benefits.

Generally, dependent children or dependent parents qualify for death benefits. A widow(er) of an insured worker can receive benefits if he or she has minor children at home, has reached 60 years of age, or has reached 50 years of age and is disabled.

Of course, the children and parents of the deceased worker must be dependent on the worker at the time of death. All of this is far more complicated

Table 19.3 Total Quarters Test
for Death Benefits

Age	Lifetime Quarters Needed
28	6
30	8
32	10
34	12
36	14
38	16
40	18
42 and over (see Table 19.2)	

than it needs to be. If someone dies, the dependents should go down to the Social Security office and find out what benefits they qualify for. Even a divorced spouse may qualify if he or she meets the "test."

Quarters Count

As noted earlier, this system is based on quarters. A person would be smart to start earning quarters of credit as soon as possible, and to earn enough in "wages" each year to collect four quarters of credit every year.

Retirement Benefits

The amount of a Social Security retirement check depends on how much persons earned in *wages* over their working life. If persons retire early, their check is reduced as shown in Table 19.1. If they wait until after 65 to retire (or 66 after 2005), their check will be increased. Before the 1983 changes, the check increased 3 percent for every year retirement was postponed. That percentage will gradually go up between 1990 and 2008. It will hit a high of 8 percent in 2008. For example, if persons could retire at age 66 in 2010 but wait three years, they will get 24 percent more per month than if they had retired at age 66. They cannot keep doing this forever. They do not get any more if they wait past age 70 to retire.

Social Security will allow retirees to earn a certain amount in wages and still receive retirement benefits (they can earn as much as they want from investments). If wages exceed the limit, the Social Security check will be reduced by one dollar for every three dollars earned over the limit. Once someone is 70, today and in the future, they can earn as much as they want in wages and still get benefits.

The general principle is that retired persons should get from 26 percent to 60 percent of their preretirement income. The lower the preretirement income, the higher the percentage until those who earned the minimum wage all their life receive 60 percent. Social Security is not set up to support retired workers in the style to which they may have become accustomed. Those who have paid off the mortgage and the car and have no debts should be able to get by on Social Security.

There used to be a minimum amount people could get from the retirement system. That is no longer true, except for members of religious orders who take a vow of poverty. These people will be eligible for a minimum amount if they first become eligible for retirement benefits before 1992.

Unmarried children under 18 (19 if still in high school), severely disabled children, a spouse over 61, or a spouse caring for a child under 16 (or a disabled child) may also be eligible for benefits when the worker retires.

The SSA has a pamphlet called *Estimating Your Social Security Retirement Check* that will take you through the calculations needed to estimate what your check will be.

Disability Benefits

Disability benefits are based on wages earned prior to disability. The actual calculation is too complicated to go into here.

The Social Security law says that the total of worker's-compensation benefits *plus* Social Security disability benefits cannot be more than 80 percent of the predisability earnings. There are several ways to calculate predisability earnings, and the worker is entitled to use the method that results in the highest amount.

A disabled person may be referred to the state vocational rehabilitation agency for help and retraining. After a person has been disabled for two consecutive years, he or she is entitled to Medicare.

Medicare

People who are eligible to receive Social Security benefits either on their own wage record or as a dependent or survivor are eligible for Medicare at age 65. Anyone who has been entitled to Social Security disability for two consecutive years is also eligible for Medicare. People who need dialysis or kidney transplants are also covered.

Medicare has two parts: hospital insurance (Part A) and medical insurance (Part B). The hospital insurance helps pay the cost of inpatient hospital care and some kinds of follow-up care. The medical insurance helps pay doctor bills and other medical expenses. The medical insurance (Part B) is paid for every month, usually by having the premium withheld from the monthly Social Security retirement check. This premium goes up every year so that the elderly pay 25 percent of the cost of this program.

On July 1, 1988, President Reagan signed into law the Catastrophic Health-Insurance Act, but it was repealed by Congress soon after because of the outcry from high-income elderly who would have had to pay more for this coverage than they were paying for private Medicare supplemental insurance. This act would have provided benefits far beyond those currently provided by Medicare, particularly in cases involving a prolonged hospital stay. Because this legislation was repealed, most elderly would be wise to carry suplemental insurance if they can afford it. There is a great deal Medicare does not pay for.

Appeals Procedure

When it comes time to file a claim, call the Social Security Administration. They will tell you what documents you need to take when you go to the Social Security office. Most people do not need a lawyer at the initial claim stage. Once you have been turned down for benefits, it is time to see a lawyer. The SSA denies benefits to over a million people each year. Less than 30 percent of those people appeal the decision. Over half of those who appeal win. Most attorneys will take the case on a contingency basis; this means they do not get any fee unless they help you get something. Their fee is limited to 25 percent of the lump-sum amount you get when the case is finally over (your back-due payments). Also, their fee has to be approved by the SSA before they can collect. Once your initial claim has been turned down, there are several stages of appeal. Generally, at each stage, you have 60 days to appeal to the next level. The 60 days runs from the time you receive the letter, but the SSA assumes you got the letter five days after they mailed it.

Reconsideration. After your initial claim has been turned down, you have 60 days to ask for reconsideration. You do not get a hearing yet, but your attorney can help you submit additional information that may convince the SSA that you are entitled to the benefits after all.

Administrative Hearing. After reconsideration, you have 60 days to ask for a hearing. The SSA's form requesting appeal has two boxes. Check the box that says you want a hearing. An administrative-law judge will preside over the hearing, look at the medical records, and listen to testimony from witnesses. This is where you are most likely to reverse the SSA and get the benefits you seek.

Appeals Council. After you receive a notice that you lost at the hearing, you have 60 days to appeal to the Appeals Council in Washington D.C. This is just a formality in most cases, but occasionally the council actually does overturn the administrative-law judge.

The Federal Courts. After the Appeals Council turns you down, you have 60 days to appeal to a federal court. The judges will overturn the SSA's decision only if they decide the SSA incorrectly interpreted the law or lacked substantial evidence to support their decision. People do win in federal court. In one recent case, all the doctors and vocational experts testified that the worker was totally disabled by back pain that would prevent any kind of employment. The SSA and the administrative-law judge denied benefits because they did not believe these experts. The Eleventh Circuit Court overturned this decision because there was no substantial evidence to support it. The SSA does not have the option of deciding that everyone is a liar and denying benefits on that basis alone (*Hale*). Also, the Social Security Administration has to consider the fact that even though no one physical problem qualifies as a severe disability, the combined effect of several physical problems do qualify (*Arnick*; *Kouril*).

Reopening a Case. Even if you have been turned down, you may be able to reopen your case later if you gain additional evidence. You will have to discuss this possibility with your attorney. Appeals from SSI, Medicaid, and Medicare are handled differently. Call the SSA to find out the details.

Common Misconceptions

The Social Security Administration used to talk about "contributions" to a "trust fund." There really was no trust fund, and the SSA does not talk like that anymore. The money paid into the system goes to pay benefits to people drawing out of the system. When you retire at some point in the future, the taxes paid by people working then will pay your benefits. During the next two decades, the SSA will actually take in more than it pays out; the surplus will be used in the next century to pay retirement benefits to the post–World War II baby-boom generation.

Another misconception is that Social Security retirement is a good deal. It is a good deal for people drawing benefits today. In most cases, people drawing benefits today receive more than they would have received if they had put that money into a private pension plan. For retirees in the next century, the opposite will be true. They will probably receive a much lower payment than they would have received if they had put 15 percent of their income into a private retirement fund every year. Some people estimate that the average worker who put 15 percent into a private pension every year would have a million-dollar fund from which to receive payments upon retirement. Also, he or she would have a million dollars to leave to descendants. It is estimated that in the year 2025, the ratio of retirees to workers will be half what it is today (for every worker there will be twice as many retirees). If that is true, then either retirement benefits will have to go down in real terms, or those workers will have to be willing to pay more of their wages in Social Security taxes.

Private Pensions

Those who want to retire in the twenty-first century and live above the poverty level had better have more going for them than Social Security. Yet many people who tried to supplement Social Security in the past ended up empty-handed because their private pension plans went broke. The United States learned in the 1930s that financial institutions work well if the federal government regulates them enough. In the 1930s, Congress put in place insurance and regulatory systems to protect the banking system. It took Congress another four decades to get around to regulating private pension funds.

Individual Retirement Accounts

Individual Retirement Accounts (IRAs) were born in 1974, expanded to allow even those with company pension funds to set them up, and then greatly curtailed in the Tax Reform Act of 1986. Why? Only upper income people were taking advantage of IRAs. Today, if your income is below a certain level, the money put into an IRA is tax deductible. The latest Internal Revenue Service (IRS) regulations should be consulted. If your income is too high, the contributions to the IRA are not tax deductible, but the income derived is not taxed as long as it stays in the IRA.

Keogh Plans

The law allows self-employed people and some people who are not covered by company pension plans to set up their own tax-free pension plans called Keogh plans. If you think you might be eligible, you should contact the IRS for information.

ERISA

The Employee Retirement Income Security Act (ERISA) of 1974 regulates private pension funds and employer benefit programs (29 U.S.C. sec. 1001). The act does not require employers to set up private pension plans or give employees any benefits whatsoever. It simply regulates these plans if employers set them up.

ERISA requires the plan administrator to file a plan description and an annual financial report with the U.S. Department of Labor and the IRS. The plan administrator must provide workers with a summary of these reports and must make the full reports available for inspection. The plan administrator must also provide workers with a summary of their individual account.

A plan must allow a worker to participate when the worker is over 21 and has worked for the company for one year. ERISA controls vesting. In most pension plans, part of a worker's income is deducted (before taxes) and invested in the plan. The employer matches this in some way. Vesting is when the employer's contributions become locked in and cannot be withdrawn. In other words, when the money the employer has put into the plan belongs to the employee, we say the money is vested.

As a result of changes made in ERISA in 1986, an employer has two choices: *cliff vesting*, which means an employee is not vested at all until after five years of service, at which time he or she becomes 100 percent vested; or *gradual vesting*, which vests 20 percent after three years and 20 percent a year thereafter until full vesting at seven years of service. Employers are free to set up more liberal vesting schedules than those required by law. It is not uncommon for employees to vest 20 percent a year over the first five years of employment.

When an employee stops working for an employer, the IRS must be notified about the employee's pension status. The IRS gives that information to the SSA. The SSA is supposed to have a record of all private pension funds.

PBGC

PBGC stands for the Pension Benefit Guaranty Corporation. ERISA created PBGC to collect premiums from all the pension funds it insures to pay benefits for plans that go bankrupt. PBGC is to pension funds what the Federal Deposit Insurance Corporation and the Federal Savings and Loan Insurance Corporation are to banks and savings and loans.

Wrongful Discharge

What if an employer fires a worker to keep him from becoming vested in the company's pension plan, or because a son's medical bills are costing the group medical plan too much money? The worker cannot sue in state court. The U.S. Supreme Court has decided that, with ERISA, Congress intended to preempt this field of law (*Mass. Mutual; Pilot Life; Met. Life*). The states can still regulate the content of insurance policies and can still control the collection of wages, but they can no longer control employee retirement and benefit plans (*Met. Life #2; Ft. Halifax*).

ERISA makes it unlawful to discharge an employee in order to interfere with "the attainment of any right to which such participant may become entitled" (29 U.S.C. sec. 1140). The act allows the worker to sue for reinstatement, attorney's fees, and more. In one case, the judge found that Bethlehem Mines had fired William Ursic just to deprive him of his pension. He had worked 29½ years for the company and needed only six months to qualify for a substantial pension. The company said it fired him because he borrowed some tools without permission. The judge found this to be a pretext and awarded William Ursic his pension (*Ursic*).

In another case, the judge found that Marriott Corporation had discharged John Folz soon after he informed Marriott that he had multiple sclerosis in order to deprive him of his benefits under the group medical and disability insurance plan. Because of the extreme hostility between Folz and the company, the judge did not order reinstatement (he could have ordered it). Instead he ordered Marriott to pay back pay from the time of discharge to the time of trial. The judge also ordered front pay, which means Marriott had to pay John Folz the salary he would have earned if Marriott had rehired him and he had worked until retirement. Marriott also had to reinstate Folz into the medical, disability, and life-insurance plans and pay him any pension, profit-sharing, and stock-option benefits to which he would have been entitled as a lifetime employee (*Folz*).

Defined-Contribution versus Defined-Benefit Plans

Whether public or private, there are two basic types of plans. A *defined-benefit plan* works the way Social Security does. Workers put in whatever is required each year and, when they retire, they get a percentage of preretirement salary until death (possibly adjusted for inflation). The amount of the benefit is defined.

A *defined-contribution plan* means that the individual worker puts in money (possibly matched by the employer). This money is in an individual account with the worker's name on it. The income from investments goes into this individual account. When the person retires, a large pool of money is available to pay retirement benefits. The amount of the retirement payments each month will depend on how much money is in the individual's account. IRAs and Keogh plans work like this, as do many private pension plans.

During the 1980s and 1990s, more and more defined-benefit plans instituted "integration" with Social Security. This means that benefits will be reduced by the amount that the retiree receives from Social Security. The result is much lower pension benefits for millions of workers.

During the last four decades, a person would usually have been better off with a defined-contribution plan. This is going to be true as long as interest rates are reasonable and inflation is stable. If inflation goes way up, a government defined-benefit plan can be modified to increase benefits accordingly. That is what happens with cost-of-living adjustments in the Social Security retirement system. A private defined-benefit plan that cannot adjust for inflation would be the worst of all possible worlds.

The ideal world might be two plans: a defined-benefit plan set up and guaranteed by government with cost-of-living adjustments (that is what Social Security is) and a private defined-contribution plan invested in stocks and bonds and allowed to grow as the economy grows. That is exactly what millions of Americans have.

The Future

While many people like to point out that in the year 2025 there will be twice as many retired people per working person as there are today, there is some good news in the future. Imagine a household at the beginning of this century: six children, a grandparent living at home, a stay-at-home wife, and one wage earner. The ratio of dependents to workers was eight to one, or 800 percent more dependents than workers. A ratio of 100 percent means that for every worker there is, on average, only one other person who is not working. This ratio has been at or below 100 percent for a decade now. If predictions hold true, it will hit an all-time low of 66 percent in 2010. It will go up to 79 percent by 2050; but over the course of the next century, it should never go above 100 percent. The big difference will be the nature of the dependents. As the twentieth century began, the vast majority of dependents were children. The majority of dependents in the next century will be elderly. This will require a tremendous shift in national resources away from things such as education and toward care for the elderly. Coping with this change will be a major task of government in the twenty-first century.

20

Conclusion:
Suing and Being Sued

Employers and supervisors have read about lawsuits throughout this book. It is only natural that some might think that anything they do might land them in court. But if you will recall most of the cases, you will realize that many of the supervisors and employers in this book deserved to be sued. Managers who follow generally accepted principles of management, and keep in mind the general dictates of the law, do not get sued.

There are some general rules that everyone—employer, supervisor, and employee—should follow:

1. *Keep a Record of Everything.* Many employers lose in court or at the unemployment-compensation office because they do not have the proper documentation. The same rule applies to employees. All employees should keep a daily logbook or diary noting who ordered them to do what, along with a record of accomplishments and complaints.

2. *Keep Your Mouth Shut.* In this book, we have seen supervisors sued for defamation and employees fired for having a foul mouth. Add to that the fact that everything people say really can be used against them in a court of law and you have a very good reason to keep quiet.

3. *Talk to an Attorney Early.* Many lawsuits could be prevented if supervisors would talk to an attorney *before* taking action. Many employees could avoid throwing their cases away if they would talk to an attorney *before* doing something stupid, like resigning or admitting guilt.

4. *Keep Pay Records.* Employees have seen throughout this book that there

are many times when they will have to prove what they are earning. A special box for paycheck stubs would be a good idea for everyone.

5. *Ask Questions*. The law is constantly changing, and no one should think definitive answers to all questions are in this book. However, both supervisors and employees should now have a better idea of the questions they need to ask when the time comes to talk to an attorney.

6. *Keep up with Deadlines*. You have seen that the law loves deadlines. An employer may have only a few days to decide whether to challenge an application for unemployment. An injured employee may have only a few days to notify his or her employer of a work-related injury. Appeals in worker's-compensation and unemployment-compensation cases must be filed in days, not months, while civil rights complaints must be filed in months, not years. The major cause for malpractice lawsuits against lawyers is that they waited past the deadline to file a lawsuit. You, as the client, should take enough interest in your own case to ask the attorney when the deadline is and make sure the lawsuit is filed on time.

7. *Do Not Accept Legal Advice from Anyone Other Than Your Own Attorney*. Many supervisors and co-workers mean well when they give free legal advice, but this kind of advice is not dependable.

8. *Tell Your Attorney Everything That Might Be Relevant*. You should now have a better idea of the kinds of things your attorney would like to know. If you are going to sue, your attorney will want to sue for everything that is reasonable under the law. The legal system wants you to do that. Once the system goes to the time and expense of a trial, the system would like you to get everything taken care of. Employers who are being sued should keep in mind that supervisors may not want to tell it all to the employer's attorney for their own personal reasons. An internal investigation may be called for and may pay off in the end.

9. *A Little Kindness Goes a Long Way*. Many of the cases in this book came about because the supervisor could not resist being mean. Some employers have the idea that they must back up their supervisors no matter what. While that may be a good general rule, there are times when exceptions are called for. Too many lawsuits come about because a supervisor has been totally unreasonable, and higher management has failed to act. Firing people who have every right to complain about the way their supervisor has treated them is a sure way to end up in court.

Here is a scene that repeats itself all too often in American business. Mary, the employee, is doing a wonderful job, so wonderful that everyone in the company respects her and calls on her for help and advice concerning her area of expertise. They do not call on her supervisor, John. John feels jealous and left out. He imposes a series of work rules on Mary that cause her more and more difficulty until she finally breaks one of the rules and John fires her. Everyone in the company is upset. Mary is very distressed because her infraction is trivial compared with the amount and quality of work she was doing. Mary is going to sue for something because she does not feel she was treated fairly by either John or the company. In most cases, she sues for either race or sex discrimination. Of course, higher management will support John, blindly and without question. When Mary files for unemployment compensation, the company will fight it. After all, isn't Mary guilty of misconduct? The company law firm explains that such a battle will be expensive and will force the company to expose much of its case to Mary's attorney, which will make it easier for him or her to prepare for the forthcoming discrimination battle. The law firm also explains that their legal fees for an all-out battle will be much higher than the increased cost to the company in unemployment taxes. If the state is New York, they will also explain that any facts decided in the unemployment hearing will be set in concrete and that the unemployment hearing is biased in favor of the worker in these kinds of cases. It is biased in that the worker is presumed not to have engaged in misconduct and the burden to prove misconduct is on the employer. Company executives say they do not care; it is the principle of the thing. Because most of the other employees feel that Mary got a raw deal, company morale sinks to an all-time low. Most of them refuse to testify for Mary unless forced by subpoena, but when subpoenaed they sound like Mary supporters, and this makes company executives even more angry. Mary's lawyer is overjoyed. He or she gets to hear all the testimony of the other side. Even in a state that does not agree with New York and does not give the facts found by the unemployment hearing officer collateral estopple effect, these people are on record and cannot change their story later in the discrimination lawsuit. In many cases, Mary gets her unemployment compensation and goes on to win her discrimination lawsuit.

Higher management should think twice about this story. While the decisions of line supervisors should be supported most of the time, blind allegiance is very costly. When you add the cost in lower company productivity because of the loss of Mary's excellent work, and the reduction of morale to the cost in legal fees and bad publicity, it is just not worth it. It also costs every other employer because judges are so outraged by the company's behavior that they twist legal doctrines to allow Mary to win. While no state requires employers to treat their employees "fairly," every employer should consider doing just that. The long-term rewards could be very great.

References

The references below will enable you to read any of the cases discussed in the book for yourself. The first number is a volume number and the second number is a page number. For example, 428 S.W.2d 98 (Tex. App. 1983) means that the case is located at volume 428 of the Southwestern Reporter Second Series at page 98. The parenthesis tells you the case was decided by the Texas Appeals Court. If the Texas Supreme Court had decided the case, only Tex. would appear in the parenthesis. Federal district court decisions are reported in F. Supp (Federal Supplement), while federal circuit court decisions are reported in F. or F.2d (Federal Reporter Second Series). If only a date appears in the parenthesis, the case was decided by the U.S. Supreme Court.

AARP—943 F.2d 996 (9th Cir. 1991)

Aasmundstad—337 N.W.2d 792 (N.D. 1983)

ABC—438 N.Y.S.2d 482 (N.Y. 1981)

Action for Boston—525 N.E.2d 411 (Mass. 1988)

Adams—597 A.2d 28 (D.C. App. 1991)

Adams County—791 P.2d 688 (Colo. 1990)

Addison—372 S.E.2d 403 (Va. 1988)

Adler—432 A.2d 464 (Md. 1981)

ADM—456 N.W.2d 378 (Iowa 1990)

Aebisher—622 F.2d 651 (2d Cir. 1980)

Aetna-Standard—493 A.2d 1375 (Pa. App. 1985)

Afroyim—387 U.S. 253 (1967)

AFSCME—770 F.2d 1401 (9th Cir. 1985)

Agarwal—603 P.2d 58 (Cal. 1979)

Aiello—818 F.2d 1196 (5th Cir. 1987)

Ainsworth—592 A.2d 871 (Vt. 1991)

Airline Stewards—573 F.2d 960 (7th Cir. 1978)

Alamo Foundation—471 U.S. 290 (1985)

Alaska Airlines—217 F.2d 295 (9th Cir. 1954)

Alcorn—468 P.2d 216 (Cal. 1970)

Allabashi—824 P.2d 1 (Cal. App. 1991)

Allegri—684 P.2d 1031 (Kan. App. 1984)

Allen—494 N.E.2d 978 (Ind. App. 1986)

Allen #2—501 A.2d 1169 (Pa. App. 1985)

Alva—750 P.2d 28 (Ariz. 1988)

Alverado—759 P.2d 427 (Wash. 1988)

Ambroz—416 N.W.2d 510 (Neb. 1987)

American Can—424 F.2d 356 (8th Cir. 1970)

American Linen—945 F.2d 1428 (8th Cir. 1991)

American Newspaper—345 U.S. 100 (1953)

Amos—483 U.S. 327 (1987)

Anchor Motor—424 U.S. 554 (1976)

Anco—693 P.2d 1183 (Kan. 1985)

Andracki—508 A.2d 624 (Pa. App. 1986)

Angelo—555 F.2d 1164 (3d Cir. 1977)

Apodaca—769 P.2d 88 (N.M. 1989)

Arabian American—111 S. Ct. 1227 (1991)

Ardestani—112 S. Ct. 515 (1991)

Arnett—416 U.S. 134 (1974)

Arnick—921 F.2d 174 (8th Cir. 1990)

Assemany—434 N.W.2d 233 (Mich. App. 1988)

Atchley—729 S.W.2d 428 (Ark. App. 1987)

Attisano—531 A.2d 72 (Pa. App. 1987)

Auddino—507 A.2d 913 (Pa. App. 1986)

Augat—565 N.E.2d 415 (Mass. 1991)

Austin—878 F.2d 786 (4th Cir. 1989)

Ayala—831 F.2d 1314 (7th Cir. 1987)

Babcock & Wilcox—351 U.S. 105 (1987)

Baker—903 F.2d 1342 (10th Cir. 1990)

Bakke—438 U.S. 265 (1978)

Baldwin—769 P.2d 298 (Wash. 1989)

Ball—731 S.W.2d 536 (Tenn. App. 1987)

Ballard—581 F. Supp. 160 (N.D. Ga. 1983)

Baltimore—504 A.2d 657 (Md. App. 1986)

Bama Tran.—732 P.2d 483 (Okla. App. 1986)

Barnes—561 F.2d 983 (D.C. Cir. 1977)

Barrett—649 F.2d 1193 (5th Cir., Unit A, 1981)

Batt—774 P.2d 371 (Kan. App. 1989)

Bauman—475 So. 2d 1322 (Fla. App. 1985)

Baxley—404 S.E.2d 554 (Ga. 1991)

Bayh—573 N.E.2d 398 (Ind. 1991)

Bayly—780 P.2d 1168 (Okla. 1989)

Beauchamp—398 N.W.2d 882 (Mich. 1986)

Belasco—510 A.2d 337 (Pa. 1986)

Bello—504 A.2d 1015 (R.I. 1986)

Belwood Nursing—505 N.E.2d 1026 (Ill. 1987)

Benjamin—390 S.E.2d 814 (W. Va. 1990)

Benoir—514 A.2d 716 (Vt. 1986)

Bergstedt—499 N.E.2d 902 (Ohio App. 1985)

Bernasconi—548 F.2d 857 (9th Cir. 1977)

Bernoudy—828 F.2d 1316 (8th Cir. 1987)

Berrutti—496 N.E.2d 350 (Ill. App. 1986)

Berube—771 P.2d 1033 (Utah 1989)

Best Lock—572 N.E.2d 520 (Ind. App. 1991)

Bethlehem Mines—529 A.2d 610 (Pa. App. 1987)

Betts—109 S. Ct. 2854 (1989)

Bever—724 F.2d 1083 (4th Cir. 1984)

Bird—740 P.2d 243 (Or. App. 1987)

Bishop Leonard—593 A.2d 28 (Pa. App. 1991)

Black—354 S.E.2d 696 (Ga. App. 1987)

Blackwell—726 S.W.2d 760 (Mo. App. 1987)

Blake—356 S.E.2d 453 (Va. App. 1987)

Blake #2—595 F.2d 1367 (9th Cir. 1979)

Blanchard—499 A.2d 1345 (N.H. 1985)

Blue Hull—393 U.S. 440 (1969)

Blue Mountain—503 A.2d 1073 (Pa. App. 1986)

BMY—504 A.2d 946 (Pa. App. 1986)

Boeing—823 P.2d 1159 (Wash. App. 1992)

Bohen—799 F.2d 1180 (7th Cir. 1986)

Boles—353 S.E.2d 286 (S.C. 1987)

Borden—825 S.W.2d 711 (Tex. App. 1991)

Borello—769 P.2d 339 (Cal. 1989)

Bouchet—730 F.2d 799 (D.C. Cir. 1984)

Boudar—742 P.2d 491 (N.M. 1987)

Bouldin—82 U.S. 131 (1872)

Boundy—514 N.E.2d 931 (Ohio App. 1986)

Bowan—107 S. Ct. 2287 (1987)

Bowers—402 A.2d 308 (Pa. App. 1979)

Bowman—331 S.E.2d 797 (Va. 1985)

Bradley—405 N.W.2d 243 (Minn. 1987)

Bradley #2—585 N.E.2d 123 (Ill. 1991)

Brady—544 A.2d 1985 (Pa. App. 1988)

Branti—445 U.S. 507 (1980)

Brennan—504 A.2d 432 (Pa. App. 1986)

Brevik—416 N.W.2d 714 (Minn. 1987)

Bridgeport—933 F.2d 1140 (2d Cir. 1991)

Briggs—630 F.2d 414 (5th Cir. 1980)

Briggs #2—746 F.2d 1475 (6th cir. 1984)

Broadrick—413 U.S. 601 (1973)

Broderick—808 P.2d 1211 (Alaska 1991)

Brown Trans.—578 A.2d 555 (Pa. App. 1990)

Bryant—722 P.2d 579 (Kan. 1986)

Bullock—444 N.W.2d 114 (Mich. 1989)

Bundy—641 F.2d 934 (D.C. Cir. 1981)

Bunkers—521 F.2d 1217 (9th Cir. 1975)

Bunnell—741 P.2d 887 (Or. 1987)

Burgess—388 S.E.2d 134 (N.C. 1990)

Burk—770 P.2d 24 (Okla. 1989)

Burlington—349 S.E.2d 842 (N.C. 1987)

Burton—803 P.2d 518 (Idaho 1990)

Bussell—498 A.2d 787 (N.J. App. 1985)

Cablevision—526 N.E.2d 240 (Ind. App. 1988)

Cagle—726 P.2d 434 (Wash. 1986)

Cahill—585 A.2d 977 (N.J. App. 1991)

Cahoon—499 N.E.2d 522 (Ill. App. 1986)

Califano—430 U.S. 199 (1977)

Callahan—534 N.E.2d 565 (Ill. App. 1989)

Callaway—832 F.2d 414 (7th Cir. 1987)

Cannon—422 N.W.2d 638 (Iowa 1988)

Caruso—506 N.Y.S.2d 789 (N.Y. Dist. 1986).

Cashdollar—595 A.2d 70 (Pa. App. 1991)

Castiglione—517 A.2d 786 (Md. App. 1986)

Castro—459 F.2d 725 (1st Cir. 1972)

Cebula—614 F. Supp. 260 (D.C. Ill. 1985)

Central Point—554 F. Supp. 600 (D. Or. 1982)

Central Telephone—738 P.2d 510 (Nev. 1987)

Cert. Question—399 N.W.2d 3220 (S.D. 1987)

Chaline—693 F.2d 477 (5th Cir. 1982)

Chapman—557 N.E.2d 256 (Ill. App. 1990)

Chavers—519 So. 2d 942 (Ala. 1988)

Chicago Magnet—534 N.E.2d 962 (Ill. 1989)

Chicago Miniature—747 F.2d 292 (7th Cir. 1991)

Chicago Teachers—106 S. Ct. 1066 (1986)

Childers—676 F.2d 1338 (10th Cir. 1982)

Chrisman—751 P.2d 140 (Kan. 1988)

Christensen—563 F.2d 353 (8th Cir. 1977)

Churchy—759 P.2d 1336 (Colo. 1988)

Cilley—514 A.2d 818 (N.H. 1986)

City Stores—479 F.2d 235 (5th Cir. 1973)

Civil Service—413 U.S. 548 (1973)

Civil Service #2—591 A.2d 281 (Pa. 1991)

Clanton—677 S.W.2d 441 (Tenn. 1984)

Clay—559 A.2d 917 (Pa. 1989)

Cleary—168 Cal. Rptr. 722 (Cal. App. 1980)

Clevenger—770 P.2d 866 (Nev. 1989)

Clifford—353 N.W.2d 469 (Mich. 1984)

Cline—352 S.E.2d 291 (S.C. App. 1986)

Cloutier—436 A.2d 1140 (N.H. 1981)

Clowes—538 A.2d 794 (N.J. 1988)

Codd—429 U.S. 624 (1977)

Coelho—544 A.2d 170 (Conn. 1988)

Coleman—520 A.2d 1341 (N.J. 1986)

Coley—561 F. Supp. 645 (E.D. Mich. 1982)

College-Town—508 N.E.2d 587 (Mass. 1987)

Collins—349 F.2d 863 (2d Cir. 1965)

Collins Foods—948 F.2d 549 (9th Cir. 1991)

Colonial Taxi—521 A.2d 536 (Pa. App. 1987)

Columbia—568 F.2d 953 (2d Cir. 1977)

Columbus Ed. Assoc.—623 F.2d 1155 (6th Cir. 1980)

Colvig—42 Cal. Rptr. 473 (Cal. App. 1965)

Coman—318 S.E.2d 445 (N.C. 1989)

Com. Bankers—516 N.E.2d 110 (Ind. App. 1987)

Com. Edison—494 N.E.2d 1186 (Ill. App. 1986)

Com. Office Prod.—108 S. Ct. 1666 (1988)

Con. Cas.—567 So. 2d 1208 (Ala. 1990)

Connick—103 S. Ct. 1684 (1983)

Cook—488 A.2d 1295 (Conn. App. 1985)

Cook #2—501 N.E.2d 615 (Ohio 1986)

Cooper—723 P.2d 298 (Or. 1986)

Cooper #2—455 N.W.2d 79 (Minn. App. 1990)

Corley—566 F.2d 994 (5th Cir. 1978)

Cornelio—243 F. Supp. 126 (E.D. Pa. 1985)

Corp. 613—510 A.2d 103 (N.J. App. 1986)

Corum—413 S.E.2d 276 (N.C. 1992)

Coston—831 F.2d 1321 (7th Cir. 1987)

Cottrell—743 P.2d 716 (Or. 1987)

Craig—721 F.2d 77 (3d Cir. 1983)

Crain—810 S.W.2d 910 (Ark. 1991)

Cross—805 S.W.2d 44 (Ark. 1991)

Crossman—825 P.2d 1330 (Okla. 1992)

Crump—576 A.2d 441 (Vt. 1990)

Cuevas—500 N.E.2d 1047 (Ill. App. 1986)

Curran—498 A.2d 51 (Pa. App. 1985)

Curtis—490 A.2d 178 (D.C. 1985)

D'Angelo—819 P.2d 206 (Nev. 1991)

Danielson—742 P.2d 717 (Wash. 1987)

Danielson Mobil—394 N.W.2d 251 (Minn. App. 1986)

Darby—312 U.S. 100 (1941)

Darneille—744 P.2d 1091 (Wash. App. 1987)

DaSilva—402 A.2d 755 (Conn. 1978)

Dean Van Horn—395 N.W.2d 405 (Minn. App. 1986)

Dearden—542 A.2d 383 (Md. App. 1988)

Dearment—932 F.2d 721 (8th Cir. 1991)

Deauville—756 F.2d 1183 (5th Cir. 1985)

DeBartolo—108 S. Ct. 1392 (1988)

DeFosse—510 N.E.2d 141 (Ill. App. 1987)

Delaney—681 P.2d 114 (Or. 1984)

Del Borrello—508 A.2d 368 (Pa. App. 1986)

Demech—400 A.2d 502 (N.J. App. 1979)

DeRose—496 N.E.2d 428 (Mass. 1986)

Derosia—519 A.2d 601 (Vt. 1986)

Desai—510 A.2d 662 (N.J. 1986)

DeSantis—793 S.W.2d 670 (Tex. 1990)

Destafano—763 P.2d 275 (Colo. 1988)

Diamond Shamrock—809 S.W.2d 514 (Tex. App. 1991)

Diaz—442 F.2d 385 (5th Cir. 1971)

Dillingham—348 S.E.2d 143 (N.C. App. 1986)

Doering—496 A.2d 720 (N.J. 1985)

Donahue—471 F.2d 475 (7th Cir. 1972)

Donato—379 F.2d 288 (3d Cir. 1967)

Downes—775 F.2d 288 (Fed. Cir. 1985)

Downslope—676 F.2d 1114 (6th Cir. 1982)

Dred Scott—60 U.S. 393 (1857)

Duldulao—505 N.E.2d 314 (Ill. 1987)

D'Ulisse-Cupo—520 A.2d 217 (Conn. 1987)

Dunkle—496 A.2d 880 (Pa. App. 1985)

Durango—614 P.2d 880 (Colo. 1980)

Durepos—516 A.2d 565 (Me. 1986)

Dwiggins—596 A.2d 1069 (Md. 1991)

Dye—781 S.W.2d 826 (Ky. App. 1987)

Easter Seal Society—815 F.2d 323 (5th Cir. 1987)

Eavenson—730 P.2d 464 (N.M. 1986)

Eckles—548 F.2d 905 (10th Cir. 1977)

Eddings—496 N.E.2d 1167 (Ill. App. 1986)

EEOC—829 F.2d 392 (3d Cir. 1987)

Eggleston—724 S.W.2d 462 (Ark. 1987)

Eib—633 S.W.2d 432 (Mo. App. 1982)

Eide—397 N.W.2d 532 (Mich. App. 1986)

Eldridge—417 N.W.2d 797 (N.D. 1987)

Elias-Zacarias—112 S. Ct. 812 (1992)

Ellett—505 A.2d 888 (Md. App. 1986)

Ellison—924 F.2d 872 (9th Cir. 1991)

El Rescate—941 F.2d 950 (9th Cir. 1991)

Elrod—427 U.S. 347 (1976)

Emanuel—897 F.2d 1435 (8th Cir. 1990)

Equitable—389 N.W.2d 876 (Minn. 1986)

Estes—856 F.2d 1097 (8th Cir. 1988)

Exxon—508 A.2d 142 (Md. App. 1986)

Exxon #2—491 A.2d 318 (Pa. App. 1985)

Ewing—861 F.2d 353 (2d Cir. 1988)

Fairmont—454 F.2d 490 (4th Cir. 1972)

Fair Oaks—729 P.2d 743 (Cal. 1987)

Fansteel—306 U.S. 240 (1939)

Farley—529 S.W.2d 751 (Tex. 1975)

Farmer's Coop.—825 P.2d 1323 (Okla. 1992)

Farwell—4 Metc. 49 (Mass. 1842)

Federated Stores—595 A.2d 1067 (Md. 1991)

Fedorenki—449 U.S. 490 (1981)

Ferraro—368 N.W.2d 666 (Wis. 1985)

Field—507 A.2d 1209 (N.J. App. 1986)

Figgie—502 N.E.2d 797 (Ill. App. 1986)

Filcek—401 N.W.2d 318 (Mich. App. 1986)

Finley—520 A.2d 208 (Conn. 1987)

Fire Protection—720 P.2d 70 (Colo. 1989)

Firestone Textile—666 S.W.2d 730 (Ky. 1983)

First Victoria—420 F.2d 648 (5th Cir. 1969)

Fisher—14 Wend. 10 (N.Y. 1836)

Flach—744 S.W.2d 690 (Tex. App. 1988)

Flesner—575 N.E.2d 1107 (Mass. 1991)

Foley—765 P.2d 373 (Cal. 1988)

Foley #2—508 N.E.2d 72 (Mass. 1987)

Folz—594 F. Supp. 1007 (W.D. Mo. 1984)

Ford—734 P.2d 580 (Ariz. 1987)

Ford Motor Co.—345 U.S. 330 (1953)

Fore—727 S.W.2d 840 (Ark. 1987)

Fortune—364 N.E.2d 1251 (Mass. 1977)

Frampton—297 N.E.2d 425 (Ind. 1973)

Francis—726 P.2d 852 (N.M. 1986)

Franklin—787 P.2d 489 (Or. App. 1990)

Frazee—489 U.S. 829 (1989)

Freidrichs—410 N.W.2d 62 (Minn. App. 1987)

French—526 A.2d 861 (Conn. 1987)

Frontiero—411 U.S. 677 (1973)

Frye—293 F. 1013 (D.C. Cir. 1923)

Ft. Halifax—107 S. Ct. 2211 (1987)

Furno—522 A.2d 746 (Vt. 1986)

Fyffe—570 N.E.2d 1108 (Ohio 1991)

Gamble—345 U.S. 117 (1953)

Gandy—531 So. 2d 381 (Fla. App. 1988)

Gannon—561 F. Supp. 1377 (N.D. Ill. 1983)

Gantt—824 P.2d 680 (Cal. 1992)

Garber—552 F.2d 1032 (4th Cir. 1977)

Garcia—105 S. Ct. 1005 (1985)

Gates—668 P.2d 213 (Mont. 1983)

Gathering—495 N.E.2d 207 (Ind. App. 1986)

Gatins—349 S.E.2d 818 (Ga. App. 1986)

Gee—139 F. 582 (S.D. Iowa 1905)

Geiser—722 S.W.2d 122 (Mo. App. 1986)

General Motors—373 U.S. 734 (1963)

Gifford-Hill—725 S.W.2d 712 (Tex. 1987)

Gilbert—429 U.S. 125 (1976)

Gilbertson—403 F. Supp. 1 (D. Conn. 1975)

Gill—574 So. 2d 586 (Miss. 1990)

Gilmer—111 S. Ct. 1647 (1991)

Gimello—594 A.2d 264 (N.J. App. 1991)

Givhan—99 S. Ct. 693 (1979)

Gladden—728 S.W.2d 501 (Ark. 1987)

Glanville—637 S.W.2d 328 (Mo. App. 1982)

Globe Sec.—520 A.2d 545 (Pa. App. 1987)

Goettler—508 A.2d 630 (Pa. App. 1986)

Golden Bear—494 N.E.2d 581 (Ill. App. 1986)

Gompers—221 U.S. 418 (1911)

Goose Creek—519 F.2d 53 (5th Cir. 1975)

Grace—395 N.W.2d 576 (N.D. 1986)

Grace Drilling—811 P.2d 907 (Okla. App. 1991)

Grant—490 A.2d 1115 (D.C. App. 1985)

Greater Cleveland—567 N.E.2d 1325 (Ohio App. 1989)

Great Plains—407 N.W.2d 166 (Neb. 1987)

Greeley—551 N.E.2d 981 (Ohio 1990)

Green—896 F.2d 801 (3d Cir. 1990)

Green #2—499 A.2d 870 (D.C. App. 1986)

Greenfield—500 N.E.2d 1083 (Ill. App. 1986)

Green Hills—514 N.E.2d 1227 (Ill. App. 1987)

Griess—776 P.2d 752 (Wyo. 1989)

Griggs—401 U.S. 424 (1971)

Grossart—758 F.2d 1221 (7th Cir. 1985)

Guffey—727 S.W.2d 826 (Ark. 1987)

Guimarales—503 N.E.2d 113 (N.Y. 1986)

Gunther—452 U.S. 161 (1981)

Hafer—112 S. Ct. 358 (1991)

Hale—831 F.2d 1007 (11th Cir. 1987)

Hamm—708 F.2d 647 (11th Cir. 1983)

Hammer—247 U.S. 251 (1918)

Hammond—498 N.E.2d 48 (Ind. App. 1986)

Hammond #2—756 S.W.2d 152 (Ky. App. 1988)

Hanson—452 N.W.2d 164 (Iowa 1990)

Hapney—579 So. 2d 127 (Fla. App. 1991)

Hardy—145 Cal. Rptr. 176 (Cal. 1978)

Harless—246 S.E.2d 270 (W. Va. 1978)

Harney—784 S.W.2d 921 (Tenn. 1990)

Harper—383 U.S. 663 (1966)

Hartford—492 A.2d 1270 (Md. 1985)

Hayes—505 N.E.2d 408 (Ill. App. 1987)

Heaser—467 S.W.2d 833 (Minn. App. 1991)

Heck's—342 S.E.2d 453 (W. Va. 1986)

Hedrick—454 N.E.2d 1343 (Ohio App. 1982)

Hegedus—443 N.W.2d 127 (Mich. 1989)

Heideck—446 A.2d 1095 (Del. 1982)

Heller—774 P.2d 1089 (Or. 1989)

Hellwig—538 A.2d 1243 (N.J. 1988)

Helmi—758 S.W.2d 219 (Tenn. App. 1988)

Helmick—543 N.E.2d 1212 (Ohio 1989)

Helvering—301 U.S. 619 (1937)

Henson—682 F.2d 897 (11th Cir. 1982)

Hentzel—188 Cal. Rptr. 159 (Cal. App. 1982)

Hepp—150 Cal. Rptr. 408 (Cal. App. 1978)

Herbert—A.C. 209, 111 (1930)

Hercules Powder—53 S.E.2d 804 (Va. 1949)

Herley—490 A.2d 979 (R.I. 1985)

Hicklin—437 U.S. 518 (1978)

Higgins #2—258 Cal. Rptr. 757 (Cal. App. 1989)

Hill—421 U.S. 289 (1975)

Hill #2—571 N.E.2d 1085 (Ill. App. 1991)

Hill #3—918 F.2d 1233 (5th Cir. 1990)

Hinson—742 P.2d 549 (Okla. 1987)

Hinthorn—519 N.E.2d 909 (Ill. 1988)

Hobbie—480 U.S. 136 (1987)

Hodge—707 F.2d 961 (7th Cir. 1983)

Hodges—811 P.2d 151 (Utah 1991)

Hoffman—512 So. 2d 725 (Ala. 1987)

Hoffsetz—757 P.2d 155 (Colo. App. 1988)

Hogan—458 U.S. 718 (1982)

Holbrook—405 N.W.2d 537 (Minn. App. 1987)

Hollenbaugh—578 F.2d 1374 (3d Cir. 1978)

Hooks—367 S.E.2d 647 (N.C. 1988)

Hopewell—528 A.2d 1082 (Pa. App. 1987)

Hopkins—490 U.S. 228 (1989)

Hopkins #2—920 F.2d 967 (D.C. Cir. 1990)

Horseman—532 N.E.2d 644 (Mass. 1989)

Howard—572 A.2d 931 (Vt. 1990)

Howard Gault—848 F.2d 544 (5th Cir. 1988)

Howard U.—484 A.2d 958 (D.C. 1984)

Hubbard—949 F.2d 453 (D.C. Cir. 1991)

Hultgren—913 F.2d 498 (8th Cir. 1990)

Hunt—4 Metcalf 111 (Mass. 1842)

Hunter—481 N.W.2d 510 (Iowa 1992)

Hurst—724 P.2d 946 (Or. App. 1986)

HV—747 P.2d 55 (Idaho 1987)

Hy-Vee—453 N.W.2d 512 (Iowa 1990)

IBP—727 P.2d 468 (Kan. 1986)

Ingersoll-Rand—542 A.2d 879 (N.J. 1988)

Intercommunity—910 F.2d 42 (2d Cir. 1990)

Intermountain—765 P.2d 619 (Colo. App. 1988)

Ithaca Ind.—846 F.2d 116 (4th Cir. 1988)

Ives—498 A.2d 297 (N.H. 1985)

Jackson—768 F.2d 1325 (Fed. Cir. 1985)

Jeffcoat—732 P.2d 1073 (Alaska 1987)

Jenks—490 A.2d 912 (Pa. App. 1985)

Jenson—468 N.W.2d 1 (Wis. 1991)

Johnson—498 N.E.2d 575 (Ill. App. 1986)

Johnson #2—107 S. Ct. 1442 (1987)

Johnson #3—408 N.W.2d 261 (Neb. 1987)

Johnson #4—745 S.W.2d 661 (Mo. 1988)

Johnson #5—105 S. Ct. 2717 (1985)

Johnson Controls—111 S. Ct. 1196 (1991)

Johnston—357 S.E.2d 450 (S.C. 1987)

Jones—392 U.S. 409 (1968)

Jones #2—508 N.E.2d 1322 (Ind. App. 1987)

Jones #3—779 P.2d 783 (Alaska 1989)

Jordan—620 F.2d 298 (5th Cir. 1980)

Justies—571 A.2d 805 (Me. 1989)

Kachinski—532 A.2d 374 (Pa. 1987)

Kalman—443 A.2d 728 (N.J. App. 1982)

Kaluza—403 N.W.2d 230 (Minn. 1987)

Kastenbaum—766 P.2d 280 (N.M. 1988)

Kater—728 P.2d 746 (Colo. App. 1986)

Katz—389 U.S. 347 (1967)

Katz #2—709 F.2d 251 (4th Cir. 1983)

Kayser-Roth—748 F. Supp. 1276 (E.D. Tenn. 1990)

Kear—517 A.2d 586 (Pa. App. 1986)

Keast—503 A.2d 507 (Pa. App. 1986)

Keay—551 A.2d 391 (Pa. App. 1988)

Keenan—731 P.2d 708 (Colo. 1987)

Kelley—479 N.W.2d 185 (Wis. App. 1991)

Kelsay—384 N.E.2d 353 (Ill. 1978)

Kem—355 S.E.2d 437 (Ga. App. 1987)

Kenall—504 N.E.2d 805 (Ill. App. 1987)

Kendrick—932 F.2d 910 (11th Cir. 1991)

Kennedy—449 F. Sup. 1008 (D. Colo. 1978)

Kerr—733 P.2d 1292 (Mont. 1987)

KGB—164 Cal. Rptr. 571 (Cal. App. 1980)

Kiehl—535 A.2d 571 (Pa. 1987)

Kiepura—358 F. Supp. 987 (N.D. Ill. 1973)

Kinney—792 P.2d 330 (Idaho 1990)

Kinoshita—724 P.2d 110 (Hawaii 1986)

Kinsey—950 F.2d 980 (5th Cir. 1992)

Kiriaka—509 A.2d 560 (Conn. App. 1986)

K Mart—732 P.2d 1364 (Nev. 1987)

Knight—714 P.2d 788 (Alaska 1986)

Kolman—412 N.W.2d 109 (S.D. 1987)

Kolstad—457 N.W.2d 728 (Minn. App. 1990)

Korean Air—863 F.2d 1135 (3d Cir. 1988)

Kotecki—585 N.E.2d 1023 (Ill. 1991)

Kouril—912 F.2d 971 (8th Cir. 1990)

Kowal—512 A.2d 812 (Pa. App. 1986)

Kozminski—487 U.S. 931 (1988)

Kowaleviocz—942 F.2d 285 (4th Cir. 1991)

Kraft—792 P.2d 1094 (Mont. 1990)

Krein—415 N.W.2d 793 (N.D. 1987)

Kreinz—406 N.W.2d 164 (Wis. App. 1987)

K-T Marine—597 A.2d 540 (N.J. App. 1991)

Kuebler—473 F.2d 359 (6th Cir. 1973)

Kuna—512 A.2d 772 (Pa. App. 1986)

Kungys—485 U.S. 759 (1988)

LaBlanc—501 N.E.2d 503 (Mass. 1986)

Laffey—567 F.2d 429 (D.C. Cir. 1976)

Lakeway—796 S.W.2d 820 (Tex. App. 1990)

LaMott—465 N.W.2d 585 (Minn. App. 1991)

Lapare—742 P.2d 819 (Ariz. App. 1987)

Lapham—519 A.2d 1101 (Pa. App. 1987)

Larimer County—727 P.2d 401 (Colo. App. 1986)

Larose—508 A.2d 1364 (Vt. 1986)

Larson—472 N.W.2d 761 (S.D. 1991)

Lavey—502 A.2d 344 (R.I. 1985)

Ledbetter—350 S.E.2d 299 (Ga. App. 1986)

Lee—401 A.2d 12 (Pa. App. 1979)

Lee #2—455 U.S. 252 (1982)

Leikvold—688 P.2d 170 (Ariz. 1984)

Leithead—721 P.2d 1059 (Wyo. 1986)

Lemons—620 F.2d 228 (10th Cir. 1980)

Lessley—727 P.2d 440 (Kan. 1986)

Leveck—498 N.E.2d 529 (Ill. App. 1986)

Levias—500 N.E.2d 370 (Ohio App. 1985)

Lewis—500 N.E.2d 47 (Ill. App. 1986)

Libby—554 A.2d 1181 (Me. 1989)

Lindsey—754 P.2d 1152 (Ariz. App. 1987)

Lingle—108 S. Ct. 1877 (1988)

Little—929 F.2d 944 (3d Cir. 1991)

Livas—711 F.2d 798 (7th Cir. 1983)

Local 28—106 S. Ct. 3019 (1986)

Local 93—106 S. Ct. 3063 (1986)

Local 397—763 F. Supp. 78 (D.N.J. 1990)

Lochner—198 U.S. 45 (1905)

Loeb—600 F.2d 1003 (1st Cir. 1979)

Loffa—738 P.2d 1146 (Ariz. App. 1987)

Lone Star—759 S.W.2d 144 (Tex. App. 1988)

Long Beach—41 Cal. 3d 937 (Cal. 1986)

Longmont—765 P.2d 1974 (Colo. App. 1988)

Lopata—493 A.2d 657 (Pa. 1985)

Lorance—490 U.S. 900 (1989)

Lorenz—823 P.2d 100 (Colo. 1992)

Loudermill—105 S. Ct. 1487 (1985)

Lovato—742 P.2d 499 (N.M. 1987)

Lovely—347 N.W.2d 752 (Mich. App. 1984)

Lovvorn—846 F.2d 1539 (6th Cir. 1988)

Lowe—207 S.E.2d 620 (Ga. App. 1974)

Luck—267 Cal. Rptr. 618 (Cal. App. 1990)

Luddie—497 A.2d 435 (Conn. App. 1985)

Ludwick—337 S.E.2d 213 (S.C. 1985)

Lueck—471 U.S. 202 (1985)

Luedtke—768 P.2d 1123 (Alaska 1989)

Lukoski—748 P.2d 507 (N.M. 1988)

Lutheran—340 N.W.2d 388 (Neb. 1983)

Lynch—454 N.W.2d 827 (Iowa 1990)

Lynn—564 F.2d 1282 (9th Cir. 1977)

Lynn #2—488 U.S. 347 (1989)

Lyon—400 A.2d 1010 (Vt. 1979)

Mackay Radio—304 U.S. 333 (1938)

Mahaffey—562 F. Supp. 887 (D. Kan. 1983)

Mallory—165 S.E.2d 913 (Ga. App. 1968)

Manatawny Manor—401 A.2d 424 (Pa. App. 1979)

Mantech—347 S.E.2d 548 (Va. App. 1986)

Marine—391 U.S. 418 (1964)

Marine Drill—535 So. 2d 1253 (La. App. 1988)

Martin—528 A.2d 947 (Pa. 1987)

Martin #2—447 A.2d 1290 (N.J. 1982)

Martin #3—949 F.2d 611 (2d Cir. 1991)

Mason—832 F.2d 383 (7th Cir. 1987)

Mass. Mutual—105 S. Ct. 3085 (1985)

Mastro Plastics—350 U.S. 270 (1956)

Matson—510 A.2d 819 (Pa. App. 1986)

Mayles—405 S.E.2d 15 (W. Va. 1990)

Mays—775 F.2d 258 (8th Cir. 1985)

MCAO—517 N.E.2d 1270 (Mass. 1988)

MCA Records—153 Cal. Rptr. 153 (Cal. App. 1979)

McCarthy—730 P.2d 681 (Wash. App. 1986)

McClanahan—517 N.E.2d 390 (Ind. 1988)

McClure—460 F.2d 553 (5th Cir. 1972)

McCoy—412 N.W.2d 24 (Minn. App. 1987)

McDaniel—350 S.E.2d 225 (Va. App. 1986)

McDonald—427 U.S. 273 (1976)

McDonald #2—789 S.W.2d 69 (Mo. App. 1990)

McDonnell Douglas—411 U.S. 792 (1973)

McGlothin—556 So. 2d 324 (Miss. 1990)

McGraw—352 S.E.2d 435 (N.C. App. 1987)

McIntosh—469 P.2d 177 (Hawaii 1970)

McKnight—908 F.2d 104 (7th Cir. 1990)

McLain—533 P.2d 343 (Or. 1975)

McLeod—408 N.W.2d 146 (Mich. App. 1987)

McMullan—65 N.W. 661 (Minn. 1896)

McMullen—658 F.2d 1312 (9th Cir. 1981)

McQuary—684 P.2d 21 (Or. App. 1985)

Medrano—416 U.S. 802 (1974)

Meeks—779 F.2d 417 (7th Cir. 1985)

Mendez—516 A.2d 806 (Pa. App. 1986)

Mendez #2—725 P.2d 584 (N.M. App. 1986)

Mercer—361 N.E.2d 492 (Ohio App. 1977)

Meritor—106 S. Ct. 2399 (1986)

Merritt—437 N.W.2d 528 (S.D. 1989)

Mers—483 N.E.2d 150 (Ohio 1985)

Met. Life—107 S. Ct. 1542 (1987)

Met. Life #2—471 U.S. 724 (1985)

MGM—728 P.2d 821 (Nev. 1986)

Michels—497 N.E.2d 586 (Ind. App. 1986)

Mignowe—525 A.2d 1297 (Pa. App. 1987)

Miller—362 S.E.2d 915 (Va. 1987)

Millison—501 A.2d 505 (N.J. 1985)

Mingachos—491 A.2d 368 (Conn. 1985)

Minwalla—706 F.2d 831 (8th Cir. 1983)

Misco—108 S. Ct. 364 (1987)

Mitchell—568 N.E.2d 827 (Ill. 1990)

Mobile Coal—704 P.2d 702 (Wyo. 1985)

Monarch Paper—939 F.2d 1138 (5th Cir. 1991)

Monge—316 A.2d 549 (N.H. 1974)

Moniodis—494 A.2d 212 (Md. App. 1985)

Monsanto—627 F. Supp. 418 (S.D.W. Va. 1986)

Moore—452 F.2d 726 (5th Cir. 1971)

Morris—513 A.2d 66 (Conn. 1986)

Morriss—738 P.2d 841 (Kan. 1987)

Mouchette—266 Cal. Rptr. 1 (Cal. App. 1990)

Mozee—940 F.2d 1036 (7th Cir. 1991)

MPI—464 N.W.2d 79 (Wis. App. 1990)

Mt. Healthy—429 U.S. 274 (1977)

Mudd—543 A.2d 1094 (Pa. App. 1988)

Mulei—739 P.2d 889 (Colo. App. 1987)

Mulei #2—771 P.2d 486 (Colo. 1989)

Mummau—687 F.2d 9 (3d Cir. 1982)

Murphree—449 So. 2d 1218 (Ala. 1984)

Myers—462 N.W.2d 734 (Iowa App. 1990)

Myrtle Springs—705 S.W.2d 707 (Tex. App. 1985)

Nash—905 F.2d 355 (11 Cir. 1990)

National Gypsum—772 P.2d 786 (Kan. 1989)

National Settlement—349 S.E.2d 177 (Ga. 1987)

Nees—536 P.2d 512 (Or. 1975)

Nemazee—564 N.E.2d 477 (Ohio 1990)

Ness—660 F.2d 517 (3d Cir. 1981)

Newark—524 A.2d 430 (N.J. App. 1987)

Newark NAACP—940 F.2d 792 (3d Cir. 1991)

Newport—462 U.S. 669 (1983)

New River—945 F.2d 1290 (4th Cir. 1991)

Nichols—729 P.2d 13 (Or. App. 1986)

Nolan—579 A.2d 1252 (N.J. App. 1990)

Northwest Foods—731 P.2d 470 (Utah 1986)

Norton—728 P.2d 1025 (Utah 1986)

Numed—724 S.W.2d 432 (Tex. App. 1987)

NYC Transit—577 N.E.2d 40 (N.Y. 1991)

O'Connor—107 S. Ct. 1492 (1987)

O'Conor—240 Cal. Rptr. 766 (Cal. App. 1987)

Odeco—532 So. 2d 453 (La. App. 1988)

Odgers—525 A.2d 359 (Pa. 1987)

Ohio Council 8—499 N.E.2d 1276 (Ohio App. 1985)

O'Hollaren—730 P.2d 616 (Or. App. 1986)

Olmstead—277 U.S. 438 (1928)

Oregon—400 U.S. 112 (1970)

Oregon Beauty—733 P.2d 430 (Or. 1987)

Ortwein—511 F.2d 696 (5th Cir. 1975)

Osterkamp—332 N.W.2d 275 (S.D. 1983)

Owen—445 U.S. 622 (1980)

Oxford—743 S.W.2d 380 (Ark. 1988)

Pacific Press—676 F.2d 1272 (9th Cir. 1982)

Pa. Labor—502 A.2d 771 (Pa. App. 1986)

Pallas—940 F.2d 1324 (9th Cir. 1991)

Palmateer—421 N.E.2d 876 (Ill. 1981)

Palmer—752 P.2d 685 (Kan. 1988)

Panto—547 A.2d 260 (N.H. 1988)

Paradise—107 S. Ct. 1053 (1987)

Parker—89 Cal. Rptr. 737 (Cal. App. 1979)

Parnar—652 P.2d 625 (Hawaii 1982)

Partello—768 P.2d 785 (Idaho 1989)

Pattern Makers—105 S. Ct. 3064 (1985)

Patterson—491 U.S. 164 (1989)

Patton—741 P.2d 301 (Ariz. App. 1987)

Payne—520 A.2d 586 (Vt. 1986)

Paynter—491 A.2d 1186 (Md. 1985)

Peeples—522 A.2d 680 (Pa. App. 1987)

Pemberton—502 A.2d 1101 (Md. App. 1986)

Percival—539 F.2d 1126 (8th Cir. 1976)

Perry—408 U.S. 593 (1972)

Petermann—344 P.2d 25 (Cal. App. 1959)

Pfenning—522 A.2d 743 (Vt. 1986)

Phillips—711 F.2d 1524 (11th Cir. 1983)

Phillips #2—400 U.S. 542 (1971)

Phipps—408 N.W.2d 569 (Minn. 1987)

Pickering—391 U.S. 563 (1968)

Pickles—492 A.2d 90 (Pa. App. 1985)

Pierce—417 A.2d 505 (N.J. 1980)

Pilot Life—107 S. Ct. 1549 (1987)

Pine River—333 N.W.2d 622 (Minn. 1983)

Piscopo—521 A.2d 846 (N.J. App. 1986)

Poll—498 A.2d 142 (Conn. App. 1985)

Polley—478 N.W.2d 775 (Minn. App. 1991)

Pollock—322 U.S. 4 (1944)

Ponderosa Villa—399 N.W.2d 813 (Neb. 1987)

Ponton—632 F. Supp. 1956 (E.D. Va. 1986)

Poole—750 P.2d 1000 (Kan. 1988)

Pope—500 N.E.2d 209 (Ind. App. 1986)

Powell—514 A.2d 241 (Pa. App. 1986)

Pranzo—521 So. 2d 983 (Ala. 1988)

Prather—918 F.2d 1255 (6th Cir. 1990)

Priest—634 F. Supp. 571 (N.D. Cal. 1986)

Priestly—3 M & W 1 (1837)

Prince—321 U.S. 804 (1944)

Puckett—725 S.W.2d 674 (Tenn. 1987)

Puckett #2—822 S.W.2d 133 (Tex. App. 1991)

Pymm—563 N.E.2d 1 (N.Y. 1990)

Quasar—950 F.2d 389 (7th Cir. 1991)

Question—443 N.W.2d 112 (Md. 1989)

Radcliffe—508 N.E.2d 953 (Ohio 1987)

Radtke—471 N.W.2d 669 (Mich. App. 1991)

Ragland—724 P.2d 519 (Alaska 1986)

Railway Express—421 U.S. 454 (1975)

Ramsay Health—560 So. 2d 746 (Ala. 1990)

Rancourt—526 A.2d 1385 (Me. 1987)

Rankin—107 S. Ct. 2891 (1987)

Rayburn—772 F.2d 1164 (4th Cir. 1985)

Rector—380 S.E.2d 922 (Va. 1989)

Redgrave—502 N.E.2d 1375 (Mass. 1987)

Reed—404 U.S. 71 (1971)

Regents—485 U.S. 589 (1988)

Reid—109 S. Ct. 2166 (1989)

Reitmeyer—602 A.2d 505 (Pa. App. 1992)

Remba—559 N.E.2d 655 (N.Y. 1990)

Renfro—948 F.2d 1529 (10th Cir. 1991)

Renny—398 N.W.2d 327 (Mich. 1986)

Republic Aviation—324 U.S. 793 (1945)

Ressler—480 N.W.2d 429 (N.D. 1992)

Reynolds—235 U.S. 133 (1914)

Reynolds #2—377 U.S. 533 (1964)

Reynolds #3—98 U.S. 145 (1878)

Rhodes—544 A.2d 562 (Pa. App. 1988)

Richards—433 N.W.2d 320 (Mich. App. 1988)

Richland Shoe—108 S. Ct. 1677 (1988)

Richmond—109 S. Ct. 706 (1989)

Richmond Memorial—349 S.E.2d 419 (Va. App. 1986)

Rieger—521 A.2d 84 (Pa. App. 1987)

Riffert—530 A.2d 906 (Pa. App. 1987)

Roberson—722 S.W. 380 (Tenn. 1986)

Roberto—571 N.E.2d 467 (Ohio App. 1989)

Roberts—757 S.W.2d 48 (Tex. App. 1988)

Robinson's Case—198 N.E. 760 (Mass. 1935)

Rodeen—733 P.2d 544 (Wash. App. 1987)

Rodriquez—763 S.W.2d 411 (Tex. 1989)

Rojo—801 P.2d 373 (Cal. 1990)

Romack—511 N.E.2d 1024 (Ind. 1987)

Ross—816 P.2d 302 (Hawaii 1991)

Roth—408 U.S. 564 (1972)

Rowe—473 N.W.2d 268 (Mich. 1991)

Rowlett—832 F.2d 194 (1st Cir. 1987)

Rudman—330 N.Y.S.2d 33 (N.Y. 1972)

Ruffiner—506 N.E.2d 919 (N.Y. 1987)

Russ—680 F.2d 97 (8th Cir. 1982)

Rutan—110 S. Ct. 2729 (1990)

Sabetay—506 N.E.2d 919 (N.Y. 1987)

Sabine—687 S.W.2d 733 (Tex. 1985)

Sacred Heart—460 N.W.2d 430 (Wis. App. 1990)

Sadler—409 N.W.2d 87 (N.D. 1987)

Safety Med.—724 P.2d 468 (Wyo. 1986)

Sage Realty—507 F. Supp. 599 (S.D.N.Y. 1981)

St. Barnabas—525 A.2d 885 (Pa. App. 1987)

St. Francis—107 S. Ct. 2022 (1987)

St. Pius—557 A.2d 1214 (R.I. 1989)

Salida Sch.—732 P.2d 1160 (Colo. 1987)

Salisbury—615 F. Supp. 1433 (D.C. Ky. 1985)

Sanchez—733 P.2d 1234 (Idaho 1986)

Sarzillo—501 A.2d 135 (N.J. 1985)

Savich—501 N.E.2d 464 (Ind. App. 1986)

Schaefer—462 N.W.2d 179 (N.D. 1990)

Schafer—728 P.2d 394 (Idaho 1986)

Schafer #2—903 F.2d 243 (3d Cir. 1990)

Scharon—929 F.2d 360 (8th Cir. 1991)

Scheduling Corp.—503 N.E.2d 806 (Ill. App. 1987)

Schlup—479 N.W.2d 440 (Neb. 1992)

Schowengerdt—944 F.2d 483 (9th Cir. 1991)

Schuermann—351 S.E.2d 339 (S.C. 1986)

Scott—409 So. 2d 791 (Ala. 1982)

Scovile—338 F.2d 678 (7th Cir. 1964)

Seaboard—347 S.E.2d 627 (Ga. App. 1986)

Seafood—861 F.2d 450 (5th Cir. 1988)

Security—460 F.2d 57 (8th Cir. 1972)

Seeger—380 U.S. 163 (1965)

Seeley—505 A.2d 95 (Me. 1986)

Seibel—752 P.2d 291 (Or. 1988)

Seiler—507 N.E.2d 628 (Ind. App. 1987)

Selcraig—705 F.2d 789 (5th Cir. 1983)

Semancik—466 F.2d 144 (3d Cir. 1972)

Shakman—722 F.2d 1307 (7th Cir. 1983)

Shannon—425 N.W.2d 165 (Mich. App. 1988)

Shaw—328 N.E.2d 775 (Ind. App. 1975)

Shebar—544 A.2d 377 (N.J. 1988)

Sheets—427 A.2d 385 (Conn. 1980)

Shenandoah Baptist—899 F.2d 1389 (4th Cir. 1990)

Sherbert—398 U.S. 398 (1963)

Sherman—500 A.2d 230 (Vt. 1985)

Shingles—513 A.2d 575 (Pa. App. 1986)

Shrimp—368 A.2d 408 (N.J. App. 1976)

Shultz—421 F.2d 259 (3d Cir. 1970)

SHV—545 A.2d 917 (Pa. App. 1988)

Siegert—111 S. Ct. 1789 (1991)

Simmons—791 S.W.2d 21 (Tenn. 1990)

Simpson—643 P.2d 1276 (Or. 1982)

Simpson #2—522 A.2d 110 (Pa. App. 1987)

Simpson #3—494 F.2d 490 (5th Cir. 1974)

Sindermann—408 U.S. 564 (1972)

Sinai Hosp.—522 A.2d 382 (Md. 1987)

Skinner—109 S. Ct. 1402 (1989)

Small—357 S.E.2d 452 (S.C. 1987)

Smith—403 S.E.2d 789 (Ga. 1991)

Smith #2—110 S. Ct. 1595 (1990)

Soliman—531 A.2d 819 (Pa. App. 1987)

Sorrells—565 A.2d 285 (D.C. App. 1989)

Soto—941 F.2d 543 (7th Cir. 1991)

Southern Pacific—729 S.W.2d 946 (Tex. App. 1987)

South Ridge Baptist—911 F.2d 1203 (6th Cir. 1990)

Southside—827 F.2d 270 (8th Cir. 1987)

Southwestern Baptist—651 F.2d 277 (5th Cir. 1981)

Southwest Gas—668 P.2d 262 (Nev. 1983)

Speckman—508 N.E.2d 1336 (Ind. App. 1987)

Spencer—501 A.2d 1159 (Pa. App. 1985)

Spinelli—515 N.E.2d 1222 (Ill. 1987)

Springer—475 N.W.2d 630 (Iowa 1991)

Sprogis—444 F.2d 1194 (7th Cir. 1971)

Staggs—486 A.2d 798 (Md. App. 1986)

Staruski—581 A.2d 266 (Vt. 1990)

State Med.—782 P.2d 1272 (Mont. 1989)

Steamatic—763 S.W.2d 190 (Mo. App. 1988)

Stebbins—442 F.2d 843 (D.C. Cir. 1971)

Steele—323 U.S. 192 (1944)

Steelworkers—443 U.S. 193 (1979)

Steelworkers #2—429 U.S. 305 (1977)

Steelworkers Trilogy—363 U.S. 564 (1960)

Steiben—932 F.2d 1225 (8th Cir. 1991)

Sterner—767 S.W.2d 686 (Tex. 1989)

Stevic—104 S. Ct. 2489 (1984)

Stewart—504 N.E.2d 84 (Ill. 1987)

Stone—522 A.2d 211 (R.I. 1987)

Stotts—104 S. Ct. 2576 (1984)

Stover—366 S.E.2d 670 (Ga. 1988)

Stowe Spinning—336 U.S. 226 (1941)

Suchodolski—316 N.W.2d 710 (Mich. 1982)

Suddarth—539 F. Supp. 612 (W.D. Va. 1982)

Sullivan—491 A.2d 1096 (Conn. 1985)

Sun Ship—447 U.S. 715 (1980)

Swan—521 N.E.2d 787 (Ohio 1988)

Sweeney—439 U.S. 24 (1978)

Swider—824 P.2d 448 (Utah App. 1991)

Swift—504 N.E.2d 621 (Mass. 1987)

Swilley—629 F.2d 1018 (5th Cir. 1980)

Swing—312 U.S. 321 (1941)

Synthetic Rubber—655 S.W.2d 489 (Ky. 1983)

Tameny—610 P.2d 1330 (Cal. 1980)

Tate—403 N.W.2d 666 (Minn. App. 1987)

Tattrie—521 A.2d 970 (Pa. App. 1987)

Taylor—413 N.W.2d 736 (Mich. App. 1987)

Teamsters—431 U.S. 324 (1977)

Terrazas—444 U.S. 252 (1980)

Terwilliger—804 S.W.2d 696 (Ark. 1991)

Texaco—729 S.W.2d 768 (Tex. App. 1987)

Thomas—577 A.2d 940 (Pa. App. 1990)

Thomas #2—450 U.S. 707 (1981)

Thompson—685 P.2d 1081 (Wash. 1984)

Thompson #2—490 A.2d 219 (Me. 1985)

Thornhill—310 U.S. 88 (1940)

Todd—784 P.2d 47 (Okla. 1989)

Todd Corp.—900 F.2d 164 (9th Cir. 1990)

Tomczak—765 F.2d 633 (7th Cir. 1985)

Tomkins—568 F.2d 1044 (3d Cir. 1977)

Toussaint—292 N.W.2d 880 (Mich. 1980)

Townley—859 F.2d 610 (9th Cir. 1988)

Tree Fruits—377 U.S. 58 (1964)

Trombetta—265 N.W.2d 385 (Mich. App. 1978)

Tron—517 A.2d 113 (Md. App. 1986)

Trotman—635 F.2d 216 (3d Cir. 1980)

Trotti—677 S.W.2d 632 (Tex. App. 1984)

True—513 A.2d 257 (Me. 1986)

Truesdale—371 S.E.2d 503 (N.C. App. 1988)

TSEU—746 S.W.2d 203 (Tex. 1987)

TWA—525 F.2d 409 (8th Cir. 1975)

TWA #2—489 U.S. 426 (1989)

TWA #3—432 U.S. 63 (1977)

Tyler—517 F.2d 1089 (5th Cir. 1975)

UFCWI—857 F.2d 422 (8th Cir. 1988)

Umbarger—404 S.E.2d 380 (Va. App. 1991)

United Methodist—815 P.2d 72 (Kan. 1991)

United Public—330 U.S. 75 (1947)

Ursic—719 F.2d 670 (3d Cir. 1983)

Usery—544 F.2d 148 (3d Cir. 1976)

Vaca—386 U.S. 171 (1967)

Va. Electric—703 F.2d 79 (4th Cir. 1983)

Vagelahn—167 Mass. 92 (Mass. 1896)

Valdes—501 A.2d 166 (N.J. App. 1985)

Vann—494 A.2d 1081 (Pa. 1985)

Velantzas—536 A.2d 237 (N.J. 1988)

Veneer—804 P.2d 1174 (Or. App. 1991)

Vermont Camping—497 A.2d 353 (Vt. 1985)

Vernon—731 P.2d 480 (Utah 1986)

Victorson—454 N.W.2d 256 (Mich. App. 1990)

Victory Tabernacle—372 S.E.2d 391 (Va. 1988)

Vigil—687 P.2d 1038 (N.M. 1984)

Visser—530 F. Supp. 1165 (N.D.N.Y. 1982)

Vlasin—455 N.W.2d 772 (Neb. 1990)

Volk—638 F. Supp. 1555 (C.D. Ill. 1986)

Von Rabb—109 S. Ct. 1384 (1989)

Wachsman—704 F.2d 160 (5th Cir. 1983)

Wagenseller—710 P.2d 1025 (Ariz. 1985)

Wagner—722 P.2d 250 (Ariz. 1986)

Walker—185 Cal. Rptr. 617 (Cal. App. 1982)

Wall-Mart—812 S.W.2d 463 (Ark. 1991)

Walters—803 F.2d 1135 (11th Cir. 1986)

Wandry—384 N.W.2d 325 (Wis. 1986)

Wanger—428 N.W.2d 242 (S.D. 1988)

Wards Cove—490 U.S. 642 (1989)

Washington Aluminum—370 U.S. 9 (1962)

Wash. Metro.—506 A.2d 1127 (D.C. 1986)

Wassenaar—331 N.W.2d 357 (Wis. 1983)

Waterbury—95 F.2d 849 (2d Cir. 1991)

Watkins—704 F.2d 577 (11th Cir. 1983)

Watson—720 P.2d 632 (Idaho 1986)

Watson #2—108 S. Ct. 2777 (1988)

Webster—118 S.W.2d 1082 (Tex. App. 1938)

Weinberger—420 U.S. 636 (1975)

Weiner—443 N.E.2d 441 (N.Y. 1982)

Weingarten—420 U.S. 251 (1975)

Weiss—546 A.2d 216 (Conn. 1988)

Welch—727 P.2d 140 (Or. App. 1986)

Welch #2—254 Cal. Rptr. 645 (Cal. App. 1989)

Wells Dairy—865 F.2d 175 (8th Cir. 1989)

West Coast Hotel—300 U.S. 379 (1937)

Western Airlines—105 S. Ct. 2743 (1985)

Westport—517 A.2d 1050 (Conn. App. 1985)

Wheeler—496 A.2d 613 (D.C. 1985)

Wheeler #2—935 F.2d 1090 (10th Cir. 1991)

White—660 F.2d 680 (5th Cir. 1981)

Whitlock—715 P.2d 1017 (Idaho App. 1986)

Whitlock #2—759 P.2d 19 (Idaho App. 1988)

Whittaker—379 S.E.2d 824 (N.C. 1989)

Whittlesey—35 FEP Cases 1089 (2d Cir. 1984)

Wiersma—401 N.W.2d 265 (Mich. App. 1986)

Wiggins—357 S.E. 2d 745 (W. Va. 1987)

Wiljef—946 F.2d 1308 (7th Cir. 1991)

Wilkes—490 U.S. 755 (1989)

Williams—552 N.E.2d 1100 (Ill. App. 1990)

Willis—376 P.2d 568 (Cal. 1962)

Wilmot—821 P.2d 18 (Wash. 1991)

Wimberly—107 S. Ct. 821 (1987)

Winters—795 S.W.2d 723 (Tex. 1990)

Wirtz—391 U.S. 492 (1968)

Wolf—443 U.S. 595 (1979)

Wood—398 S.E.2d 110 (Va. App. 1990)

Woods—515 A.2d 1262 (Pa. App. 1987)

Woodson—407 S.E.2d 222 (N.C. 1991)

Woolley—491 A.2d 1257 (N.J. 1986)

Wright—589 N.E.2d 1241 (Mass. 1992)

Wygant—106 S. Ct. 1842 (1986)

Wyndham—354 S.E.2d 399 (S.C. App. 1987)

Yamavchi—638 P.2d 1253 (Wash. 1982)

Yarbrag—409 S.E.2d 835 (Ga. 1991)

Young—572 So. 2d 378 (Miss. 1990)

Zabkowicz—589 F. Supp. 780 (E.D. Wis. 1984)

Zadworny—404 N.W.2d 7 (Minn. App. 1987)

Zamboni—847 F.2d 73 (3d Cir. 1988)

Zeman—911 F.2d 107 (8th Cir. 1990)

Zimmerly—816 P.2d 1179 (Or. App. 1991)

Index